Resurrecting Eve
Women of Faith Challenge the Fundamentalist Agenda

Resurrecting Eve

Women of Faith Challenge the Fundamentalist Agenda

Roberta Pughe, Ed.S.
Paula Anema Sohl

White Cloud Press
Ashland, Oregon

White Cloud Press
PO Box 3400
Ashland, Oregon 97520
www.whitecloudpress.com

Cover and interior design: Christy Collins, Confluence Book Services
Cover image: Lilith, 1887 (oil on canvas) by Collier, John (1850-1934)
Atkinson Art Gallery, Southport, Lancashire, UK/ The Bridgeman Art Library

Printed in the United States of America
First edition: 2007

Library of Congress Cataloging-in-Publication Data

Pughe, Roberta Mary. Resurrecting Eve : women of faith unveil
the fundamentalist agenda / Roberta Mary Pughe, Paula Anema Sohl.
-- 1st ed. p. cm.
ISBN 978-1-883991-70-8(pbk.)
1. Fundamentalism. 2. Women in Christianity. 3. Christian women--
Religious life. 4. Feminism--Religious aspects--Christianity. 5. Eve (Biblical
figure) I. Sohl, Paula Anema. II. Title.
BT82.2.P84 2007
277.3'083082--dc22
                                          2007006217

To Zach, Josh, and Millo, without you, this book
would not have been written.
—Roberta

For my family: you continue to touch me and teach
me every day.
—Paula

Contents

Introduction

Roberta

The Bible says that I shall know the truth and the truth shall set me free. In my life, however, the Bible and the Christian religion have not set me free. Instead, they have been primary sources of suppression. Christian "authorities" taught me that their truth was the only truth. I was far too young to know otherwise. Their truth became ingrained in me: that I was weak and inferior because I was female. Christian families, Christian churches, Christian people — all claiming to be followers of Jesus — used positions of power and authority to exert their needs for control and domination at my expense. Today this is the truth my soul must speak.

As a little girl, I knew instinctively who held the power: God — a male; pastor — a male (like God); Dad — again, a male (like God). Not me, not Mom, not female. Men, big men, always had the ultimate divine say over me. Because I was female, I knew I could not belong to myself. What was legitimately and divinely created as mine — my mind, my body, my soul — was the property of others. A possession, I did not own myself. I was theirs — their female, their child, their object.

As an innocent, vulnerable, and gullible child, I believed them. I believed they knew best. I believed their God was big, and mighty, and powerful, and male. Anyone who disagreed with Him and His rules would be sent straight to hell. I did not disagree. I did not question. He was God. He was male. He was authority. He was power. I was child. I was female. I was subject. I was powerless.

In the thirty or so years since a conservative Christian movement declared war on secular humanism, we have seen the Christian Right exercise increasing political influence on U.S. policy, with the stated intention of preserving "traditional family values." This effectively marketed agenda, with the domination of women at its core, has affected many through the use of the pulpit and the family. In reality, this movement is an extreme and distinctive form of sexism, operating within a religious subculture that claims to follow in the tradition of Jesus.

Closed hierarchical systems are by nature exclusive and resistant to change, and this one purports to function with a mandate from God. Christian fundamentalism is notable for its emphasis on a male God, its discriminatory view of women, and its lack of women in leadership roles. For today's Christian fundamentalists, limiting women's freedom and suppressing the feminine in both women and men are the true primary "traditional family values."

As women who came of age in the midst of this thrust and who look to Jesus as a teacher and friend, we challenge the misguided assumptions that have created the current psychological and political atmosphere. These principles and doctrines are contrary to Jesus' message of equality and inclusiveness. Jesus' associations with women blatantly challenged the cultural norms when he clearly validated women as equals and honored children as models. His work was filled with the ministrations of the traditional, stereotypic feminine — tending, feeding, healing, touching, and encouraging. Rather than an apocalyptic Jesus, a conquering warrior, he was a man marked by naked vulnerability both in his infant arrival and in his tortured end. This is the Jesus we know from the sacred writings and through our personal experiences of his spirit.

This book is designed to explore the repression of women and the feminine as the motivating force behind fundamentalist and dominionist dogma. We expose the insidious effects of this insensitivity to women and the destruction of the feminine expression of power as we examine how women and their dreams are progressively deadened. We do not mean to ignore how this system impacts men. In fact, the many women's stories in this book clearly reveal the tragic effects on men and children as well. While we hope that many men will read the book and see the parallels between the male perspective and the female experience, we've chosen to focus on how fundamentalism treats and affects women.

We will analyze the systemic influence of this wounding on the couple, on the family, on the church, and on the culture. We will offer internal and external supports as well as a healing skill set for women who want to reclaim their voices, rejuvenate their bodies, and resurrect their souls. And we will emphasize body awareness and movement through expressive dance as powerful tools for transformation.

The myriad ways in which the feminine has been devalued have saddled women with profound burdens and interrupted their spiritual, emotional, and professional self-expression. Male domination of the church has left them voiceless, depressed, and conflicted about the church they love and often want to stay connected with. A culture of fear and judgment keeps them from developing or sharing their opinions, wisdom, and talents. They suffer, their families suffer, and the whole world community suffers.

Many women have lost appreciation for and connection with the deepest aspects of their feminine, intuitive, instinctual, and authentic selves. We define "authentic self" or "soul" as the integrated center where a woman's physical, intellectual, emotional, sexual, and spiritual dimensions merge to guide her in the physical world. In this place, she is able to make contact with and express fully her needs, her desires, and her female creative power. We'll use these terms interchangeably. Through Christian fundamentalist teachings regarding the Good Woman role, women have learned to separate from their souls, even die to them.

Often in repressive systems, a public façade hides a subversive private agenda. The belief named publicly by the system is often the polar opposite of what is privately going on. Although unspoken, the underlying message is tolerated by the ffected individual and internalized as truth. Her personal experience becomes subordinate to the mind of the system; the dogma of the system replaces her own reality. An example is the way in which motherhood is framed as a highly respected calling. Yet, "just a housewife" continues to be the practical status and the experienced reality of the homemaking professional who receives no pay, little honor, and, in fundamentalism, not even a voice. Mothering is certainly not a recognized career when welfare rolls are being purged.

This framing tactic is used constantly in the political arena and affects policy of every sort. George Lakoff describes how the words *healthy, clean,* and *safe,* for example, are used whenever possible, "even when talking about coal plants or nuclear power plants. It is this kind of Orwellian weakness that causes a piece of legislation that actually increases pollution to be called the Clear Skies Act."[1] George Monbiot of the *Guardian*, describes how the media has been co-opted into promoting this deception.

The role of the media corporations in the US is similar to that of repressive state regimes elsewhere: they decide what the public will and won't be allowed to hear, and either punish or recruit the social deviants who insist on telling a different story. The journalists they employ do what almost all journalists working under repressive regimes do: they internalise the demands of the censor, and understand, before anyone has told them, what is permissible and what is not.[2]

In our years of clinical experience in therapy and working with women from Christian/religious backgrounds, we have met women well schooled in this same self-censoring. They have no idea of the fullness of who they are as females, having lived their entire lives internalizing the censor. Some are depressed and unfulfilled. Others wonder why they are unhappy despite seemingly perfect lives. Many struggle with an inner critic that paralyzes their effectiveness in one or more areas of their lives. Some have been physically, sexually, and emotionally fragmented and hurt, often by male relatives, families, and churches. All have suffered a specific form of tyranny (covert and overt) hidden beneath the cloak of "Christian" dogma.

While we are focusing in this book on women who have had direct experience with Christian fundamentalism, these attitudes have bled through the entire culture, and all women would benefit from examining the influential role that patriarchal religious traditions have had in shaping their lives. In fact, Merlin Stone speaks of "the far-reaching effects that centuries of Church power continue to have on each of us today, no matter how far removed we may be from the actual pulpit or altar." He notes that it is the rare family that can trace back beyond two or three generations and not find that their predecessors were deeply immersed in the attitudes and values of one of the male-oriented religions. These attitudes and values are transmitted generationally in the forms of behaviors and actions within the family. It is for this reason that religious pressures are not as far from us as we might prefer to think."[3]

As we explore how and why some forms of Christianity actively suppress women and the feminine, we realize that, for women raised or nurtured in the church, the foundation and the support for healing functions best when it comes from a spiritually based system — ideally, the church. A psychological or humanistic perspective alone does not always satisfy the need for integrated healing. A feminine re-visioning of Jesus' life, message, and model of resurrection allows women to welcome and value their true feminine selves, experiencing renewal as the blessings of the feminine find new balance with the masculine. We call the institution of the church to this same renewal.

Also valuable for self-affirmation and healing is a reexamination of the Biblical character Eve. While Jesus was a historical person and Eve a mythical figure, in Christian fundamentalism Eve is treated as if she were historical. Growing up as conservative Christians, we believed that the events detailed in the Book of Genesis occurred in real time and space. Our tradition taught literalism, with specific focus on texts that emphasized repression of women and condemnation of homosexuals. We have since found great support for learning to read the Bible in its historical context. Theology ought to be flexible, dynamic, and, most importantly, accessible to all, not just the province of a few "experts." It certainly should not be the sole domain of men. The study of the nature of God and religious truth must include women and women's experiences in order to reflect the fullness of divinity.

Throughout this book we will synthesize what we can learn both from Jesus as a historical figure and from Eve as a mythical figure. With the help of Eve and Jesus, we propose an alternate agenda for Christianity. In the spirit of consciousness and truth-telling, and an honoring of the body — the very temple (in the Greek, *naos*, "a dwelling place or inner sanctuary")[4] of the living God — we draw from a variety of wisdom traditions while relying on our own knowledge and womanly intuition.

When we as women allow ourselves to honor our own intuitive sense, we only have to look within our families to know what is true. Do people thrive on judgment or on grace? Do we nurture abundant life through violence or through support? Do we foster balance and sustainability through domination or through cooperation? From our experiences of the realities of our relationships, we know the answers to these questions. Yet we have looked to male religious leaders and to women who voice the patriarchal agenda to tell us how to dominate our children, submit to our husbands, and vote for candidates who would serve the interests of hierarchical power structures. In fact, we have facilitated this agenda.

Jesus' message was clear: we cannot serve both God and *mammon*. *Mammon* is an Aramaic word that speaks not just of money, but of the whole package of power, privilege, wealth, and domination. We are serving *mammon* when we support the hierarchies that perpetuate domination. Charlotte and Harriet Childress describe such systems in their book *Clueless at the Top*:

hierarchies,

the object of the
game is to climb up ladders

"higher" people are accountable to
channel power and resources to themselves

"lower" people support and hold up hierarchies,
send their power and resources to "higher" people
and look to the top for direction, permission, approval

"problems" such as deception, inequity, fear, greed, scarcity,
violence, and war keep hierarchies healthy and participants engaged[5]

In reclaiming our wholeness as women, our challenge is to actively withdraw our support from such systems of domination, finding our direction, permission, approval, and power from within.

John Perkins, in his book *Confessions of an Economic Hit Man*, describes his experiences working within what he calls the "corporatocracy" to secure U.S. interests while creating economic dependency in developing nations. He shows how this system is driven by "a concept that has been accepted as gospel: the idea that all economic growth benefits humankind and that the greater the growth, the more widespread the benefits. This belief also has a corollary: that those people that excel at stoking the fires of economic growth should be exalted and rewarded, while those born at the fringes are available for exploitation."[6]

This Old Boy's Network of influence is enmeshed with patriarchal religion. The National Prayer Breakfast, which meets annually in Washington, D.C., is organized by a religious group called the Fellowship. Charles Colson once suggested that about 20,000 Americans participate in this loose and secretive coalition of powerbrokers, who through money and political connections have world-wide access and influence. Jeff Sharlet who reported on their activities in *Harper's* magazine in March 2003 and in an interview with Anthony Lappé, said,

> I think they are definitely a force for fascism. I think a lot of the way the world looks is a result of their work. They were instrumental in getting U.S. government support for General Suharto [Indonesia], for the generals' juntas in Brazil. Just take those two countries alone, they are two of the biggest countries on Earth.

Those countries might have been progressive democracies a long time ago had it not been for U.S. support for those regimes… This is about maintaining a certain kind of power, a certain view of how power should be distributed. The Episcopalian Old Boys Network was a lot more easygoing than this. This is a lot more militaristic. Really at its fundamental core, almost monarchist. We would be told time and time again, "Christ's kingdom is not a democracy." This is their model for leadership. They would often say, "Everything you need to know about government is right there in the cross — it's vertical not horizontal.[7]

Patriarchal power is unevenly distributed and hierarchies exist to maintain the privilege of a few. As Jesus taught, this love of *mammon* is incompatible with love for God. Jesus' message did not concern gay marriage, the criminalization of abortion, the promotion of capitalism, or the shaming of female sexuality. To allow these issues to define the Christian agenda is to support the privilege of domination. We cannot serve two masters. We will either "hate the first and love the second, or be attached to the first and despise the second" (Luke 16:13). According to this text, if we remain attached to our wealth and privilege, we are in fact despising God.

The time has come for a new reformation within the Christian church for the sake of the world, for the church itself, and for all the men and women whose lives have been limited by religious fundamentalism and the current movement toward a Christian dominionist agenda.

Although many Christian denominations would not call themselves fundamentalist or dominionist, the attachment to hierarchy and the specific attitudes and attributes we will explore continue to influence much Christian language and practice as well as society at large. They echo through every culture and belief system in which women and girls learn that they matter less than men and the wisdom and gifts of the feminine are trivialized.

The apostle John tells in Revelation 21–22 of his apocalyptic vision of the new heaven and the new earth, when the nations come together to live in peace. *Apocalypse* means "unveiling," and it is a soulful unveiling of the feminine that will usher in this new reality. The incarnation of the feminine in all its beauty and giftedness, as women live more fully in their bodies and effectively express their wisdom, will move us toward this peaceable realm. We discover the wholeness of God's image in the fullness of female and male humanity, working together in mutual honor and mutual respect. It is only in this wholeness that we can face the challenges of this day. The revelation of God's domination-free order (the kingdom of God) that Jesus proclaimed will unfold as the historic values of the feminine are brought into balance with masculine values in all world cultures.

Christian history reveals ongoing efforts to squeeze out the feminine dimension of God's image ever since the collection of the biblical canon. The church has been dragging its feet in the critical endeavor of assimilating a corrective feminist interpretation of scripture. Meanwhile, the whole creation groans as the insights and interests of women go unheeded, and warring and environmental devastation go unchecked. It is time for the voice of the feminine to be resurrected from this soul-death for the preservation of our planet and the future of our children.

We need to be open to new information if we are to understand the full nature of Jesus' message. Increased consciousness is essential to promoting change and growth in the individual and in the larger system. The redemption required in the body of Christ (the church) also is required in the bodies of women as they release the pain of this wounding and discover anew the goodness and resources of their whole created selves. As the body of the woman heals, the body of her intimate relationships heals as well. The body of her family will grow in wholeness. The body of her church, if it is safe for her to stay, will mature with her. The body of the whole church, the family of humanity, the earth itself will rise up from paralysis — walking, leaping, and praising.

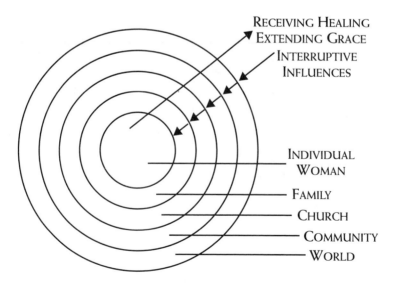

RECEIVING HEALING
EXTENDING GRACE
INTERRUPTIVE
INFLUENCES

INDIVIDUAL
WOMAN
FAMILY
CHURCH
COMMUNITY
WORLD

Interruptive influences on women have been multilayered, compounding their power and ability to silence and deaden the individual. The circles of expanding influence, as the individual woman receives healing and extends grace to those in her extended spheres, is a powerful force of unlimited effect.

Women who inhabit their bodies with authority and celebrate them through dance can promote profound healing and change, not only for themselves, but also for the world. For those Christian women who are seeking spiritual growth, this book may serve as a catapult out of conservative oppression and into greater freedom and awareness. We hope to help women resurrect their souls, revive their dreams, and reclaim their lives.

By analyzing the subtle and powerful influence of the Christian fundamentalist system, we will shed light on the pathology of other closed hierarchical systems. The principles presented here — for developing awareness and fostering healing — can be used by those living under any repressive regime.

Men may find this book significant for the insight it provides into the experiences of women. They may notice as well how the lack of respect for women's ways in the culture causes them to dismiss and dishonor the feminine dimension of their own psyches. They may develop courage and confidence for supporting feminine expression. This book will also be a valuable tool in the therapist-client relationship. Therapists who have not themselves grown up under Christian fundamentalism will gain an understanding of the paralyzing Christian fundamentalist dynamics that often keep women from moving forward in their therapy and in their lives. The Greek word *egeiró*, to raise up or arise,[8] is often used in the New Testament to describe healing and resurrection. This language is rooted in the physical experience of waking and standing up. The resurrection we envision is the rising up — in healing and wholeness, in seeing and hearing, in speaking and acting — that we hope to support through this work.

The clients whose stories we share in this book have given their permission for us to do so. When requested, we changed names and altered details to protect confidentiality. In a few cases, when themes paralleled one another in women's stories, we created composite characters. Other clients asked that we name them boldly so that they may speak their truth with clarity and pride. We have honored these requests and are grateful for the richness each story provides. We also share vignettes from our own lives and have received grace and healing in doing so.

Some may choose to hold fast to a theology of male supremacy, but as women, we have lived and died in that paradigm. Each day we are born again to the possibilities of God's full intention for our lives — for each and every life.

Paula

My daughters don't understand why I am working on this book. The world they have known is so unlike the one in which I grew up. Sure, they still have to do the internal editing when they hear a minister say, "In him was life, life that was the light of men" (John 1:4). (Does that mean men, or both women and men?) And when they were small, on the trip to the firehouse when the chief talked about the "firemen," I would clarify for us all, "Now, is it only men who can be firefighters?" Because they have always been listened to, it would be impossible for them to sit back in class and not insist on their turn to be recognized in a discussion. They have not been threatened with hell as punishment for not accepting the mystery of God and the message of Jesus distilled into four simple laws. Their bodies, their choices, their faith, and their passions have been honored and respected since their infancy, so they move in the world in an entirely different way than I did.

I have learned much from watching their journeys as they have freely explored their interests, spoken their truths, and grown into their bodies with grace and strength. I grieve my own missed opportunities to fully develop and discover my gifts. As parents, we teach by how we live, regardless of the rhetoric we offer. I know that the limitations of my voice and confidence have affected my daughters. But I know that my movement toward a more whole and integrated self also teaches them and inspires their unfolding, just as my own mother's ongoing journey to her own expression strengthens mine.

Still, I feel like David preparing to meet Goliath in trying to describe how fundamentalism terrorizes the souls of women. I'm a stay-at-home mom challenging a huge, organized, well-financed effort to subjugate women in the name of God, and I must protest. I remember a dream of another giant from when I was about seven. The giant was chasing me up a flight of stairs. Each step was higher than my entire body and it seemed impossible to escape. I awoke terrified of being overtaken and overwhelmed by the giant. As I lay awake, too frightened to return to sleep, I realized I could alter my dream. I decided I could choose to see the giant as friendly and save myself from destruction — or at least from my fear. Then I could go back to sleep . . . which I did.

Now I understand this dream as a metaphor for the way in which, at an early age, I chose to go to sleep and yield, unknowingly cooperating with a dominating and disempowering system. I did this for the sake of my own preservation. I just didn't realize I was asleep for so long.

Notes

1 George Lakoff, *Don't Think of an Elephant* (White River Junction, VT: Chelsea Green, 2004), 23.

2 George Monbiot, "A Televisual Fairyland," *The Guardian*, 18 January 2005, www.guardian.co.uk/comment/story/0,3604,1392770,00.html.

3 Merlin Stone, *When God was a Woman* (San Diego, CA: Harcourt Brace Jovanovich, 1976), 239.

4 Robert Young, *Young's Analytical Concordance to the Bible* (Nashville, TN: Thomas Nelson, 1981), 966.

5 Charlotte Childress and Harriet Childress, *Clueless at the Top: While the Rest of Us Turn Elsewhere for Life, Liberty, and Happiness* (Fort Bragg, CA: Cypress House, 2005), 2.

6 John Perkins, *Confessions of an Economic Hit Man* (San Francisco: Berrett-Koehler, 2004), xii.

7 Anthony Lappe, "Meet 'The Family'," *Guerilla News Network*, www.alternet.org/story/16167/ (accessed June 13, 2003).

8 Robert Young, *Young's Analytical Concordance to the Bible* (Nashville: Thomas Nelson, 1981), 49, 792.

1

History . . . Herstory

My Father's World

This is my Father's world
And what a state it's in
The jets take flight in dark of night
To rout out "evil men"

This techno-lethal game
To shock and awe the theme
Who gave the right to cause this blight
On earth and living things?

The God of grace and truth
Is blamed by men provoked
Whose thirst for power has seized the hour
While children's embers smoke

These men who never face
Themselves the fatal loss
Their sons deferred, their lives preserved
At other families' cost

'Twas never meant to be
This dominion travesty
To bring forth life instead of strife
Is our true destiny

This is my Father's world
Of warring and disgrace
It's not too late to heal the hate
As mothers take their place

And as the women rise
We'll make a different choice
The wisdom of all mothers' love
To every child gives voice

In partnerships of power
To balance we are called
Let justice guide instead of pride
To find the good for all

A new day we'll then see
Our God will not forsake
Behold the light, new eyes, new sight
New courage we will take

One day we'll live in peace
A little child will lead
With hearts renewed, our faith will prove
How love has sown the seed

Paula

In February 2003, my son and I traveled on a drafty school bus with friends to San Francisco to protest the planned invasion of Iraq. We made signs and marched and sang. We later realized that people like us were standing up to have their voices heard all over the world, but to no avail. After years of supporting Saddam Hussein, then causing the deaths of countless Iraqis through U.S.-imposed sanctions, our government was moving forward with plans to attack under the false pretense of finding weapons of mass destruction. The people in charge, it seemed, had no sense of the futility and madness of war. (Or perhaps they had all too clear a sense of the profits of war.) At the protest, a friend of mine displayed a poster reading, "You can bomb the world into pieces but you can't bomb it into peace." Another more graphic sign we saw that day said, "Bombing for peace is like fucking for virginity."

As those bombs began to drop I wrote this poem in my anger and frustration. All I could think was this: Who do these men think they are? When are the mothers of the world going to say, "enough"? When will we mobilize nonviolent ways to resolve conflict? It seemed a world devoid of the collaborative wisdom and peacemaking leadership of women. Indeed, throughout the world the voices and needs of women are often disregarded. As a woman of incredible privilege in the United States who has been silent too long, I must raise my voice to say, "Together, we can find better ways, as women wake up and stand up."

The administration has justified this attack in defense of "freedom loving people." The U.S. Constitution still ensures freedom of speech, and the Christian church preaches freedom in Christ, but Christian fundamentalist women are far from free. In their families and churches, they look for spiritual guidance and support for their life's direction; instead, they find debilitating control and domination. Holy writings are used to rationalize this repression. Religious leaders create narrow interpretations, declare them the word of God, and insist that these beliefs should never be questioned or changed. Doctrine becomes fixed and static, not adapting to changing times and needs, no longer subject to natural and organic processes of development and growth, inoculated from ongoing reformation. Women remain limited in their expression, incarcerated by the regulation of dogma.

Why are these hierarchical structures still so powerfully promoted within so much of Christianity when they are clearly unjust and, in fact, deadly to women and other living things? What exactly is the fundamentalist church teaching to and about women? What beliefs prevent women from living free and fully expressed lives, as intellectually, emotionally, sexually, and spiritually integrated human beings?

The fundamentalist church continues to treat women as the inferior, incomplete, invisible gender. Consequently, new interpretations of the Bible are as essential today as in 1895, when Elizabeth Cady Stanton's *The Woman's Bible* first appeared. In the century following the presentation of her ideas, so many changes have taken place, but there is still much to be done regarding the church's attitude toward women. Stanton's three arguments in favor of a scholarly and feminist interpretation of the Bible within the Christian church, including all its denominations, are valid still today:

1. Throughout history and especially today, the Bible is used to keep women in subjection and to hinder their emancipation.

2. Women are the most faithful believers in the Bible as the word of God. Not only for men, but also for women, the Bible has a numinous authority.

3. No reform is possible in one area of society if it is not advanced in all other areas. One cannot reform the law and other cultural institutions without reforming biblical religion, which claims the Bible as Holy Scripture. Because "all reforms are interdependent," a critical feminist interpretation is a necessary political endeavor, although it might not be opportune. If feminists think they can neglect the revision of the Bible because there are more pressing political issues, they do not recognize the political impact scripture has on churches and society — and on the lives of women.[1]

Christian fundamentalists refuse to interpret the Bible and other holy writings through the lens of history, cultural context, or woman's experience. They ignore Jesus' egalitarian treatment of women and continue to participate blindly in irresponsible and ungodly treatment of women. They continue to legitimize the domination of women. Women need to question, reevaluate, speak out against, and at times, reframe the sexist religious traditions and biblical interpretations of gender relations, which are used to limit their wholeness and wound their souls. Christian fundamentalism attempts to keep women in bondage through religious teachings and political power. Too often, women continue to cooperate with this oppression, just as they did in Stanton's day.

> The canon law, church ordinances and Scriptures, are homogeneous, and all reflect the same spirit and sentiments. These familiar texts are quoted by clergymen in their pulpits, by statesmen in the halls of legislation, by lawyers in the courts, and are echoed by the press of all civilized nations, and accepted by woman herself as "The Word of God." So perverted is the religious element in her nature, that with faith and works she is the chief support of the church and clergy; the very powers that make her emancipation impossible. ... A few of the more democratic denominations accord women some privileges, but invidious discriminations of sex are found in all religious organizations, and the most bitter outspoken enemies of woman are found among clergymen and bishops of the Protestant religion.[2]

As we study the early historical and cultural developments of what we today call Christianity, we see a thread common to most historical movements interested in reformational and revolutionary change. They are reactionary protests rooted in polarized ideology. Looking at the early developments in Judaism, Judeo–Christianity, early Christianity, and Christian fundamentalism, we can see that they developed as protests against the dominant culture around them, each rejecting the view of reality taken for granted by prior religious and sociopolitical establishments.

Early Judeo–Christian patriarchal doctrines were antithetical to even earlier origin myths, which celebrated the life-giving creativity of the female. In *The Creation of Patriarchy*, Gerda Lerner outlines "historical evidence from the fourth millennium forward derived from myths, rituals, and creation stories" wherein the "Mother–Goddess is virtually universal as the dominant figure in the most ancient stories."[3] The newer myth, developed within Judeo–Christian religious thought, reversed the form of this earlier held reality. In the common telling of the Genesis story, a male God gives birth to Adam, and Eve is birthed by the man — not from a womb, but from the man's rib. Eve's birth from a male's body altered the tradition of women's power, influence, and their essential equality.

The Christian church has used this story as evidence and justification for male power and supremacy over women and promoted this message throughout church history. As the power and influence of this patriarchal religious system grew, always equating the male gender with God, men's supremacy in everyday life became legitimized and divinely sanctioned. Men could victimize, dominate, abuse, even kill women in the name of God and in the name of righteous, divine authority. The church's burning of influential women as witches is perhaps the most blatant attack on the feminine in the name of God and male authority, while the ongoing abuse of women in the home is certainly the most persistent.

John Calvin, the French theologian so influential in the reformation, had some insight into the church's abuse of power, which he described as "unbridled tyranny":

> Scripture must be confirmed by the witness of the spirit; ... and it is a wicked falsehood that its credibility depends on the judgment of the Church. ... Scripture has its authority from God, not from the Church. ... Thus these sacrilegious men, wishing to impose an unbridled tyranny under the cover of the Church, do not care with what absurdities they ensnare themselves and others,

provided they can force this one idea upon the simpleminded: that the Church has authority in all things.[4]

Calvin held that the church, in its abuse of power and authority, had "exercised upon souls the most savage tyranny and butchery"[5] as he recognized how corrupt the church had become in its business and political influence. He condemned the church for claiming authority in the judgment of the scriptures rather than relying on the witness of the spirit. Modern Christian fundamentalism perpetuates this same tyranny.

Just as many early Judeo–Christian traditions developed in reaction to the surrounding "pagan" culture, so the emergence of Christian fundamentalism was a reaction to its environment, an evolving secular culture. Fundamentalism owes its primary beginnings to widespread nineteenth-century suspicion of and resistance to radical theological, scientific, and social changes. It roots can be found in seventeenth-century Puritanical thought, with the notion of America as a covenanted nation.[6]

A turn-of-the-century movement, fundamentalism emerged in the United States just after World War I as a reaction to perceived liberal theological thought, which touted the Bible as historically inaccurate. The movement began with a series of twelve paperback volumes of Protestant writing, *The Fundamentals*, published between 1910 and 1915 by oil millionaires, Lyman and Milton Stewart.[7] Their brand of fundamentalism was designed to carry on the "essential principles of faith" — especially the insistence on the literal truth of every word in the Bible. Christian fundamentalism, with its marriage to literalism, used the Bible not as a classic piece of literature, or even as a sacred text, but as a primary political weapon, especially against the struggle for women's rights.

Consider the assessment of Nancy Ammerman, a professor of sociology and religion at Hartford Seminary in Hartford, Connecticut, and one of the scholars on the *Fundamentalism Project*. Ammerman notes, "Fundamentalism has been most politically active and culturally visible in times following periods of major cultural unsettlement."[8] It's no wonder that an extremist religious movement rooted in the domination of women took hold at that time. Social systems were changing radically; women were gaining influence. After seventy-two years of defeat, the nineteenth Amendment finally passed in 1920, granting women the right to vote. Then came the Roaring Twenties, when women cut their hair, shortened their skirts, and started smoking and drinking alcohol in public places. This free-spirited and educated generation of young women would soon perpetuate their new ideas in educational programs promoting much more than manners and needlepoint.

Because modern Christian fundamentalism was basically a fear-based reaction to rapidly changing times, the movement easily became belligerent, attempting to outlaw the teaching of evolution in schools. In 1925, the "Scopes Monkey Trial" brought the conflict between science and religion to the legal arena. This debate is fresh again as religious conservatives today seek to promote "intelligent design" as a scientific rather than a religious theory in public school curricula.

More recently, the radical changes of the 1950s and 1960s mobilized fundamentalists to develop new strategies to defend against feminism, homosexuality, humanism, public schools, easy divorce, rock music, and women in the work force. These and other "mortal enemies of the family/forces of evil," are outlined by Tim LaHaye in his 1982 book *The Battle for the Family*.[9]

Literalism was the hallmark of Christian fundamentalists from the beginning, and continues to characterize fundamentalism today. Consider these current requirements for chartering a Mothers of Preschoolers (MOPS) group, a Christian support program for women of young children:

> Churches/parachurches and individual MOPS ministry leaders must embrace and agree on the basic, orthodox truths of the Christian faith and the essential issues of salvation. We believe the Bible is the foundation for these truths. It is God's Word, uniquely and fully inspired by the Holy Spirit, and is authoritative on all matters on which it speaks. MOPS International is committed to telling the truth of the saving work of Jesus Christ, of God's grace to mankind, of the reality of the Trinity, and the role of the Church in God's plan for the world. These foundational Christian beliefs are reflected in many of the historic church creeds.[10]

This language is quite standard and the nuances subtle. The carefully selected words — mankind, authoritative, and orthodox — reveal the intentional insensitivity to inclusiveness in language, the rigid requirement for compliance, and the bias of static literalism in the Bible and the creeds.

Walter Wink in his short book, *The Bible and Homosexuality*, warns against such "bibliolatry" as he succinctly reframes this critical issue of biblical interpretation. Rather than referring to the Bible as "authoritative on all matters on which it speaks," he calls us rather to develop:

> an interpretive theory that judges even scripture in the light of the revelation of Jesus. What Jesus gives us is a critique of

domination in all its forms, a critique that can be turned on the Bible itself. The Bible thus contains the principles of its own correction. We are freed from bibliolatry, the worship of the Bible. It is restored to its proper place as a witness to the Word of God. And that Word is a Person, not a book.[11]

Within fundamentalist systems, religious tenets are literally taken to the extreme, with members' lives becoming unbalanced. For these followers, life is a constant reaction. Contradictions, paradoxes, and life's mysteries are explained away with narrow, simplistic answers. The pain and loss of life's disappointments are minimized and interpreted as God's necessary discipline toward wayward children. Many fundamentalist leaders speak as if they alone are privileged to know precisely what God intends.

Fundamentalists, who perceive themselves as an elect group, become a subculture based on the foundational notion that they are joining Christ in a war against secular culture. They view the world through a polarized lens and consequently often respond from an antisocial position. By adhering vigilantly to their self-proclaimed "higher laws," they place themselves in a position of superiority, over and above those below. Join them and you are righteous. Question them, and you are suspect. Refuse to join — or worse, leave them — and you are fallen, evil, apostate, hell-bound.

In a 1992 article in the *International Journal for the Psychology of Religion*, Bob Altermeyer and Bruce E. Hunsberger offered this definition of fundamentalism:

1. The belief that there is one set of religious teachings that clearly contains the fundamental, basic, intrinsic, essential, inerrant truth about humanity and deity;

2. that this essential truth is fundamentally opposed by forces of evil which must be vigorously fought;

3. that this truth must be followed today according to the fundamental, unchangeable practices of the past; and

4. that those who believe and follow these fundamental teachings have a special relationship with the deity.[12]

In terms of Christian fundamentalism, we would add to the list three more distinguishing characteristics: biblical literalism, the masculinization of God, and the suppression of women. A primary target of fundamentalism is feminism itself. LaHaye has repeatedly made hostile remarks about feminists, calling them:

[A] group of radicals who claim to speak for the American woman but in truth misrepresent her and use womanhood to advance the cause of homosexuality, lesbianism, and radicalism. …Many feminists look more like blocking ends in the NFL than women. … The woman whose unfeminine feminism drives men away in her youth by making them feel insecure around her is doomed to spend her life in lonely solitude.[13]

LaHaye's wife, Beverly, founded Concerned Women for America in 1979. It is an anti-homosexual, anti-feminist think tank, which works "to protect and promote Biblical values for women and families." James Dobson, psychologist and founder of Focus on the Family, keeps up the attack against feminism. In his July 2004 newsletter article "Radical Feminism Shortchanges Boys," he writes: "The influence of feminist ideology … began to rip and tear at the fabric of the family… Not only do radical feminists tell us that men are fools, but that boys are fools too … the proponents of these misguided and harmful ideas have become social engineers who are determined to reorder the way children think."[14]

In terms of social engineering, consider the following manipulative tactics described in Focus on the Family's April 1996 newsletter. Dobson was responding to the following questions: How can Christians evangelize a society as complex and spiritually confused as North America in the 1990s? How do we break through to people here and around the world who no longer fear hell, are unconcerned about what God thinks, and even reject the existence of absolute truth or objective standards of right and wrong? "In scheduling our radio broadcasts, for example, we select highly practical topics that will interest people with no particular Christian commitment. Tucked within these discussions are elements of what we believe, although the presentation is subtle and inoffensive."[15]

Implicit in Dobson's "what we believe" are rigid fundamentalist interpretations of gender roles described as reinforcements for "marital harmony and other principles of family living from a biblical perspective," and fundamentalist parenting principles of physical discipline rooted in a power-based, domination-over philosophy, including the promotion of spanking, otherwise referred to as teaching and reinforcing the "fundamentals of child discipline." When the general public tunes in to radio broadcasts seeking to receive solid psychological and spiritual guidance, too often they receive the fundamentalist political agenda stated in the Focus on the Family mission statement: "To cooperate with the Holy Spirit in disseminating the Gospel of Jesus Christ to as many people as possible, and, specifically, to accomplish that objective by helping to pre-serve traditional values and the institution of the [traditional] family."[16]

Their new motto, Nurturing and Defending Families Worldwide, updated in April, 2005, reflects the "desire to nurture families through helpful advice and resources in areas such as parenting, discipline, and marriage, while at the same time defending the family by working to preserve the institution of traditional marriage, protect the lives of preborn babies, combat the anti-family forces in pop culture and the government, and other important issues."[17]

The brief 2005 financial report for this organization, available on the internet (and audited by Capin Crouse LLP) reports annual expenditures of $26,238,237. Seven million dollars reportedly goes to "public policy awareness."[18] Large donors to this organization include the Richard and Helen DeVos Foundation (Amway) and the Edgar and Elsa Prince Foundation. Focus on the Family's ability to wield political power not only in the U.S. but throughout the world is especially frightening in light of the following:

> Dr. Dobson is heard daily on more than 3,400 radio facilities in North America, in 15 languages, on approximately 6,300 fa-cilities in 164 countries. Dobson's estimated listening audience is over 220 million people every day, including a program transla-tion carried on all state-owned radio stations in the Republic of China. In the United States, Dobson appears on 80 television stations daily.[19]

> Our daily 30-minute radio program is the second most widely syndicated show in America. ...Our videos are shown in more public schools than in churches. ...We specialize in both the micro (helping a single mom in Ohio find the courage to face another week) and the macro (advising Congress about its family policies).[20]

This ongoing radio broadcasting into millions of homes around the world calls to mind the warning of 2 Timothy 3:5–6: "Of the same kind, too [they will keep up the outward appearance of religion but will have rejected the inner power of it], are those men who insinuate themselves into families in order to get influence." [21]

The Purpose Driven Life, or the "blueprint for Christian living" by Rick Warren, applies a more subtle approach. Many readers have joined small groups for forty-day studies of this book, creating opportunities for building community and perhaps applying peer pressure. It is important, however, to evaluate the author's underlying beliefs and presuppositions to appreciate the intentions and potential effects of such a book.

Leading up to the 2004 election, the website of the author's church revealed the following litmus tests for evaluating political candidates' voting records: abortion, stem cell research, homosexual marriage, human cloning, and euthanasia. Followers were urged to vote in accordance with Warren's "Purpose Driven Agenda."

Some issues directly under attack in this ongoing agenda are women's reproductive health and freedom, support for homosexual marriage, and the right to death with dignity. What are tacitly defended are male supremacy and the repression of feminine expression. Some of the things this book subtly shames are babies, defending oneself, valuing reason and emotion, self-reflection, dissent, and influential women in the Bible.

The book gives little or no attention to issues of justice, aid to the poor and the marginalized, protection of the environment, respect for all living things, and the defense of civil and human rights. Nothing is said about working toward eliminating violence in homes, schools, the country, and the world. The book makes no mention of living wages, adequate schools, or accessible health care. Yet Jesus' agenda was certainly driving in these alternative directions.

Of particular concern today is the movement termed *Dominionism* or *Christian Reconstruction* and what might be called a growing "theocracy" in the United States. Dominion theology is "the belief that the church is to exercise rule over every area of society, people as well as institutions, before Christ returns." Christian Reconstruction refers to "the moral obligation of Christians to recapture every institution for Jesus Christ... godly dominion will be mediated through the church."[22] Theocracy is from the Greek words *Theos*, "God" and *kratos*, "power, rule". We will not attempt to explore all the nuances of these various influences, but we do want to emphasize the domination of women as a convergence of mutual intention.

LaHaye's *Left Behind* series of apocalyptic novels gives us another glimpse into the assumptions of these theologies and their strategies for gaining influence. The Left Behind Games website reports that the books have sold over sixty-three million copies and have been translated into more than thirty languages. The Left Behind Video Game, available for $39.95 in time for Christmas 2006, invites the player to "wage physical and spiritual warfare: using the power of prayer to strengthen your troops in combat and wield modern military weaponry throughout the game world." Players may command the Tribulation Force or the AntiChrist's

Global Community Peacemakers (part of a "one world government seeking peace for all mankind").[23] Apparently, the peacemakers are the "bad guys."

The popularity of these books may help us understand why millions of Christian fundamentalists actually believe that "environmental destruction is to be welcomed — even hastened — as a sign of the coming apocalypse." In the October 2004 issue of *Grist* magazine, environmental writer Glen Scherer examined this theology:

> Christian dominion will be achieved by ending the separation of church and state, replacing U.S. democracy with a theocracy ruled by Old Testament law, and cutting all government social programs, instead turning that work over to Christian churches. Reconstructionists also would abolish government regulatory agencies, such as the U.S. EPA, because they are a distraction from their goal of Christianizing America, and subsequently, the rest of the world.[24]

George Grant, who was the executive director of Coral Ridge Ministries for many years, explained the intentions of the theocratic right in *The Changing of the Guard, Biblical Principles for Political Action:*

> Christians have an obligation, a mandate, a commission, a holy responsibility to reclaim the land for Jesus Christ — to have dominion in civil structures, just as in every other aspect of life and godliness.
>
> But it is dominion we are after. Not just a voice.
>
> It is dominion we are after. Not just influence.
>
> It is dominion we are after. Not just equal time.
>
> It is dominion we are after.
>
> World conquest. That's what Christ has commissioned us to accomplish. We must win the world with the power of the Gospel. And we must never settle for anything less. ... Thus, Christian politics has as its primary intent the conquest of the land — of men, families, institutions, bureaucracies, courts, and governments for the Kingdom of Christ.[25]

This alarming mission has taken shape through effective use of the electoral system and has gained momentum by rallying voters with hot-button issues such as abortion and gay marriage. In violation of this "holy responsibility," however, this conquest threatens to dismantle the representative democracy on which America was built. Katherine Yurica, an author, reporter, and publisher of the *Yurica Report*, has paraphrased what she calls the "four immoral principles" of the Dominionist movement:

1. Falsehoods are not only acceptable, they are a necessity. The corollary is: The masses will accept any lie if it is spoken with vigor, energy, and dedication.

2. It is necessary to be cast under the cloak of "goodness," whereas all opponents and their ideas must be cast as "evil."

3. Complete destruction of every opponent must be accomplished through unrelenting personal attacks.

4. The creation of the appearance of overwhelming power and brutality is necessary in order to destroy the will of opponents to launch opposition of any kind.[26]

The confirmation of these principles is evident in the unfolding of recent political strategy and is strangely similar to the characteristics and commandments of fundamentalist systems, as we will describe them. This ideology is seeded in the churches and homes where men, women, and children are ruthlessly indoctrinated into a shamelessly arrogant authoritarian interpretation of what ought to be honored as a sacred text.

This brief history outlines the development of the current climate of patriarchal Christianity, rigorously defended by those who would happily call themselves fundamentalists. What follows is the beginning of a story depicting the powerful and insidious way this climate can wound and diminish women. The conclusion of the story is found at the end of the book.

Eva's Dance — The Beginning

Once a baby girl was born with a dancing and singing heart. She smiled and laughed and wiggled as babies do. She danced her hands and arms and legs in the air, and after she learned to walk, she began to dance on her feet. What else is the way we move our bodies but our dance? What else is the way we express our unique selves but our song? Eva enjoyed hers immeasurably, singing and dancing freely every day.

When Eva turned three, she had a birthday party, and her mother made her a crown of purple construction paper and glitter that said "queen" — and that is exactly what Eva thought she was. She was regal, benevolent, and beautiful, and she loved wearing purple.

While queen, she heard the voice of her Fairy God Mother — no, wrong story, it was her Fair Mother God speaking to Eva's heart. "A queen you are, Eva. Dance like a queen and share your queenly goodness and remember above all that a queen must rule herself: Queen Mother advice, which Eva happily received.

Eva went to church with her family and one day started Sunday school. She loved it there. There were snacks and crafts and friends and music and flannel boards. (No dancing in those days.) She loved the pictures and the stories about Jesus, especially Jesus with children on his lap, Jesus healing, Jesus feeding the hungry, Jesus in the wilderness, Jesus welcoming Martha and Mary and all his friends, Jesus challenging the rich and powerful, Jesus living simply — Jesus, the prince of peace. She heard the voice of her Mother God affirming, "You are Jesus' friend Eva. Listen to Jesus' call to follow. Become all you are meant to be, just as Jesus did."

Eva learned to pray to "Our Father, Hallowed be thy name," and she became confused. She had never before thought of God as a man. It was the voice of her Mother God she knew. "Deliver us from evil." She shuddered to wonder what evil that might be. She sang, "Oh, be careful little hands what you do … mouth what you say … feet where you go, for the Father up above is looking down in love." She sang, "I am weak but he is strong … the Bible tells me so," and learned enough about hell to be careful to avoid every evil she could imagine.

Eva worked hard to understand. She was intuitive and perceptive, always watching, listening, and integrating. She wanted things to make sense. She wanted to make people happy. She wanted to belong. She wanted to go to heaven. The voice in her heart wasn't quite as loud, but still she could hear, "Eva, remember who you are. Keep paying attention. Keep speaking up. Remember your dance and your song."

Eva loved to wear dresses, especially purple, twirling ones. There was, however, the problem of her underwear showing. So, she wore tights; but having no hips to hold them up, she had to lift her dress to pull them up when they slipped down. This met with disapproval and shame. What was wrong with underwear showing anyway? She heard quietly from her Mother God, "Keep on twirling, Eva. Your body is beautiful. Your dance is exquisite." Some mothers think everything their children do is precious.

Eva saw a performance of dance students one day and longed to be part of a dancing show. Her parents were concerned about what the church people might think about her dancing, so they didn't arrange for dance classes. So, Eva did most of her dancing in private. Besides, her parents were quite busy with her brothers' sporting activities. She took piano lessons, but made a lot of mistakes at recitals. She could barely hear the soft voice saying, "Your performance need not be perfect, Eva. Just keep dancing and making music, and invite others into their own music and their own dance. Each person's expression is to be treasured."

In church, in school, and at home, Eva began to notice that boys were given more respect for their ideas and initiative as well as more privileges. In school, she could tell it would be better not to be too bright or to sparkle too much if she wanted to fit in. In language, the preference for males was clear. Often "people" were referred to as "men." At times that meant just men; other times, it meant both men and women. It was very confusing, but she tried hard to sort it out right. All the language about God seemed to suggest that God was a man, and in her church only men had authority. They had all the important jobs — except, of course, the really important job: teaching Sunday school. Women usually did that. That's where Eva kept learning those stories about Jesus, how much he loved children and loved to tell the truth and was never afraid to speak up, even to people in power.

In school, Eva learned about the sciences. She began to wonder about the seven-day creation story. When she asked how her new understanding of science fit in with the stories of the Bible, she was encouraged not to think about it too much. She should just believe the words of the Bible and realize that to have faith was to believe in what one could not understand or explain. It was a simple answer for such a complex concept. Eva gradually put aside her questions, accepted the answers she was given, and looked for guidance in the Bible. She heard the faintest whisper of her Mother God saying, "Where are you, Eva? I can hardly see your dance, or hear your song, or recognize your voice." Mothers know when their children are slipping away. But Eva could see no other way to go or to be. She loved her family and her church and she wanted to belong, so she paid careful attention and followed the rules and expectations very well.

Before long, Eva developed into a young woman. She got hips, so tights were less of a problem, and by then girls had permission to wear pants. But she also got breasts, and there was a lot of attention about those. She was reminded to keep them covered up as much as possible so she wouldn't bother boys and men. She began to feel bad about her breasts, and she wore baggy clothes to hide her discomfort and fear. Her dance became awkward and inhibited. She stopped wearing purple. She listened to the little bits of information she could get about her budding sexuality, summed up in the phrase, "Just say no." She did the best she could. She couldn't hear the voice any more, and she paid little attention to the world at large. Without even knowing, she had given in to the powers above her.

Eva didn't feel like a queen anymore, but she tried hard to fit in with her church and Christian youth programs. She read her Bible every day and memorized lots of verses. She told her friends they must believe in Jesus or go to hell. She forgot most of what she used to know about dancing and being a queen. She forgot about making music in her heart. She could hardly remember having her own voice and thinking for herself. She had lost the confidence to offer her own gifts and wisdom to the world.

Notes

1 Elisabeth Schüssler Fiorenza, *In Memory of Her: A Feminist Theological Reconstruction of Christian Origins* (New York: Crossroad, 1987), 12.

2 Elizabeth Cady Stanton, *The Woman's Bible* (New York: European Publishing, 1898), 8, 13.

3 Gerda Lerner, *The Creation of Patriarchy* (New York: Oxford University Press, 1986), 147-148.

4 John Calvin, *Institutes of the Christian Religion* (Louisville, KY: Westminster John Knox, 1559/1977), 74-75.

5 Ibid., 1179.

6 George M. Marsden, "Defining American Fundamentalism," in *The Fundamentalist Phenomenon: A View From Within, A Response From Without*, ed. Norman J. Cohen, 22-37 (Grand Rapids, MI: Eerdmans, 1990).

7 Don Lattin, "Apocalypse Now?" *Common Boundary* (May/June 1996), 32-38.

8 Ibid.

9 Tim LaHaye, *The Battle for the Family* (Grand Rapids, MI: Revell, 1982), 26-27.

10 Mothers of Preschoolers...Because Mothering Matters, "Faith Position Statement," www.mops.org/page.php?pageid=79&srctype=linklist&src=78.

11 Walter Wink, *Homosexuality and the Bible* (New York: Fellowship Publications, 2003), 13. www.forusa.org/articlesandresources/wink-homosexuality.html.

12 Bob Altermeyer and Bruce E. Hunsberger, "Authoritarianism, Religious Fundamentalism, Quest, and Prejudice," *International Journal for the Psychology of Religion* 2 (1992): 113-133.

13 Tim LaHaye, *The Battle for the Family* (Grand Rapids, MI: Revell, 1982), 140-145.

14 James Dobson, "Radical Feminism Shortchanges Boys," *Focus on the Family*, www.family.org/docstudy/newsletters/a0032398.cfm (accessed July 2004).

15 James Dobson, *Focus on the Family Newsletter* (April 1996): 3. www.family.org/welcome/aboutfof/a0005554.cfm.

16 James Dobson, *Focus on the Family Newsletter* (April 1996): 3. www.family.org/welcome/aboutfof/a0005554.cfm.

17 Focus on the Family, "What is focus on the family's motto?" http://family.custhelp.com/cgi-bin/family.cfg/php/enduser/std_adp.php?p_faqid=22397&p_created=1116430029&p_sid=kTdcElsi&p_accessibility=0&p_lva=22397&p_sp=cF9zcmNoPTEmcF9zb3J0X2J5PSZwX2dyaWRzb3J0PSZwX3Jvd19jbnQ9M-SZwX3Byb2RzPSZwX2NhdHM9JnBfcHY9JnBfY3Y9JnBfcGFnZT0xJnBfc2VhcmNoX3RleHQ9bW90dG8*&p_li=&p_topview=126 : www.focusaction.org/pdfs/FOFA_2005_AnnualReport.pdf

18 Capin Crouse LLC, "Annual Report 2005," Focus on the Family Action, Inc., www.focusaction.org/pdfs/FOFA_2005_AnnualReport.pdf (accessed January 26, 2007).

19 Right Wing Watch, "Right Wing Organizations: Focus on the Family," People for the American Way, www.pfaw.org/pfaw/general/default.aspx?oid=4257.

20 James Dobson, *Focus on the Family Newsletter* (Colorado Springs, CO: Focus on the Family, April 1996): 1, 5, 6.

21 All biblical references will be from the *New Jerusalem Bible* (Doubleday, 1990); any references to Kingdom of God will appear as God's domination-free order.

22 H. Wayne House and Thomas Ice, *Dominion Theology: Blessing or Curse?* (Portland, OR: Multnomah, 1988), 418-419.

23 Left Behind Games, Home Page, Left Behind Games Inc., www.leftbehindgames.com.

24 Glenn Sherer, "The Godly Must be Crazy," *Grist Environmental News & Commentary*, www.grist.org/news/maindish/2004/10/27/scherer-christian/ (accessed October 27, 2004).

25 George Grant, *The Changing of the Guard: Biblical Principles for Political Action* (Ft. Worth, TX: Dominion, 1987), 50–51.

26 Katherine Yurica, "Conquering by Stealth and Deception: How the Dominionists are Succeeding in their Quest for National Control and World Power," *Theocracy Watch*, www.theocracywatch.org/yurica_weyrich_manual.htm (accessed September 14, 2004).

2

Eve

"Eve, *Havvah* ... the mother of all who live." (Genesis 3:20)

Roberta

As a young girl, I was vibrant and carefree. My life was full of spontaneity and passion. My father endearingly referred to me as "the Bucking Bronco that needed to be tamed." Fort Lauderdale, Florida — the land of bikinis, vacations, sun, and fun — was my playground from the time I was six until I was eighteen. This parkland was the perfect setting for all sorts of adventurous explorations. In sixth grade, I tested, bent, and even on occasion, broke many rules.

Unfortunately, I consistently got caught — for smoking, for kissing, for having too much fun. My parents enrolled me in piano, tennis, and modeling courses all at the same time, hoping they might subdue my reckless spirit. They didn't — until one day, a "miracle" happened. The summer after my sophomore year at the public high school, I decided to be "born again."

During my preteen and early teen years, I had defied anybody and everybody, including my parents, school authorities, even the elders at church. Although I was unaware of why I was doing this, I knew my family was experiencing constant turmoil and stress. I felt as if there was nowhere to get the support I needed. My mother had been seriously ill for years with polycystic kidneys, and my dad's presence was minimized because of his heavy business and travel commitments. At sixteen, I found myself looking for solace, good parenting, and the extended family support a church could provide. Suddenly, much to my own surprise,

I willingly made the choice to become an active member of the conservative Protestant church that for so long I had mocked.

People from the church convinced me that my dad was right: I was a wild bronco and I desperately needed to be tamed. They told me to break all my dearly loved heathen records and listen only to Christian music. I was told to reserve my lips for God and the man I would marry someday. They admonished me to quit my successful modeling career and surrender my life fully to Jesus. Modeling, they told me, would lead me to temptation and an ungodly life. Without realizing it, I was learning that in order for me to survive, my authentic self had to die. I knew the only option for me was to settle down and become a good girl.

I especially remember a teen outing at the beach sponsored by the church. I asked some of the older Christian women what type of bathing suit I should wear. I wanted their approval. They told me to wear a one-piece suit, loose fitting, like a jumpsuit. Their description reminded me of one of those suits with a full skirt that came halfway down my thigh — the sort of suits I had seen only on senior citizens.

Before I was "born again," I'd been proud of my body. I was fit, making regular workouts at the gym a priority. Estrogen had kicked in, and my girlish body had developed womanly curves that attracted attention everywhere I went. This was a new experience for me, and I loved it. I was tanned from spending so much time on the beaches, prior to the days of sun block. I had always worn a bikini, though one that was modest by today's standards. When I broached the subject of wearing my old suit, I received a little lecture about "causing men to lust." I wouldn't want to be the reason some poor man "fell into sin," would I?

That night, I threw my white bikini into the garbage, feeling ashamed of myself for having worn such a skimpy suit the previous summer. Even admitting I'd owned such a sinful garment would make me suspect to the good Christian ladies of my church. From then on I became very, very careful about how I dressed. Like any teenage girl, I was obsessed with my appearance, but now my main concern was to look modest and correct. I learned to feel bad about looking good, guilty about having a fit body, ashamed of my breasts and curves, humiliated at being female.

Sin ... clothing ... my body ... men — all were somehow carelessly entangled with saving my soul. And I, a young Eve, already a temptress, already guilty of causing innocent men to sin, needed a bridle.

Eve has long been blamed for the act of original sin. In Christian tradition, Eve has been portrayed as a sensual, assertive, inquisitive woman who shamefully seduced Adam into eating from the tree of the knowledge of good and evil. For this, Eve and all women were to be punished for generations to come. Women would have to endure pain during childbirth and be dominated by their husbands. Men would have to work the soil to earn their food until they returned to the dust. The Genesis texts unfold as follows:

> God (*Elohiym*: plural of *elowahh'*; gods in the ordinary sense; but specifically used of the supreme God)[1] said, "Let us make [humans] in our own image, in the likeness of ourselves." ... God created [humans] in the image of himself, in the image of God he created him, male and female he created them. (Gen. 1:26–27)

In this first account of creation, the humans came last — after the lights and the fish and the birds and the animals and the plants. They were to be masters of all the animals, and God blessed them, saying, "Be fruitful and multiply." This creation myth outlines the classic seven-day creation story and gives a clear picture of male and female together as the image-bearers of God, the crowning glory of creation. They were authorized to be sexual and to procreate.

Following this, there is another creation myth, quite distinct from the first, beginning in Genesis 2. Of course, the first question for the literalist is, which account is to be believed? In this second story, the Lord (Yhovah: the self-existent or eternal; Jehovah, Jewish national name of God)[2] God (Elohiym) made the human first, even before there were plants or rain or anyone to till the soil. In his article "Eve and Pandora Contrasted," William E. Phipps describes how "the divine potter shapes clay and animates it by blowing breath into its nostrils." He points out that "the human" *ha-adam* was created from the earth, the definite article *ha* indicating that "adam" was not being used as a personal name. Next, the garden was created and the human was settled there with this command: "You are free to eat of all the trees in the garden. But of the tree of the knowledge of good and evil you are not to eat; for, the day you eat of that, you are doomed to die." Phipps explains,

> Realizing that solitary life and work is less than ideal, Yahweh [*Yhovah*] forms other animal species for human companionship. However, satisfaction does not arrive until a second divine experiment is completed. Simultaneously the male (ish) and the female (ishshah) are created from adam. Each sex then seeks the missing part of the divided body. Soon the naked male and female rejoin and "become one flesh."[3]

In this divine experiment, the Hebrew word interpreted as rib, *tsela*, suggests not just a bone, but a portion, as in a side of flesh or a plank or even a chamber. Apparently, the feminine dimension of this being was removed and the tender flesh wound closed up. A remnant of the feminine remained, however, in the genetic code. Every cell of a male bears an X chromosome along with the male determining Y. The new being was built (*banah*) into an XX creature of the selfsame bones and same tender flesh and the two were not disappointed or confused (*buwsh*).

Now the snake (the serpent), "the most subtle of all the wild animals," asked the woman, "Did God really say you were not to eat from any of the trees in the garden?" She, having been present as part of the composite human when the command was given, explained about the tree in the middle of the garden, clarifying that God had said,

> You must not eat it, nor touch it, under pain of death." Then the snake said to the woman, "No! You will not die! God knows in fact that the day you eat it your eyes will be opened and you will be like gods, knowing good from evil." The woman saw that the tree was good to eat, and pleasing to the eye, and that it was enticing for the wisdom that it could give. So she took some of its fruit and ate it. She also gave some to her husband *who was with her* and he ate it. Then the eyes of both of them were opened and they realized that they were naked. (Genesis 3:3-7; emphasis added)

The man, who was with her, had not participated in the conversation. After addressing what had been done, God sentenced the snake to life on its belly and the humans to their respective labors. Then "the man named his wife 'Eve' because she was the mother of all those who live." God made clothes for them of animal skins and said, "Now that the [humans have] become like one of us in knowing good from evil, [they] must not be allowed to reach [their hands] and pick from the tree of life too, and eat and live forever!" So, they were sent forth from the garden with no further access to the tree of life. Eve, and Adam with her, chose divinity; they chose the wisdom of knowing good from evil and the mortality that would eventually come with that, over their naked garden-variety life with free access to the tree of eternal life.

Of course, this is not the way we, or our children, have heard the story. As a myth, this story can be considered in many ways. It explores the questions of where we came from, why we die, why life is hard, why labor is painful. What does it mean that no children came until after the exodus? Had Adam and Eve been in the garden for just a moment or for a millennium? Did Eve's choice actually usher in the fullness of human experience even as she and Adam became "like gods"? Could the fruit have been a metaphor for the fruit of the womb as Eve ventured first into the consciousness-raising experience of mothering through the death experience of giving birth? Why did Adam say nothing in the conversation with the serpent, and then say that Eve was to blame? Was he even blaming, or was he giving credit? (Genesis 3:12) Clearly the writer of Genesis did not frame Eve as more to blame than Adam.

Furthermore, the snake is a curious element in the story, considering the animal's mythical association with the feminine: the womb that sheds its lining each month is a reflection of the snake's shedding of its skin. Lerner suggests that "in the historical context of the time of the writing of Genesis, the snake was clearly associated with the fertility goddess and symbolically represented her."[4] "[A]t the dawn of civilization the snake was a positive symbol of feminine energy ... a beneficient, vital creature intimately associated with feminine sexuality, and, by extension, with life," adds Leonard Schlain in *The Alphabet Versus the Goddess*.[5] The snake curiously appears again in Exodus and in the New Testament: "As Moses lifted up the snake in the desert, so must the son of man be lifted up (John 3:10)." What exactly might Jesus' association with the snake suggest?

This pregnant tale affirms the richness of what the story offers, as we are invited to wonder on the mystery for ourselves without being told what we must believe it means. When this invitation into the mystery is rejected, this second myth of creation solidifies into the Christian theologies of original sin, Satan as the snake, woman as the temptress, all women as subordinate, and hell as punishment for sin, although only death and leaving the garden are mentioned in the texts (Genesis 2:17, 3:3, 3:24).

As a result of this theological perspective, Eve-like qualities would be forever suspect. By blaming and taming women, pious Christians would vainly attempt to reenter the garden. If only Eve — and consequently, all women — were more submissive, less questioning, less daring, and less thirsty for knowledge. If only she — and all women — were less autonomous. If only she — and all women — weren't so curious and desirous, humanity might not have fallen and the world would not be in such a mess. If only Adam, like a good Promise Keeper, had kept a tighter rein on his wife. If only he were more of a leader in the relationship, and she — along with all other women — more compliant, we would all be experiencing the bliss of the garden today. If only ...

After Genesis 4, Eve is not mentioned again in the Hebrew scriptures except in the apocryphal book of Ecclesiasticus. In 25:24-26 we read,

"Sin began with a woman and thanks to her we must all die. Do not let ... a spiteful woman give free rein to her tongue. If she will not do as you tell her, get rid of her." The persistent blaming of Eve in the church tradition began early, as reflected in this writing from Tertullian, one of the early framers of Christian orthodoxy, around 190 CE:

> And do you not know that you are an Eve? The sentence of God on this sex of yours lives in this age; the guilt must of necessity live too. You are the devil's gateway ... the first deserter of the divine law; you are she who persuaded him whom the devil was not valiant enough to attack. You destroyed so easily God's image, man. On account of your desert — that is, death, even the Son of God had to die.[6]

Augustine (354-430 CE), Western Christendom's most influential theologian, wrote "Whether it is in a wife or a mother, it is still Eve the temptress that we must beware of in any woman."[7]

In a sixteenth-century church report, used to justify the execution of witches we read: "Woman is more carnal than man: there was a defect in the formation of the first woman, since she was formed with a bent rib. She is imperfect and thus always deceives. Witchcraft comes from carnal lust. Women are to be chaste and subservient to men."[8]

Separatist Rev. John Robinson (1575-1625) gave this description: "[T]he Pilgrims in Plymouth, Massachusetts, for instance, enjoined a "reverend subjection" of the wife to her husband, adding that she must not shake off the bond of submission, but must bear patiently the burden, which God hath laid upon the daughters of Eve."[9]

As recently as 1966, William Barker, in his book *Everyone in the Bible*, echoed similar sentiments about Eve, placing on her the entire responsibility for trouble in the world.

> Her name in Hebrew means "life-giving," and she was named "Eve" because she was the mother of all living men. ... Eve rebelled against God and put her own plans and wisdom ahead of God's. Her disobedience triggered Adam's, and produced the chain reaction of anxiety and guilt in every person, and the estrangement between man and God, man and woman, brothers, nations and races, that continues to this day.[10]

Despite the passing of time, Christian fundamentalism remains obsessed with the central belief that woman is not just tempted but, like the snake, a temptress. Fundamentalists are still preaching the same sermon that the early church fathers did: that sin and death entered the world by means of a woman. They are quick to agree that the fall of humanity was Eve's fault. The following comments come from an article entitled "God and the Genesis of Gender: The Trustworthy Biblical Design of Man and Woman" by Folke T. Olofsson. It was published in *Touchstone* magazine in September 2001 and reprinted on the website of the Council on Biblical Manhood and Womanhood as a resource for pastors.

> It is not possible to understand the Christian view of man's grandeur and misery if one does not focus on Mary, the Mother of God, as contrasted with Eve. Mary is the representative of mankind, as is also Eve, and in a human sense, Mary reverses the disobedience of the Fall. She is more like Christ and unlike Eve when she does not try to grasp equality with God on her own terms… [Eve] did not accept her position in the God-given hierarchy; she perverted her role as a helper by luring her husband to transgress God's command and thereby brought ruin upon herself and mankind.[11]

Within Christianity, female sexuality, sinfulness, and death all merged, justifying religious customs rooted in the domination of women. Eve was the origin of the church fathers' fear and hatred of women; she became identified with death. Her identification with birth was taken away, and the creation of life credited to the Father God. The Virgin Mary has become an anti-Eve, one not tainted by sin. Mary was portrayed by the early church as the favored woman, hand-picked by God. Mary would be the passive vessel miraculously penetrated by God, used to birth the sinless male savior who would forever remind the world that maleness, not femaleness, was the source of life.

Through the centuries, Christian theology has portrayed women as temptresses, the descendants of Eve, the inheritors of a wicked, seductive sensuality that could only be tempered through subordination to strong men. Women continue to be depicted as weak creatures, easily prone to deception. Although she is known as the first woman and the "mother of all who live," the church has chosen to emphasize Eve's role as a rebellious woman who defied God and tempted man, representing how good women ought not to act. Her bold, autonomous pursuit of consciousness and knowledge has been interpreted and condemned by the Christian church as sinful, shameful, deceptive, even eve-il. Thus, she represents Christianity's archetypal woman, the temptress in need of reform. Eve and all the wild women who followed would have to be trained in appropriately womanly tasks, drilled in what they should say and how they should say it. They would learn obedience, chastity, meekness, and subordination to the male of the species.

Many biblical passages that seem to recommend restraints upon women are thought to have been written by the apostle Paul. The challenges of these texts are highlighted in 2 Peter: "Our brother Paul, who is so dear to us ... wrote to you with the wisdom he was given... In all his letters there are of course some passages which are hard to understand, and these are the ones that uneducated and unbalanced people distort, in the same way as they distort the rest of scripture" (2 Peter 3:15–16).

In her book *Sexual Shame: An Urgent Call to Healing*, Karen McClintock explores further the challenges of Paul's teachings:

> The apostle Paul's writings tended to confuse the church on issues of sexuality and spirituality. For example, Paul considered that love of Christ must always preempt sexual love and that the two were opposed to one another. Thanks to Paul and the early church fathers, a dualism arose that claimed that love of God and human sexual love were incompatible. They taught that holiness required reining in one's sexual desire, thereby pitting a life of faith against a life of active sexual expression. Dualism focused on the fall as the source of sexual lust and cited the virgin birth as proof that women chosen by God are to be pure, chaste virgins. Dualism also used the celibacy of Paul and Jesus as proof that the renunciation of sex is the only way of life that pleases God and that those who engage in sex sink to an inferior spiritual level. Paul's contribution to the issue of sexual shame cannot be denied. His writings reinforced slavery and racial injustice and limited women's voices in the church for thousands of years. His words now reinforce the dominant culture's bent toward shame. Only when Paul is seen as a man struggling with his own sexuality in light of his commitment to serving the church do we manage to set his comments in context and understand them fully.[12]

Only once in the New Testament does the blaming of Eve over Adam occur. It appears in 1 Timothy and is attributed to Paul, but it may have been written decades after his death . It says, "I give no permission for a woman to teach or to have authority over a man. A woman ought to be quiet, because Adam was formed first and Eve afterwards, and it was not Adam who was led astray but the woman who was led astray and fell into sin" (1 Timothy 2:13–14).

Don Williams, in *The Apostle Paul and Women in the Church*, in his evaluation of this text, points out that although Eve had "priority in deception (2:13,14), this is erased in 2:15: ... 'Yet she will be saved by the childbearing (or the birth of the child)' ... all women are united corporately to Eve in redemption."[13]

Even more to the point is Rosemary Radford Reuther's scholarly interpretation of this passage: "The teachings of 1 Timothy about women keeping silence appear, not as the uniform position of the New Testament church, but as a second-generation reaction against widespread participation of women in leadership, teaching, and ministering in first-generation Christianity."[14]

Eve is maligned once again in I Corinthians 11:3. "But I am afraid that, just as the snake with his cunning seduced Eve, your minds may be led away from single-minded devotion to Christ." Again, in looking at the Old Testament passages with new eyes, religion professor Kang-Yup Na rather describes her as the first decision maker, "an observing, thinking, deliberating and deciding moral agent" who "freely explores the divinely given power to think and choose."[15]

Once, Eve lived as the woman who moved with the wind. Now mute, she stands as a symbolic mannequin, frozen in time for all womankind. Her story, told from generation to generation, is designed to bridle young girls and grown women. The voice others have given her speaks of the destruction and the curse that will befall a woman who acts freely in a self-chosen, spontaneous manner. Even today, her story delivers a familiar message: It was the woman's fault. She gave me of the tree. She is the temptress responsible for my actions. She is the temptress in need of control. She is the woman worthy of punishment.

Eve's story has been sexualized into "the woman who caused the man to lust." The story, promoted throughout the centuries, leaves in its trail the unmistakable aroma of a woman who, following her wild, earthy, animal instincts, asserted herself and exercised her female power and inquisitiveness. Like inquiring women who have walked in her footsteps, Eve found herself not only doomed to eternal exile but held accountable for damning others as well.

Christian women and men alike have stood in awe of her, secretly admiring her power to act boldly in the face of God and man. And yet, we have been taught to fear her, for she is the first independent woman. Her crime? Self-expression and self-determination: a testimonial for all. She was a woman courageous and powerful enough to assert herself in the face of pure, male authority.

Christianity has hallmarked Eve as the archetypal female in order to send a message to any daring woman: if you even consider acting on your own power or equating yourself with that seductress Eve, there will be hell to pay. And hell, in fundamentalists' culture, is a heinous reality. The church will make life hell on earth for the woman who defies its law, and then assures her an eternal afterlife in hell as well, where there will be weeping, wailing, and gnashing of teeth. Eve is portrayed as the sexually powerful female. The poor, innocent male, Adam, becomes a passive participant in evil due to woman's godlike powers of seduction, capable of rendering him impotent and powerless to act. Her power is, at the same time, secretly revered and feared.

In the fundamentalist subculture, man and his needs are central. Both the woman and her sexuality are to be man's possessions. Women exist as creatures for men's pleasure and domination. And yet, when the woman brings this dichotomy to light and the unspoken agenda becomes transparent, the woman is the one shamed and judged, labeled the harlot, the impure woman, the seductress.

This contradictory response to Eve's desired yet feared sexuality fragments women. As a result, the individual woman's perception of her own sexuality is replete with internal contradictions, confusion, and conflict. The fundamentalist woman is expected to play out these binding sexual twists. As case studies throughout this book will illustrate, she is told to be seductive yet innocent, attractive yet invisible, titillating yet tame. Women are expected to take their place willingly under men as submissive, secondary creatures, believing their personhood (including their sexuality) is divinely designed for man's domination and control. In fact, according to biblical scholar R.C. Sproul, "[T]he general principle is that a woman is to bend over backwards to defer to the leadership and authority of her husband. She is not free to disobey simply because she disagrees or because she finds herself inconvenienced by what the husband requires."[16]

Fundamentalism glorifies the Good Woman role, as opposed to Eve, who symbolizes what every good woman should *not* be. Eve's sin, was a compound of self-assertion, curiosity, and intuition. She did not act as a man's inferior or possession. She behaved as if her life (and, by extension, her body) was hers to control. She assumed equality with Adam (encouraging him to eat the fruit and gain knowledge with her). She acted independently in strength, trusting her own perceptions. Wishing to gain knowledge, she was brave, authentic, and willing to rebel, or at least to disregard an edict she could not abide.

The Good Woman role demands that a woman live out her life in pain and sorrow. She must recreate herself in ways that promote falsehood, fragmentation, and isolation, ultimately separating her from the truth of her soul. Internally disillusioned and confused — and most likely mildly depressed — she blames herself for her emotional state. Many adult women struggle to feel the freedom and wholeness that were destroyed when they were younger. For a fundamentalist Christian man, life is a great journey, a challenge. For a fundamentalist Christian woman, life is a box. This condition is the tragic and sad fate of all Eves.

The most confusing message the Christian fundamentalist church preaches to women is this: "You are Eve. Be not Eve." As seed of her seed, flesh of her flesh, and daughters of the mother of all who live, how can we not have her blood running through us? How can we not be her? The church, even today, reminds us that as females we are inferior, we are shameful; we are deceivers; we are Eves. The irony is that we are taught not to be like Eve, yet she exists within each and every one of us when we are curious, when we are sexual, when we are creative. Therefore, when we aspire as women not to be like her, we are cut off from a primary source of our womanly power, from a deep part of ourselves — that instinctively daring, aggressive, and autonomous woman that exists in each of us.

As it is told in Christian fundamentalist circles, the creation myth has one primary theme: Eve, the bad woman, induced humanity's fall. Could it be that Eve's partaking of the fruit was her attempt to birth and create knowledge for all, within a patriarchal system wherein only men could create? Let us imagine for a moment that when Eve partook of the fruit of the tree of the knowledge of good and evil, her choice was actually one in favor of self-growth and self-consciousness for all; that somewhere within her intuitive, instinctual self she knew her autonomous action would yield knowledge and growth — not only for herself, but for all generations to come.

We suggest that Eve's biting of that juicy fruit stands as an invitation to all women to disbelieve, even to disobey, the rules of the script as an act of faith into the unknown. Eve's actions metaphorically represent the option to doubt and discover, to come out on the other side, a conscious and evolved woman.

Like Eve, Jesus also modeled authentic freedom apart from the law and convention that was radical in his time. He broke Sabbath laws, allowing his disciples to pick and eat ears of corn (heads of grain) when they were hungry (Matthew 12:1–8). He broke the purity laws by touching lepers and eating with outcasts (Mark 1:40, 2:15). He broke up money-changing tables and business as usual (Matthew 21:12–13). His responses to women were repeatedly and radically non-hierarchical, as when he affirmed Mary's role as disciple (Luke 10:38–42).[17]

Jesus described himself as the "son of the man" (*ho huios tou anthropou*) who came eating and drinking. (Luke 7:34) This odd Greek idiomatic phrase, which means "human being" or "child of the human," is one Jesus repeatedly used to refer to himself. Walter Wink, in *The Human Being: Jesus and the Enigma of the Son of the Man*, explores this phraseology as it is used throughout the Bible. He holds that "the 'son of the man' functioned as a catalyst for personal and social transformation." Among other conclusions, he describes the value of encountering Jesus "to be delivered from a stunted soul, a limited mind, and an unjust social order."[18]

"The wind blows where it pleases, you can hear its sound, but you cannot tell where it comes from or where it is going. So it is with everyone who is born of the Spirit." (John 3:8)

Being "born of the Spirit" implies fluidity, unpredictability, free-formness. These words of Jesus remind us that leading a truly spirit-filled life is as unchartable as where the wind blows — a life lived by faith rather than by prescription. Through their autonomy and authenticity, both Jesus and Eve brought enlightenment and a new consciousness to their respective audiences. As a mythical mentor, Eve did not act based on the literalism of God's command; as a historical figure, Jesus did not act according to the literalism of his day. In *The Powers That Be*, Wink notes, "In his subversive proclamation of a new order in which domination will give way to compassion and communion, Jesus brought to fruition the prophetic longing for the 'kingdom of God' — an expression we might paraphrase as God's domination-free order."[19]

Both Eve and Jesus (as the protagonists of their own stories) disobeyed the law of the land and consequently redefined the possibilities. In fact, both acted in opposition to external authority, judging for themselves what was true, and both threatened the religious and the social order. Both affirmed a spiritual practice that empowered women and brought conscious knowledge to all who were willing to partake. Through their liberating acts, both aroused the fierce antagonism of men, and ultimately, both were banished from their communities. Within Christian fundamentalism, the man, Jesus, in spite of his disobedience, became the hero. But the woman, Eve, because of her disobedience, became the outlaw, identified for all time as temptress.

As with nearly all consciousness-raising experiences, Eve's independent choice ruined the imagined bliss of the garden, altering idyllic perceptions about what should be — instead bringing to light what is. Perhaps that's why fundamentalists loathe her so. She unveiled the fundamentalist illusion that divinity is gained as humanity is denied and displayed that it is in the pursuit of self-knowledge and self-growth that one truly meets God. Eve demonstrated — as did Jesus — that divinity is incarnated as humanity is embraced. Partaking of the fruit brought awareness to the nakedness of their humanness. That nakedness brought them closer to their own sacredness, their vulnerability, their God-likeness, the divinity in their humanity (just as the snake said it would).

We declare it good that Eve was curious. Acting as an independent, intuitive thinker, her display of courage brought knowledge and awareness both to herself and to all humanity. With this action came individuation and maturation. Expanding consciousness, much like labor, is a painful experience, yet painful experiences can often give birth to a blessing. Eve's eating of the fruit was a blessing. We acknowledge and reclaim her as a mentor and suggest that aspects of her essence are heard consistently in women's diverse voices. Eve's spirit needs re-imagining in today's culture — she communicates a universal spiritual wisdom to women. Eve, the mother of all who live, desires to nurture all of her daughters, to impart empowering spiritual and practical truths, plucked from the tree of knowledge.

Notes

1 Strongs Hebrew Bible Dictionary; Bible Software by johnhurt.com http://www.htmlbible.com/

sacrednamebiblecom/kjvstrongs/STRHEB4.htm#S430

2 Strongs Hebrew Bible Dictionary; Bible Software by johnhurt.com http://www.htmlbible.com/

sacrednamebiblecom/kjvstrongs/STRHEB30.htm#S3068

3 William E. Phipps, "Eve and Pandora Contrasted," *Theology Today* 45, No.1 (April 1988): 35.

4 Gerda Lerner, *The Creation of Patriarchy* (New York: Oxford University Press, 1986), 196.

5 Leonard Schlain, *The Alphabet Versus the Goddess* (New York: Penguin Putnam, 1998), 54.

6 Vern L. Bullough, *The Subordinate Sex* (Chicago: University of Illinois Press, 1973), 114.

7 Augustine. *The Literal Meaning of Genesis, Vol. II, Book 11.* (New York: Newman, 1982), 176.

8 Merlin Stone, *When God was a Woman* (San Diego: Harcourt Brace Jovanovich, 1976), 227-228.

9 Randall Balmer, "American Fundamentalism: The Ideal of Femininity," in *Fundamentalism & Gender*, ed. John Stratton Hawley, 49 (New York: Oxford University Press, 1994).

10 William P. Barker, *Everyone in the Bible* (Grand Rapids, MI: Revell, 1966), 103.

11 Folke T. Oloffson, The Council on Biblical Manhood and Womanhood, "God and the Genesis of Gender: The Trustworthy Biblical Design of Man and Woman," *Touchstone Magazine*, www.cbmw.org/resources/articles/genesis_gender. php (accessed September 2001).

12 Karen McClintock, *Sexual Shame: An Urgent Call to Healing* (Minneapolis: Fortress, 2001), 64.

13 Don Williams, *The Apostle Paul and Women in the Church* (Los Angeles: BIM, Inc., 1977), 113.

14 Elizabeth Langland and Walter Grove, eds., *A Feminist Perspective in the Academy* (Chicago: University of Chicago Press, 1983), 56.

15 Kang-Yup Na, "About Eve..." *Presbyterians Today* (September, 2006): 42.

16 R.C. Sproul, "Christian Submission: Eph. 5:21-33," *The Purpose of God: Ephesians* (Fearn, Scotland: Christian Focus Publications, September 2002); www.cbmw.org/resources/articles/christian_submission.php.

17 Marcus Borg, *Meeting Jesus Again for the First Time* (New York: HarperCollins, 1994), 57.

18 Walter Wink, *The Human Being: Jesus and the Enigma of the Son of the Man* (Minneapolis: Augsburg Fortress, 2002), 16, 22.

19 Walter Wink, *The Powers That Be: Theology for a New Millennium* (Minneapolis: Augsburg Fortress, 1998), 64.

3
Light for the World

"Arise, shine out, for your light has come." (Isaiah 60:1)

"You are light for the world." (Matthew 5:14)

"The lamp of the body is the eye. It follows that if your eye is clear, your whole body will be filled with light. But if your eye is diseased, your whole body will be darkness. If then, the light inside you is darkened, what darkness will that be?" (Matthew 6:22–23)

"See to it then that the light inside you is not darkness. If therefore, your whole body is filled with light, and not darkened at all, it will be light entirely, as when the lamp shines on you with its rays."
(Luke 11:35, 36)

Each of the next seven chapters will examine (1) the *characteristics* of fundamentalist systems; (2) the associated unwritten *commandments* used to control women; and (3) the opportunities for the *creation* of new thinking, behaving, and living the resurrection. Each creation is rooted in Jesus' teaching of God's domination-free order for the kindling of the light within. Each chapter will end with some ideas for movement and dance that will help to explore the concepts in body (incarnate) experience.

What does it mean that we are to be light for the world? In her book *Beyond Belief*, biblical scholar Elaine Pagels examines the image of light in the Gospel of Thomas:

> God created us in the image of the primordial light. Like many other readers of Genesis, Thomas suggests that what appeared in the primordial light was "a human being, very marvelous," a being

of radiant light, the prototype of the human Adam, whom God created on the sixth day. This "light Adam," although human in form, is simultaneously in some mysterious way also divine. Thus Jesus suggests here that we have spiritual resources within us precisely because we were made "in the image of God," ... hidden within each of us, secretly linking God and all humankind.[1]

Jesus himself appears as a light image in Revelation 1:12–16. The writer describes hearing a loud voice and turning to see a radiant vision of "one like a son of man, dressed in a long robe," with a face "like the sun shining with all its force." Later in Revelation 4:1–3, the writer sees a door open in heaven and hears the same voice, then sees flashes of lightning coming from a throne encircled by a rainbow. The rainbow in Genesis 9:12–16 represents the "sign of the covenant ... between me and the earth ... between myself and you and every living creature, in a word, all living things. ... When the bow is in the clouds I shall see it and call to mind the eternal covenant between God and every living creature on earth, that is all living things." This vivid symbolism and imagery of light, color, sun, lightning, and covenant awakens our wonder about the nature and interplay of humanity, divinity, and the physical world.

In imagining ourselves as light, a lamp, a candle, or fire for the world, we might visualize the spectrum of refracted light as a color overlay for the body. Each color rests on a physio-spiritual energy center, or *chakra*, of the body that also correlates to one or more of the glands of the endocrine system. According to Dr. Richard Gerber: "The endocrine glands are part of a powerful master control system that affects the physiology of the body from the level of cellular gene activation on up to the functioning of the central nervous system. The chakras are thus able to affect our moods and behavior through hormonal influences on brain activity."[2]

"*Chakra* is a Sanskrit word from ancient India that means 'wheel' or 'disk' or 'spinning vortex.' A chakra is a place of intersection and can be any coming together of energy forces, be it a fingertip, a flower bud, a spiral galaxy or a traffic jam."[3]

To enhance awareness of our body and spirit we will use this model of seven chakras, represented by the seven colors of the rainbow, a glorious symbol of grace and promise. By incorporating this tool, we hope to demonstrate an integrative approach and the value of learning from the wisdom of other traditions and understandings. Theologian Matthew Fox calls learning the chakra tradition and bringing the wisdom of the

East together with the wisdom of the West, "Deep Ecumenism."[4]

These concepts may be new and unfamiliar, but we hope you can move past any resistance you may feel for the pleasure of exploring and enjoying this colorful, imaginative, ancient, and helpful tool.

The Bible offers several examples of such imagery. In imagining chakras as flowers, we might envision a gradual and graceful opening into fragrant fullness. The Greek word *dianoigo* means "to open completely." This word is used in the New Testament to describe the opening of eyes, ears, tongues, hearts, understanding, awareness, even the womb. The correspondent Hebrew word, *pathach*, refers to the opening of flowers, of the heavens, of the barren womb, and in the Song of Songs we see it in the phrase, "Open to me, my sister, my beloved, my dove, my perfect one" (5:2).

The concept of spinning wheels brings to mind Ezekiel's description of the whirling wheels in his vision (Ezekiel 1). We might also imagine the chakras of "the son of the man" as further described in Revelation 1:12-16:

Hairs of his head, snow white as wool	Crown chakra
Eyes as a flame of fire	Third eye chakra
Voice of many waters	Throat chakra
Hands with seven stars	Heart (Arms, Hands) chakra
Girdle of gold	Solar Plexus chakra
Oriface with "two-mouthed" sabre	Sacral (Womb/Phallus) chakra
Feet like burnished brass[58]	Root (Legs, Feet) chakra

Once again, in Ephesians 6, we enjoy a graphic description of physical images and body centers as we consider the "panoply of God." This regalia that we may imagine wearing, often referred to as the "armor of God," is meant to empower us in our struggle against spiritual powers of evil. The items in this list correlate closely both to the chakras and to the description of Jesus in Revelation. See Table 1, page 37.

Our intention is not to fully explore the chakras, but to use this model as a way to focus attention on one of the body's physio-spiritual centers at a time, considering what each may represent. We have related each chakra to the particular creative inheritance of women that is violated by fundamentalist indoctrination. By facilitating awareness of the life energy that has been blocked by repressive training, we'll explore how the light in us has been darkened. As each of these centers opens in the individual, her relationship to her external environment is transformed as she more effectively shares the light of her being through her self-expression.

In the Christian tradition, we celebrate the powerful indwelling of the Holy Spirit so visually described at Pentecost as fire: "[A]nd there appeared to them tongues as of fire; these separated and came to rest on the head of each of them. They were all filled with the Holy Spirit and began to speak different languages as the Spirit gave them power to express themselves." (Acts 2:3–4)

The immediate result of this outpouring of the Spirit was the ability to communicate and connect with others in a powerful communion of diversity and renewal. Our longing for such astonishing experiences of joy and generosity persists. Through music, poetry, story, dance, and case studies, we will unfold the myriad tapestries of women's lives, inviting reflection, validation, clarification, and initiation into the supportive community of women in resurrection.

Energy and emotion live in the body and are housed in certain body localities. In fundamentalism, women become fragmented and alienated from their bodies. As we have personally observed and experienced the healing power of body awareness in our own lives, we have come to value the primitive wisdom and ancient healing arts that have existed throughout a variety of cultures. While a fundamentalist mindset is exclusionary and narrow, we hope to model an integrative, inclusive, holistic approach. A one-way mentality causes a void in a woman's "skill set." As she neglects relevant and valuable information, she loses the ability to expedite her healing. As you work with this material, we believe that you will experience healing and integration of your own energetic presence.

Through the movement and dance opportunities at the end of each chapter, you will be able to explore Jesus' rich metaphor of light in your own body. What might it mean for us to be women of light? How do we shine our radiance in the midst of darkness? How might Jesus have shone his light? How might Eve enlighten our awareness? What darkness have we allowed when we failed to shine our brightness? What makes our eye clear or diseased? The Greek words are helpful in illuminating the Matthew text. The lamp (*luchnos*, "light, candle") of the body (*somatos*, "animated body") is the eye (*ophthalmos*, "sight, view, paradigm"). If your eye is clear (*haplous*, "single, sound, liberal, bountiful"), your body will be full of *photeinos*, "light." When your eye is diseased (*poneros*: evil, malicious, bad, wicked, hurtful), your body will be full of *skoteinos*, "darkness." We can wonder about how we let light in and how we are affected in our bodies by our point of view, our paradigm.

The exercises are designed to facilitate embodied experiences of healing and resurrection. They can be adapted for use in families, in women's or youth groups, individually, or for couples. They may unlock new insights or forgotten truths. Recorded instrumental music by a variety of artists is an important resource for facilitating movement experiences. To begin a collection of music, we suggest *Secret Garden: White Stones* (Philips), Jami Sieber: *Lush Mechanique* (Out Front Music), and Thomas Newman: *American Beauty Soundtrack* (Dreamworks). These pieces can be used to accompany the dance exercises described.

Tables 2 and 3 outline the relationships between the various colors, chakras, creations, characteristics, and commandments. At the conclusion of the next seven chapters, we'll look again at Jesus as light, exploring how he honored children and the feminine, his use of story, and his commitment to truth. In the final chapter, we'll reaffirm dance and ritual in support of healing and transformation, the physical practice of incarnating new light.

Notes

1 Elaine Pagels, *Beyond Belief: The Secret Gospel of Thomas* (New York: Random House, 2003), 55.

2 Richard Gerber, *Vibrational Medicine* (Rochester, VT: Bear & Co., 1996), 369.

3 Matthew Fox, *Sins of the Spirit, Blessings of the Flesh* (New York: Harmony Books, 1999), 94, 98.

4 Jay P. Green, Sr., ed., *Interlinear Greek-English New Testament* (Grand Rapids, MI: Baker Books, 2004), 742.

Table 1: Chakras in the Bible

Colors/Chakras/Creations	Panoply of God in Eph. 6	Jesus in Revalation 1
Violet (or White) Crown Chakra: Spirituality **Marvel in Mystery**	*Perikefalaia* 4030* (encircle the head) with *Soterion* 4992 (rescue, safety, health, salvation, defense)	Hairs of his head, snow white as wool
Indigo Third Eye Chakra: Intuition **Recognize Your Authority**	*Agrupnew* 69 (be sleepless, keep awake, watch) in *Proskarteresis* 4343 (persistency, perseverence)	Eyes as a flame of fire
Blue Throat Chakra: Speaking and Being Heard **Creative Expression**	*Macaira* 3162 (sword) of *Pneuma* 4151 (breath, spirit) *Rhema* 4487 (utterance) of *Theos* 2316 (a deity, esp. supreme Divinity, God)	Voice of many waters
Green Heart (Arms, Hands) Chakra: Love for Self and Others **Find Your Heart**	*Thureos* 2375 (shield, portal, entrance, door, gate) of *Pistis* 4102 (assurance, belief, faith, fidelity)	Hands with seven stars
Yellow Solar Plexus Chakra: Power to Act **Support / Balance**	*Thorax* 2382 (chest, corslet, breast-plate) of *Dikaiosune* 1343 (equity, justice, righteousness)	Girdle of gold
Orange Sacral(Womb/Phallus) Chakra: Sexuality **New Covenant / Naked Truth**	*Perizonnumi* 4024 (gird all around) your *Osphus* 3751 (loins, hips, procreative power) with *Alethia* 225 (truth, not hidden, or ignorant, or unaware)	Oriface with "two-mouthed" sabre
Red Root (Legs, Feet) Chakra: Belonging **Ancestral Inheritance**	*Hupodeo* 5265 (put on shoes or sandals) of *Euaggelion* 2098 (a good message, gospel) of *Eirene* 1515 (peace, rest, set at one again	Feet like burnished brass

* James Strong's numbering system for Greek words; www.htmlbible.com/

Table 2: Colors, Chakras, Creations

Colors	Chakras	Creations
Violet (or White) Chapter 4 Like a Little Child	**Crown Chakra** Top of head Connect human to divine Spirituality, knowing Gland: Pineal	**Marvel in Mystery** Matthew 18:3 Mark 10:14–16 John 8:32
Indigo Chapter 5 Reclaiming Awareness	**Third Eye Chakra** Eyes, ears To value intuition Awareness Gland: Pituitary	**Recognize Your Authority** Luke 12:57
Blue Chapter 6 Exploring Self-Expression	**Throat Chakra** Throat To speak and to be heard Expression Glands: Thyroid, Parathyroid	**Open to Creative Expression** Ephesians 6:19–20 Matthew 12:35
Green Chapter 7 Unveiling Authenticity	**Heart Chakra** Heart, arms, hands To love and to be loved Authenticity Gland: Thymus	**Find Your Heart** 1 Chronicles 17:2 Mark 12:31 1 John 4:18
Yellow Chapter 8 Dance of Balance	**Solar Plexus Chakra** Gut, core To mature and to act Empowerment, equality Glands: Pancreas, Adrenals	**Support / Balance** James 2:5–9, 12–13
Orange Chapter 9 Domination of Female Sexuality	**Sacral Chakra** Sexual, reproductive organs To give birth to, to create Sexuality, feeling Glands: Ovaries, Testes	**New Covenant** Luke 22:17–20
Red Chapter 10 The Cost of Belonging	**Root Chakra** Base of spine, legs To connect to earth and tribe Belonging Glands: Adrenals	**Ancestral Inheritance** Isaiah 60:1 1 Kings 21:3

Table 3: Fundamentalist Characteristics and Commandments Followed by New Creations from Crown to Root

Characteristics	Commandments	Creations
Original sin is emphasized; children are dominated, devalued, and rigidly controlled	You will bear and train good, obedient children	"I will welcome children and child-likeness; become like a little child; truth will make me free" *Marvel in Mystery*
Fear, guilt, manipulation, and literalism interrupt awareness	You will not be aware of or value your intuition; you will believe what you are told	"I will judge for myself what is true and just" *Recognize Your Authority*
Women's voices are silenced, then co-opted for promotion of the system	You will fit in and not express your uniqueness	"I will speak up fearlessly; tell my own stories; develop my own art; own my voice" *Open to Creative Expression*
Role is valued over authenticity	You will be forced to be what others need you to be; you will not be selfish	"I will discover authenticity; love others; also love myself; believe in the power of love" *Find your heart*
Exclusive language; women are not permitted to act powerfully or be ordained in the church; injustice is legitimized	You will not act independently or become a mature woman	"I will exercise the power to act; realize female and male in partnership; consider the disempowered; move in God's domination-free order" *Support/Balance*
Relationships are hierarchical; traditional marriage; devaluation of the feminine; anit-gay; anti-choice	Your sexuality is not your own and will be controlled and appropriated by men; your emotions are not important	"I will bless the body; bless the cup; bless the feminine; bless and respect my sexuality and emotionality" *New Covenant*
Us against them mentality; insistence on rigid adherence to the law; rooted in judgment	You must keep up appearances and not be an embarrassment; you will only belong if you are judged obedient	"I will create circles of welcome and grace; born of spirit; embodying truth; secure in the family of God; willing even to die" *Ancestral Inheritance*

4

Like a Little Child

Crown Chakra: Spirituality

When a Baby Comes to You

When a baby comes to you
To love you
To adore you
To depend on you
She will show you how wonderful you are
In case someone never told you
Or showed you
Or loved you
Like a baby

But a baby requires all your care
She demands more than you may want to share
She shows you just what's inside you
Because there's no way
You can hide you
From your baby

You may invest more
Than you thought you could give
You may risk it all
So your baby can live
It's a novel exchange here
This flirtation with danger

As you welcome this stranger
And you see what she'll do
For your baby will change you
You'll discover a strange you
This mystery will arrange you
Into someone new

You will find if you let her
Your baby will do
All of this
For you

Characteristics: Original sin is emphasized; children are dominated, devalued, and rigidly controlled; projection is practiced at the expense of truth.

While Christian fundamentalist doctrine teaches that children are given as a blessing from God, there is a covert devaluing of children's worth within the system's hierarchical ordering and in the concept of original sin, which implies that children are born sinful. This system also promotes the belief that children want and need physical discipline (spanking), and that this form of punishment will teach them obedience and respect for the hierarchy. Some theologians explain that we are "born in sin," or "totally depraved," or "bound to sin," as seen in the behavior of infants, who are "self-centered." Rick Warren teaches in *The Purpose Driven Life*, "Babies by nature are completely selfish. They think only of themselves and their own needs. They are incapable of giving; they can only receive."[1] Babies certainly have needs, but it is a lie to say they are incapable of giving. This negative and false view of children justifies adult attempts to correct their "wicked" selfishness and demand their obedience.

Children are certainly born into an imperfect world; some situations are tragically more imperfect than others. The human condition, endlessly explored by artists, philosophers, and scientists, is as rife with potential for truth, beauty, goodness, and love as it is for hatred and destruction. We are born into this paradox: our culture can nurture our best or worst manifestation, but this damning notion of "original sin" need not be foisted upon newborns. Rather, the birth of a cherished child is often welcomed as a singularly miraculous and wondrous event of a lifetime. The engaging presence of a new baby is experienced by many as riveting, even mystical.

The recurrent theme in James Dobson's (Focus on the Family) parenting advice is domination: the obedience of the child to the authority of the parent. In addition to "I love you," Dobson recommends parents give this primary message to their young children, "Because I love you so much I must teach you to obey me."[2] "When that nose-to-nose confrontation occurs between generations, it is *extremely* important for the adult to win decisively and confidently"[3] because "deliberate disobedience involves the child's perception of parental authority and his obligations to accept it."[4] Dobson teaches "a spanking is to be reserved for use in response to willful defiance *whenever it occurs*."[emphasis in the original].[5] In answer to a parent's question about why spanking didn't seem to help, one of his explanations is that "the spanking may be too gentle. If it doesn't hurt, it doesn't motivate a child to avoid the consequence next time. A slap with the hand on the bottom of a multidiapered thirty-month-old is not a deterrent to anything. Be sure the child gets the message — while being careful not to go too far."[6]

This type of disciplinary advice is even being exported to developing nations as evidenced by this excerpt from Pat Robertson's weekly column in the *Sunday Vision* Uganda newspaper:

> A self-willed, indisciplined child who grows up to be a husband or wife is a danger to society. When a child flies into a rage, or breaks something, or displays behaviour that is obviously malicious and wrong, there is nothing wrong with smacking him sharply once or twice on his bottom. That is much better than berating him for an hour verbally. It is much better to administer punishment and get the matter out of the way than to let the thing fester or to let the child think he can get away with doing something wrong.[7]

Swiss object-relations therapist Alice Miller, in her book *For Your Own Good*, addresses the dangers of harmful child-rearing practices. She describes the injustice, humiliation, and coercion that children experience as a compulsive repetition of the exercise of power. She says that consciously, we hardly know what was done to us as children and why.

> Any mistreatment was held up to us as being necessary for our own good. Even the most clever child cannot see through such a lie if it comes from the mouth of his beloved parents, who after all show him other loving sides as well. He has to believe that the way he is being treated is truly right and good for him, and he will not hold it against his parents. But then as an adult he will

act the same way toward his own children in an attempt to prove to himself that his parents behaved correctly toward him. ... The child's intense anger at the parents, being strictly forbidden, is simply deflected onto other people and onto himself, but not done away with. Instead, because it is permissible to discharge this anger onto one's own children, it spreads over the entire world like a plague.[8]

Rigid control of children is abusive and produces lifelong damaging effects as it takes away a child's sense of distinct identity and subsumes it as an extension of parental will. Children learn to rely on false selves that mirror their parents' feelings and needs and to respect the powers of authority and dominance, rather than their own feelings and needs. If we are adults who were raised this way, we continue to function with these limitations and pass them on to our children unless we are able to uncover and resolve this wounding. Without direct access to our own feelings and the ability to express them, intimacy is impossible.

Dobson minimizes the wounding of spanking even as he acknowledges the uncanny awareness of little children. He reports that after being spanked by parents reading his book *Dare to Discipline*, a three year-old girl put the book in the toilet.

> That darling little girl had done her best to send my writings to the sewer, where they belonged.... Another child selected my book from an entire shelf of possibilities and threw it in the fireplace.... I am apparently resented by an entire generation of kids who would like to catch me in a blind alley on some cloudy night. [9]

Dobson's comment about the children who would like to catch him in a blind alley is an example of projection. Projection is the mechanism whereby people, in order to distance themselves from what may be judged as unacceptable, project their own fears, insecurities, disowned desires, aggression, and internal conflicts onto others. When evil is framed as a completely external phenomenon, projection is a defense mechanism that allows people to avoid looking at what might be their own feelings or failings. This behavior affects not only their view of the world but also their perceptions and treatment of children. Since adults were once children, it is important for them to consider the messages absorbed in preconscious and precritical years.

We have all watched the grocery store scenarios wherein children are victims of projection. A tired, hungry little one, who would be much happier at home napping, begs for treats, whines, or acts out. The child's parent, embarrassed by the reflection on his or her ability to ensure better market behavior, threatens the child with punishment, which is all too often delivered violently. The parent's discomfort and anger is disowned and then projected onto the needy and annoying child who is blamed as "disobedient." The child is the one who is punished. We have also seen the child perfectly behaved, with scripted responses, living in terror of irritating or embarrassing her or his parent. Swiss object-relations therapist Alice Miller, discusses how parents project onto their children in her book *You Shall Not Be Aware*, "The younger the child, the stronger the parents' projection, for the child is not yet able to show them the absurdity of their projections."[10]

As newborns, we arrive without filters. We trust our physical awareness implicitly. We regularly comment in some way on the reality of our present experience, by rooting, or squirming, or screaming. Our whole world revolves around surviving and securing that blissful state of homeostasis: a full belly, a dry bottom, a welcoming bosom, and a responsive presence that seems to say, "You are absolutely perfectly beautiful; what a miracle you are!" Perhaps that's the better part of what we all still long for.

Children's connection to the truth of their own experience is too often extinguished early by parents who insist on the validity of their truth over and above the child's. Children who speak candidly to their parents often are answered with a denial of their truth.

Table 4: How Parents Deny Their Children's Truth

Child says:	Parent responds:
It hurts.	That doesn't hurt.
I'm not hungry.	You must eat anyway.
I'm not cold.	You need to wear a jacket.
You're not listening.	Sure, I'm listening
I can do it myself.	No, I'll do it for you.
I don't want to.	You will do as I say.
Stop yelling at me.	I'm not yelling!

In denying children their truth, punishing harshly, and projecting the concept of original sin onto them, the fundamentalist system perpetuates itself at the expense of the wholeness of children, true spirituality, and truth itself. Children are taught at an early age that the reality they are coming to discover through their experiences is not true, but truth lies in a set of beliefs imposed upon them. The lie that is exchanged for their truth is this: the truth of those who they are required to obey is more valid than our own, and their understanding of God must come from the system rather than their own direct connection.

Biblical scholar Arthur J. Dewey suggests that the first encounter with the truth of God is when the newborn learns to negotiate the breast. In order to survive, the infant must make an effective connection with this source of life and sustenance. Believing really is about, and comes from, the basic experience of trust. He suggests that this perspective may shed light on our culture's difficulty with viewing the human breast in a public non-sexual display, "Perhaps it is because we are afraid of God."[11]

Commandment: You will bear and train good, obedient children.

Adam and Eve's story is the first testimonial destroying the fantastical belief that families must always be blissful gardens. This story as promoted by fundamentalists is used to remind all good women and men that family members must live life in rigidly fixed stereotypical gender roles and that the Christian life, the family life, can be problem-free, even divinely blessed, if the woman obeys and submits to God and man. Everything else will then fall into place.

The role of women as child bearers is focal. The individual's needs are insignificant compared to the needs of the group, because the system's mission is to perpetuate itself and populate the world with believers. Consider the words of Dobson, who defends the necessity of women having babies. Note the familiar doubletalk. Initially he seems to support a woman's choice in the matter, yet as he continues, his true beliefs become evident:

> It is a woman's prerogative not to have a baby, so I would not be so foolish as to try to force that decision on anyone. *However,* there's something ambiguous about insisting on a "right" which would mean the end of the human race if universally applied! If women wearied of childbearing for a mere thirty-five years on earth, the last generation of mortals would grow old and die, leaving no offspring to reproduce. What godlike power is possessed

by the female of the species! [This is what fundamentalist men apparently fear.] She can take the bit in her mouth and gallop down the road to oblivion with a wagonload of humanity bumping along behind. No hydrogen bomb could destroy us more effectively, without bloodshed or pollution.... .

What I'm saying is that sex-role attitudes are closely related to the survival of a society. What will happen, for example, if the present generation reaches retirement age and still outnumbers the younger workers? Who would support the social security system when today's adults become too old to earn a living? Who would populate the military when America is threatened from abroad? What would happen to an economy that is based on decreasing returns rather than growth from productivity? Yes, the liberated woman will have had her way — her "right" to abortion and childlessness. She will have proved that no one could tell her what to do with her body. But what a victory![12]

Dobson dramatically associates a woman's right to choose whether or not to have children with the destruction of all humankind. Her godlike power could decimate the Social Security system, depopulate the military, even cause the decline of our economy. His views support the fundamentalist script promoting the notion that women's primary function and fulfillment is in having children. Clearly, this script is by nature fixed, unable to accommodate a changing world or the uniqueness of the individual.

Fundamentalists covertly promote the belief that if only women would obediently follow the requirements of the Good Woman role — and, of course, produce babies — we could get back to that utopia again, back to the garden: if only the women of today would learn from Eve's mistake and remember that it was her departure from the script with her improvisational, independent behavior that ruined paradise for all.

Added to the expectation that women produce children is the assumption that they must be told how to raise those children. Granted, new mothers and fathers often are hungry for support when traveling the uncharted waters of parenthood. But much of the "Christian" advice they receive is frightening. It is alarming that Dobson, a psychologist — whom many unsuspecting listeners trust to be disseminating solid, psychological advice — promotes the practice of spanking so readily rejected in mainstream psychology today.

When spankings occur, they should be administered with a neutral object; that is, with a small switch or belt, but rarely with the hand. I have always felt that the hand should be seen by the child as an object of love rather than an instrument of punishment. ... Should a spanking hurt? Yes, or else it will have no influence. A swat on the behind through three layers of wet diapers simply conveys no urgent message. However, a small amount of pain for a young child goes a long way; it is certainly not necessary to lash or "whip" him. Two or three stinging strokes on the legs or bottom with a switch are usually sufficient to emphasize the point, "You must obey me."[13]

This is but one among many horrifying examples of how Christian fundamentalists — this one a psychologist — preach their fear-based agenda over and above the well-being and psychological health of the individual, especially the pure in spirit and diaper-ridden. If the hand should be seen as an "object of love rather than an instrument of punishment," that same hand ought not be gripping the switch or belt performing the heinous punishment.

In the May 1996 issue of the *Focus on the Family* newsletter, John Croyle, the founder of Big Oak Ranch, a Christian home in Alabama for abused, orphaned, and neglected children, outlines fundamentalist parenting principles in "Four Things Every Parent Should Know," excerpted from his book, *Bringing Out the Winner in Your Child:*

Remember: Children want discipline. We had one small boy, Michael (at Big Oak Ranch), who stood in front of me one day and stomped on our flowers.

"Michael, if you stomp on those flowers one more time, I'm going to spank you," I warned.

He looked up at me — I must have seemed like a giant to him because I'm 6 feet 6 — and looked back down at the flowerbed. Then he raised his foot and smashed the flowers into the ground.

"Okay, come on inside," I said. I took a ping pong paddle and gave him three licks, but when I got through, he wasn't crying.

"You done?" he asked.

"Yeah, but why did you deliberately stomp on those flowers?"

"Because I didn't think you'd spank me."

"Really?"

His answer was in his eyes. They were saying, "No one's loved me enough to discipline me and keep their word."

> Sometimes parents are afraid to discipline because they fear their children won't love them afterward. It's like going to the grocery store and hearing a mother say, "Josh, if you touch that cereal box again, I'm going to punish you." When the youngster continues to pull cereal boxes off the shelves, the mom threatens him — again and again. You feel like saying, "Hey, lady, will you just go ahead and do it?"
>
> You see, a broken promise is a lie to a child, and if you promise him that you're going to do something, he'll test you to see if you're going to keep your word.[14]

Focus on the Family describes and recommends such physical acts of discipline in their publications, demonstrating how essential these abusive principles are to the system's maintenance: the threat of physical punishment is the mortar cementing the fundamentalist framework. The justifications used for spanking Michael are ludicrous: that it's a lie to not follow through with a threat of spanking (a threat that should never have been made) and that striking a child with a ping pong paddle is a way to let him know you love him. How hard would it have been for Mr. Croyle to redirect Michael into a constructive activity like watering the flowers or playing catch rather than instigating a power struggle in his attempt to control Michael's behavior with threats of physical violence? We don't hit adults when they don't do as we say. Why should we hit children?

It is ironic that the setting for this incident is a Christian home for abused children, where one would hope non-abusive loving principles would be practiced. Was Michael's problem really that he had not had enough love, or could it be that Michael had never experienced nonviolent parenting? Perhaps because he had endured hitting and spanking previously, Michael had learned how to garner attention negatively, believing that a punitive response was better than no attention at all. The fact that Michael did not cry could be evidence that abuse was so normal for him that he had learned he must present a tough, "I'm-not-afraid-of-you" façade in order to survive. Who knows, in his world he may have been taught, "If you cry, I'll really give you something to cry about."

When Michael said to John Croyle, "I didn't think you'd spank me," maybe he meant, "I hoped you would be different. I thought that this was a safe place and so I decided to test you to see if you might be unlike all the other authorities in my life … but I guess not. The only way for me to survive is to defy, to fight for my life."

None of us really knows Michael's inner truth; and it seems that Croyle did not try to understand Michael's interpretation of the situation. Instead, Croyle placed his fundamentalist equation over and above Michael's subjective experience, suggesting that he knew exactly what Michael was thinking and feeling and needing. Perhaps Croyle was denying his own anger and embarrassment over Michael's testing of a six-foot six-inch not-so-jolly giant, even as he remained deaf to Michael's silent cry. Really, when Michael (and every other child at the Big Oak Ranch) obediently follows the rules, the staff's job is made easier, just as a fundamentalist parent's job is made easier with an obedient, authority-fearing, silent child. Less time must be spent listening to and understanding the child's inner experience and thought processes. But at what cost to the wholeness of both parent and child?

Fundamentalist interpretations about Christian parenting offer a quick-and-easy answer guide with simplified equations for every potentially troublesome dilemma. The child's perceptions are viewed as unimportant and are consequently discounted because the parent assumes to know what the child is thinking. This unspoken belief, supporting the parent's hierarchical authority over the child, rescues the parent from wrestling with the ambiguities and complexities of careful discipline and makes a relationship of mutual respect and equality impossible. In a religious system that presupposes that all are born sinful and operate from devious, deceptive motives, children in particular are suspect. Their strong wills must be broken and their spontaneous urges curbed.

Just as Michael "smashed the flowers into the ground," so did Croyle's act of "loving discipline" smash Michael into the ground. One used a foot, the other a ping pong paddle. Imagine being Michael and having an adult tell you it's wrong to physically harm a plant but it's okay to physically hit another human being. How does a child learn not to smash when he himself is smashed? Both killed the beauty of the flower, potentially disrupting its ability to blossom again. An eye for an eye ... a tooth for a tooth ... a flower for a flower.

Fundamentalist disciplinary concepts are self-serving, meeting the needs of the system, not those of the individual child. Taught to fear authority figures early on, many grow up without ever really growing up, becoming good, obedient, law-abiding children in adult bodies, quick to unquestionably obey the authority of the church, secretly terrified to do otherwise. Obedience is a central requirement in this system, regardless of the cost to healthy psychological development.

The widely accepted view in the mental health field is that hitting (including spanking) does not promote the development of emotionally healthy adults. In fact, in her book *The Bully, The Bullied, and the Bystander*, Barbara Coloroso points out, "Studies of the background of bullies and their most vulnerable targets conclude that physical punishment (or neglect) played a big role in the lives of both."[15] Yet, spanking is advocated by countless fundamentalist Christians, who inflict physical pain on small children in the name of discipline and love. As such children grow, they will try to hide their actions, fearing the response that may follow if they are found out. Deception as a way of life becomes second nature. They may live their entire lives with a deep core sense of shame, unsure why they don't feel quite right about who they are. They may act out their deep-seated hostilities and resentments on others.

The American Academy of Pediatrics highlights several negative effects of spanking. When aggressive behavior is modeled as a solution to conflict, increased aggression in preschool and schoolage children has been noted. Spanking alters parent-child relationships so that discipline is more difficult when children are adolescents. Reliance on spanking makes other types of discipline strategies less effective to implement. And most alarming, because of the relief from anger that spanking provides to parents, they are likely to sustain or increase this disciplinary pattern. In conclusion, this report recommends that parents be encouraged and assisted in developing disciplinary methods other than spanking.

> Parents who spank their children are more likely to use other unacceptable forms of corporal punishment. The more children are spanked, the more anger they report as adults, the more likely they are to spank their own children, the more likely they are to approve of hitting a spouse, and the more marital conflict they experience as adults. Spanking has been associated with higher rates of physical aggression, more substance abuse, and increased risk of crime and violence when used with older children and adolescents.[16]

The fabled biblical "rod," sometimes used to justify spanking, would not have been an instrument of punishment; rather, the staff of a shepherd caring for sheep. In biblical times, the shepherd used a staff to gently prod the sheep in the right direction, not to strike out in retaliation for disobedience. The intent of the metaphor, in light of the teachings of Jesus, would be to encourage parents to gently instruct, offering their children guidance and nurturing love while lifting them out of potentially dangerous situations. Jesus' parable of the lost sheep evokes the image of such a shepherd, tenderly devoted to the care and rescue of every last lamb. Parents who routinely slap or strike their children are handing them instead a model of physical violence to imitate and to justify.

Coloroso offers three useful tenets for developing a philosophy of parenting and evaluating parenting techniques:

1. Kids are worth it.

2. I will not treat a child in a way I myself would not want to be treated.

3. If it works and leaves a child's and my own dignity intact, do it.[17]

It is time that Christians take seriously Jesus' honoring of children. His words for those who would offend a child are extremely harsh. "Anyone who welcomes one little child like this in my name welcomes me. But anyone who is the downfall of one of these little ones who have faith in me would be better drowned in the depths of the sea." (Matthew 18:5–6)

Jesus' vision of the family was not rigid, hierarchical, or abusive, but instead was flexible, egalitarian, and loving. Similarly, Jesus' vision of women was empowering and life-affirming. He would not have supported the family values espoused by the fundamentalist church and its political allies. Fundamentalist systems, at their core, are unjust. Jesus, on the other hand, was a justice seeker. We also are called to be lovers of justice, to be mutually related in Godbeingness with all other Godimages, including children, women, men, and all other living things.

Like adults, children flourish in environments of love and nurture with firm yet flexible limits, and they will follow the example of those who inspire affection, admiration, and mutual respect. Likewise, adults flourish in an environment where children are valued and honored, learning as much as they teach.

Creation: "I will welcome children and child-likeness;
become like a little child; truth will make me free."

Marvel in Mystery

"In truth I tell you, unless you change and become like little children,
you will never enter God's domination-free order." (Matthew 18:3)

"Let the little children come to me; do not stop them; for it is to
such as these that God's domination-free order belongs. I tell you the
truth, anyone who does not welcome God's domination-free order like
a little child will not enter it." Then he embraced them, laid his hands
on them, and gave them his blessing. (Mark 10:14–16)

"You will know the truth and the truth will make you free."
(John 8:32)

To "become like a child," and to "know the truth," both point to mysteries
that we reach to understand. Conceptions of "spirituality" are as diverse
as the individuals who incarnate them. We understand spirituality as that
which expresses the true spirit of the authentic self and nurtures the connection to what is beyond. This otherworldly reality may be described
as the presence or revelation of the numinous: creative, psychic energy
reflecting divinity or spirit. So, what is the connection between spirituality, childlikeness, and knowing truth?

As we ponder what Jesus is suggesting in these texts, let's begin with
the crown chakra, at the top of the head. This physio-spiritual center relates to consciousness, transcendence, connection to God, and knowing
beyond the physical world. The color for this chakra is violet, (sometimes white). Explore your level of comfort with the mystery. Embrace
your potential to be transformed. Notice the wisdom of children. How
might you better listen to children and pay loving attention to them,
supporting them in being their spontaneous, authentic selves as much as
you can? Imagine the inherent goodness and the incredible gift of a tender newborn. Ponder how you might become like a child and so enjoy
God's domination-free order. Think about the child you once were and
whose wounds may live inside you still. Offer the same quality of honor
and welcome to this child that is you.

Consider Native American philosophies of raising children. Ed
McGaa, author of *Native Wisdom: Perceptions of the Natural Way*, discusses
how the Northern Plains tribes raised their children: "Children were
highly regarded by the tribe. Any form of child abuse could easily
draw the death penalty or banishment."[76] McGaa expresses the Native
American belief that the focus of communication of beliefs (the education of children) ought to be more on the purity and innocence of
children's playful natures. Children's "work" is play; it is through their

play that they creatively explore and interact with their environment and hence gain a healthy sense of self. Maybe if more attention were given to the value of play, there would be less need to focus so much on the issue of discipline.

Apache philosopher, Viola F. Cordova, describes her understanding of native practice in the nurture of children.

> We discourage competitiveness and encourage co-operativeness; we frown on selfish behavior and encourage perceptiveness of the other; we correct by offering alternatives rather than through threat or admonitions; we encourage laughter and camaraderie— there is no one "out there" waiting to "get us." We transmit these values through loaning our attitudes to our children.[19]

Effective parenting or mentoring requires careful listening and watching and the offering of support for each child's individuality. Parents must balance the needs of their children with their own, as they provide thoughtful and flexible limits to ensure their safety and development. This type of parenting helps children remain connected to what is going on inside of them, in touch with what they feel and need. Although as babies we are initially quite good at expressing our needs and feelings directly, Marshall Rosenberg describes in *Non-Violent Communication* how we have been trained to use language

> that encourages us to label, compare, demand, and pronounce judgments rather than to be aware of what we are feeling and needing. A life-alienating mode of communication is rooted in views of human nature that have exerted their influence for several centuries. These views stress our innate evil and deficiency, and a need for education to control our inherently undesirable nature. Such education often leaves us questioning whether there is something wrong with whatever feelings and needs we may be experiencing. We learn early to cut ourselves off from what's going on within ourselves.

> Life-alienating communication both stems from and supports hierarchical or domination societies. Where large populations are controlled by a small number of individuals for their own benefit, it would be to the interest of kings, czars, nobles, etc. that the masses be educated in a way that renders them slave-like in mentality ... When we are in contact with our feelings and needs, we humans no longer make good slaves and underlings.[20]

Perhaps this explains why children have been targeted by fundamentalist parenting dogma with its emphasis on obedience. A movement intent on "defense" and "combat" and "dominion" and "world conquest" needs well-trained foot soldiers for its operations. In studying the writings of several men who surrounded Hitler, Alice Miller was unable to find a single one among all the leading figures of the Third Reich who did not have a strict and rigid upbringing. She exposes the danger inherent in the unquestioned obedience to authoritarian parenting.

> If a father misuses his power by suppressing his children's critical faculties, then his weaknesses will stay hidden behind these fixed attributes (uniqueness, bigness, importance, and power). ...And so, when a man comes along and talks like one's own father and acts like him, even adults will forget their democratic rights or will not make use of them. They will submit to this man, they will acclaim him, allow themselves to be manipulated by him, and put their trust in him, finally surrendering totally to him without even being aware of their enslavement.[21]

The emotional health and integrity of children requires that they not be rigidly controlled, but supported in discovering their gifts. In addition, the compassionate nurture of children can foster profound spiritual and personal growth. The opportunity in parenting, or other caretaking relationships with children, is to remember one's own childlikeness. In the welcoming of the child, one may welcome herself anew. She may reconnect to some part of her own beautiful truth and purity — when she was delivered fresh from God. She may remember the ways in which her feelings and needs were discounted, and, through the grieving of her losses, begin to offer herself new options. She may discover new meaning, glimpse a reality beyond a set of beliefs, and experience renewed connection to the source of mystery. These dimensions of spirituality are lost to both children and parents in authoritarian family systems.

Systems of domination are maintained at the cost of our own spirituality as we miss opportunities to touch what is beyond ourselves and transform us. Through the influence of the fundamentalist church, women have been conscripted with mandatory childbearing and oppressive childrearing to perpetuate domination at the family level. The church's primary influence on culture is through the family, the one institution small and manageable enough for the church to directly control. By setting up specific guidelines of "good" behavior for each family member (especially for the woman) and by emphasizing a strict need for gender assignment, rigid roles, and obedience, the church enrolls family members in a partnership, with the repression of feminine authority as the common denominator. The fundamentalist family is the primary institution enforcing fundamentalist values, and it is the primary place where girls learn "not to be like Eve."

In a young girl's mind, with a limited experience of the world, her family is her entire life and her only means of survival. If, as a youngster, she acts feisty, free, and independent, she is expected to succumb to the external pressures and become a "good girl." It is in the family system that the girl first learns the experience of being locked into role, of doing what others expect rather than knowing what she really wants. This subjugation is accomplished so early that we are quite unconscious of how effectively we have been trained and how automatically we cooperate.

Strong-willed children are gifts to us as parents who have work to do and lessons to learn about ourselves and the parenting journey. The less compliant the child, the more opportunity exists for us to hear authentic and wonderful words of truth about how our child experiences the world and us. We can find encouragement for our own path toward greater truth and understanding from the mouths of our babes. Children's unconditional love, trust, and acceptance of us as parents, especially in the early years, also can be a great support. They have confidence in the best in us. No wonder Jesus said you must be like one of these little ones to enter God's domination-free order.

Children truly can be agents of our own growth and change. The authenticity of their emotional reality reminds us of how we once were, what we once knew. When given permission to do so, children offer uncensored accounts of their perceptions and experiences. Their truth telling is an invitation for us to acknowledge with them the realities of our lives together in the stories of each day. The grace offered by a child to a weeping parent is nothing less than divine. In such moments we can access deep spirituality and transformation.

Children come to us as the fruits of life, bearing gifts in the same way that the fruit of knowledge came to Eve. Both her humanity and her divinity emerged when she partook of the fruit. In much the same way, children are delicious consciousness-raising creatures, ripening our awareness of both our humanity and our divinity, if we are willing and courageous enough to learn from them. Conversely, both the child's and the adult's humanity and divinity are suppressed and wounded by warped and distorted perceptions of hierarchical order: men first, women next, children last. In this pecking order, children cannot teach parents, children cannot know more than parents, and children cannot bring spiritual truths to their parents.

As she is willing to examine her own life and experience, a woman grows in truth. Truth encompasses ambiguity, paradox, and mystery; it rarely shows up as black and white. Our habits of maladaptive behaviors cannot remain intact in the light of truth. A willingness to be truthful with one's self and about one's life supports growth and movement, for as we live in truth we open up more fully to life. Children enhance this journey as they lovingly remind us that we are dynamic beings, capable of daily growth and change. We can be born again into childlikeness. Children provide an opportunity for deepened spiritual growth and enriched insight if we are willing to be open to them as our divine teachers, as ones who embody the spirit of Jesus. As Alice Miller hoped:

> Someday we will regard our children not as creatures to manipulate or to change, but rather as messengers from a world we once deeply knew, but which we have long since forgotten, who can reveal to us more about the true secrets of life, and also our own lives, than our parents were ever able to. We do not need to be told whether to be strict or permissive with our children. What we do need is to have respect for their needs, their feelings, and their individuality, as well as for our own.[22]

Our childrearing philosophies in this culture might be transformed if women were valued as the "experts" they are as mothers. What a positive trickle-down effect this would have on their mothering! Imagine if women, without the distorting influences of domination, were honored for their generational wisdom, springing from their feminine heritage as life-givers and primary caretakers. They might remember together and re-imagine an ancient past when women trusted their hearts and their intuitive instincts as authoritative, fully supported by their partners and their communities. Envision the day when women are respected for their powers to birth, to create, to mother, to be.

Women can invite men also into this womb of genesis. As women share the fruit of awareness with men, and as men allow it to be born in them as well, we will more brightly reflect God's female/male image as we create lives of mutuality. Men can become "experts" at honoring women as co-creators and co-defenders of humanity and humane earth- keeping, stewards together with women rather than dominators in an abusive hierarchy. By learning from children, we can discover the value and benefit of play, welcoming the wonder and marveling in the mystery.

Paula

Roberta asked me once, when our children were very young, how I hoped they would turn out, what values and characteristics I expected to instill. In the moment I said, "Well, I guess I hope they are like their dad and me. I like us. I like our values. I am teaching them our beliefs." As I have reflected further, in awe of their surprising moral integrity, their individual uniquenesses, and their amazing attachment to us as parents, I have become convinced of deeper realities. I now recognize my role in supporting and witnessing each of their journeys of self-discovery. I realize my responsibility for living more intentionally, more in line with my own values, so as to create less confusion for them and to enhance their experience of congruence. Finally, I have come to acknowledge the sacred trust of their dependence on us as parents — knowing that, for a while at least, we have represented God to them. My hopes for their development are now less certain, yet much more secure. The parenting journey I now witness breathes in the "assurance of things hoped for, the reality of things unseen."

Dance: Choose a piece of music that speaks to you of childlikeness, wisdom, mystery, and wonder. Wear a violet dress or tie a violet scarf around your head. Invite a baby or a child to share a moment of movement. Give yourself permission to embody your crown chakra through the beauty and mystery of your dance.

Playing with Wonder: Starting at the crown of your head and moving down, allow different parts of your body to be the impetus for your movement. Begin by following your head for one minute or so. How many ways might your head inspire you to move? Next, let your shoulders instigate your moving, then go on to different body parts in the same way (elbows, hands, chest, hips, knees, feet). Strive for childlike abandon and appreciate the creativity and novelty of your own way of moving.

Playing with Wonder with a Partner: With a partner you can do the same process but with added surprise. One person touches the other on a hip or shoulder (or wherever) and that becomes the body part that guides the movement. When the first person is finished, (30 seconds or however long it takes for that body part to finish the dance it is directing) she will stop and touch her partner and that person will then dance. Pass the touching and moving back and forth in this manner throughout the song you have chosen. If you would like another level, try touching two or three different body parts at a time.

Giving Honor: This process is for use in a group, but the attention you develop in it can be practiced everywhere. While music is playing, allow group members to dance amongst each other with the intention of giving honor to each other. Imagine that each person you pass is some exalted royal being. Allow your movements and your countenance to communicate your reverence. Notice how others respond to such attention. Notice what it brings forth in yourself.

Healing

We fail our children when we
Ignore their wisdom
Fear their confrontation
Deny their truth
But even more, we fail ourselves

We enrich our children when we
Allow them to move us
Suspend our judgment
Welcome their differentness
But even more, we enrich ourselves

We heal our children when we
Confess our failings
Listen to their stories
Cry them through their disappointments
But even more, we heal ourselves

Notes

1 Rick Warren, *The Purpose Driven Life* (Grand Rapids, MI: Zondervan, 2002), 182.

2 James Dobson, "James Dobson Answers Your Questions." (Focus on the Family: August 1995), 5.

3 James Dobson, *The Strong-Willed Child* (Wheaton, IL: Tyndale 1978), 32.

4 Ibid., 37.

5 Ibid., 36.

6 Focus on the Family, "Does the Spanking Approach Fail with some Children?" *Focus on the Family*, http://family-topics.custhelp.com/cgi-bin/family_topics.cfg/php/enduser/std_adp.php?p_faqid=781.

7 Pat Robertson, "Does the Bible Allow You to Cane Your Child?" *Sunday Vision*, April 2, 2006.

8 Alice Miller, *For Your Own Good* (New York: Noonday Press, 1990), 247-248.

9 James Dobson, *The Strong-Willed Child* (Wheaton, IL: Tyndale 1978), 30.

10 Alice Miller, *You Shall Not Be Aware* (New York: Noonday Press, 1981), 128.

11 Arthur J. Dewey, "The Future of Religion," Conference Presentation, The Jefferson Center Summer Institute, Ashland, OR, August 1-3, 2005.

12 James Dobson, *Marriage and Sexuality* (Wheaton, IL: Tyndale House Publishers, Inc., 1982), 45-46.

13 James Dobson, *Dr. Dobson Answers Your Questions* (Wheaton, IL: Tyndale, 1982), 153.

14 John Croyle, "Four Things Every Parent Should Know" *Focus on the Family Magazine*: May 1996, 2, 4.

15 Barbara Coloroso, *The Bully, the Bullied, and the Bystander* (New York: HarperCollins, 2003), 103.

16 American Academy of Pediatrics, "Guidance for Effective Discipline." *Pediatrics* Vol. 101, No. 4 (April 1998): 723-728. http://aappolicy.aappublications.org/cgi/content/full/pediatrics;101/4/723.

17 Barbara Coloroso, *Kids Are Worth It* (New York: Avon Books, 1994), 11.

18 Ed McGaa, "Domestic Violence, Untruth, and Racism," *Wildfire ó Networking Journal of Native American Spirituality* 7, (Summer 1996): 13.

19 V.F. Cordora, "Ecoindian:A response to J. Baird Callicott," Ayaangwaamizin: International Journal of Indigenous Philosophy (1:1): 33-34

20 Marshall Rosenberg, *NonViolent Communication: A Language of Life* (Encinitas, CA: PuddleDancer, 2003), 23.

21 Alice Miller, *For Your Own Good* (New York: Noonday Press, 1990), 74-75.

22 Rita Nakashima Brock, "And a Little Child Will Lead Us: Christology and Child Abuse," in *Christianity, Patriarchy, and Abuse: A Feminist Critique*, eds. Joanne Carlson Brown and Carole R. Bohn, 50 (Cleveland: Pilgrim Press, 1989).

5

Reclaiming Awareness
Third Eye Chakra: Intuition

Thinking for Yourself

"No, you can't do this.
No, you can't be that.
How could you think that, anyway?"

When I heard these words,
Something inside me died,
Something being born again each day,
Now that I'm thinking for myself.

The One who knows me best,
Whose words can stand the test of truth,
Speaks to my heart.

The One who wants us all to
Listen to the call to love
Always reminds me:

Just keep on thinking for yourself.
You may not change the world,
Maybe not a single mind,
But you have become different from before.
You've found your way to love
And your way to speak your truth
And so the world has changed.
Nobody else can do your thinking for you.
Just keep on thinking for yourself.

Characteristics: Fear, guilt, manipulation, and literalism interrupt awareness.

The architects of the current traditional family philosophies have been busy these last several decades with indoctrination programs such as Bill Gothard's Institute in Basic Youth Conflicts, Family Life Seminars, Promise Keepers, MOPS, and Focus on the Family. An entire generation of fear-ridden and easily manipulated voters is in full flower, well trained to submit to authority and to think and vote however they are told. The dauntingly complex political landscape is distilled into two or three voting issues.

Meanwhile, those who operate outside this system may have little appreciation that members' greatest fear may be that of dissent against the "God-ordained chain of command." This fear and insecurity is instilled very early. Consider *On Becoming Babywise*, from a series of books called "Raising Kids God's Way." It's a book about breastfeeding and training babies to sleep through the night. "Utilized by one million parents world wide," it promotes a philosophy of training children through punishment to adapt to the needs of the parents.

Authors Gary Ezzo and Robert Bucknam recommend that a mother's "responses be rational and purposeful instead of emotive." Automatically offering the breast to a crying baby, they say, is "blocking the cry" rather than giving responsive comfort and nurture.[1] These ideas dramatically show an intent to supplant women's most basic intuitive and maternal wisdom. When mothers respond in this proscribed way, babies are trained to doubt their own ability to elicit a life-supporting response, perhaps fearing for their very survival.

A further level of fear is established in Sunday schools with songs and stories about the devil and hell. These primal childhood fears are largely unconscious, but they are viscerally present and easily activated. Such fear, along with the silencing of women and the pressure on men to dominate and align with power, leave both sexes ill equipped to behave autonomously in their own authority. Women and men often are terrified of thinking independently, of considering alternatives, of speaking or even discovering their own truths.

Fear-based tactics are foundational to Christian fundamentalism. They are useful in controlling members, especially those who are female. The emotion of fear can and does keep grown adults stuck in a childlike mentality, often for a lifetime. As Ronald M. Enroth wrote in *Churches That Abuse*:

Another effective control mechanism employed by abusive churches is fear; fear of not measuring up, fear of exclusion if one does not follow the rules, fear of losing out with God if one leaves the group, and fear of spiritual failure. As one observer colorfully described it, an incredible environment of fear is created where the hens huddle together within the walls to protect themselves from ravenous wolves, while allowing weasels to guard their chicken coop.[2]

Fundamentalist systems disguise their desire for power over women while effectively maintaining patriarchal power's superior position. There are many ways in which churches control women, both directly and indirectly, using guilt, manipulation, and fear.

Manipulative cuing is one indirect form of communication to which members subject one another. These are the spoken and unspoken, subtle and yet unmistakable signals that reinforce the rules about how members should act, feel, and think. One method of manipulative cuing is the indirect leading question. For example: You're not married? You don't have children yet? When are you going to start a family? Do you really think you should be working so hard in your own career? How is your husband adjusting? How are your children holding up with you working so much outside the home? How can we pray for you? How has God been at work lately in your spiritual life? What is God's plan for your family life? These questions, framed as expressions of concern and often delivered in condescending tones, clearly deliver the underlying message that you are not conforming to the system's standards. The words *God, the Lord, spiritual,* and *prayer* intensify the effect.

Condemnation of the lifestyles of the wayward provide a clear outline of behaviors not to be tolerated within the fold. Members may not remember being told directly what they should or should not do or be, but the public discourse and critique of the sins of others communicates effectively to each individual the system's restrictions and expectations.

Another covert method frequently used by fundamentalist institutions is the prayer chain, which all too easily becomes the gossip vine. A member of the chain calls another, asking for "prayers for some poor soul who has lost her way." Then, the caller ever so gracefully spills the juicy details. Having received such highly personal information about the woman in need of prayer, other members are now privy to potentially damaging details that can be used on a whim. This becomes an effective way to dominate, shame, and control.

Loving generosity, cordial politeness, even friendly smiles and warm hugs can be used to exert covert control. These actions are not always what they appear to be on the surface; often there is a hidden agenda. The expectation of the fundamentalist Christian church is that these subversive tactics of guilt and manipulation will create the fear of God in the souls of young girls and women, thereby keeping them in line.

Case Study: The Clarity of Pain

Jennifer's story reveals how her fundamentalist church family tried to manipulate her through guilt and fear:

A friend of Jennifer's described her as looking like "a feminist librarian." In fact, she's a bit of both. For years she was her church's librarian. There's a clear determination in her eyes that announces her intelligence and her independence, qualities her friend translated into "feminism." She wears her thick red hair pulled back in a ponytail, dresses in long sweaters, and floral skirts in muted colors. Her dark-rimmed glasses and the pencil that is usually poked through her ponytail contribute to the librarian look. She sees herself as a no-nonsense type with a strong artistic streak, and she finds no contradiction in that.

Jesus had always been important to Jennifer, both as a child and later as a mother of two girls. But, ideas she had previously and passively accepted — ideas about women in the ministry, women in the world, women in family life — had recently come into serious question with the birth of her first daughter. As she tried to raise her daughters to be competent, full human beings, she found herself uneasy about taking them to her church, with its fundamentalist Sunday school class. Did she really want her daughters to believe women couldn't be ministers? Did she want her daughters believing that girls and women couldn't be significant contributors in the world? Did she want them to believe they had to define their lives solely in terms of marriage and children?

Jennifer herself had never worked outside the home. Her husband had died when her daughters were small, and she was fortunate to have been left financially secure. She had painted, collected antiques, volunteered at the church, cared for her children, and created and maintained a rich home life. Although she missed her husband, she enjoyed her life and would not, in fact, be disappointed if her daughters pursued the same choices she had. The church had been a warm community for her and her girls. She felt guilty thinking about leaving, but she was becoming uncomfortable at the prospect of teaching her daughters to limit their aspirations. They might develop passions and interests beyond the domestic sphere. She didn't want them thinking they shouldn't try to be everything they could be, everything God created them to be, whether they chose a career, homemaking, or both. She wanted them to be able to support themselves if they someday found themselves alone without the financial security she had known.

As she was questioning these attitudes of her fundamentalist church, Jennifer's father, who had suffered from cancer for years, became terminally ill. Her church and her family opposed her father's wish to be allowed to die with dignity, insisting instead that he and Jennifer both submit themselves to God's will and pursue medical heroics, for God would guide the doctors. Jennifer was appalled that she alone stood with her father in supporting his demand that no extraordinary measures be taken to prolong what had become a life of agony. She was relieved when her father died quickly and life support never actually became an issue, but through the struggle over her father's right to die, she came to see her church in a new light.

As she entered her period of grieving, Jennifer decided to put some distance between herself and the church. She decided to take a break from church, needing time for herself to question and explore. She wrote a letter to her minister announcing her intention, assuring him that her absence would probably be temporary.

Barely a day passed between the writing of her letter and the first visit. In the weeks that followed, Jennifer's tastefully decorated drawing room saw a steady parade of church visitors: the pastor, elders, the director of church education, the head of the library committee, even her daughters' Sunday school teacher came. They acted as though they were coming to console her, but Jennifer knew that wasn't quite true. They didn't show any genuine interest in listening to her expressions of her loss or explorations of her doubts.

They came to pressure her and to shame her into returning: "What kind of example does this set for your children?" they admonished. "You should think of them first. Everyone has doubts and yours will pass. You surely won't feel better if you're not attending weekly services. It sounds to me like your emotions are overtaking you and leading you into sin. Don't listen to them! Turn off your feelings and tell Satan to leave you alone! You are making yourself more vulnerable to the evils of the world. This will only get you into trouble. God will punish you for this, Jennifer."

She had stayed in the church for years, despite her doubts about its teachings on women, because the community had given her comfort and spiritual sustenance. It had seemed like the idyllic extended family she had dreamed of but never experienced as a child. Now she saw that the comfort gained was completely conditional on her behaving in a rigidly prescribed manner, a manner that excluded questioning. Her temporary hiatus became permanent.

Three years later, Jennifer has not returned to the church. She is certain her decision to leave was a lifesaver not only for her but for her daughters as well. Through therapy, she learned how to process her feelings of guilt and has gained greater insight and understanding into the beliefs that trigger her guilt. She came to recognize false guilt and saw it as a tool the church had used to manipulate her. She learned not to allow others to control the intimate decisions of her life or the lives of her beloved daughters. She now sees her daughters expressing themselves with confidence and creativity. She has learned to create a circle of supportive friends, apart from the church. From her friends, she receives genuine listening, comfort, and acceptance for who she is today as an evolving, growing woman. She experiences these friends as her church and says that she feels "more whole and more spiritually mature" than ever before.

The emphasis on Biblical literalism is an invitation to stop thinking and merely look to the Bible as "authoritative on all matters." *The Purpose Driven Life* offers this advice: "Decide that regardless of culture, tradition, reason, or emotion, you choose the Bible as your final authority. Determine to first ask, "What does the Bible say?" when making decisions. Resolve that when God says to do something, you will trust God's Word and do it whether or not it makes sense or you feel like doing it."[3]

In contrast, in his work *The Fourth Day*, physics and astronomy professor Howard Van Till describes the practice of taking the Bible seriously:

> Failing to recognize a given literary form correctly will most likely make it impossible to determine the intended meaning of any kind of literature, biblical literature included. If we try to read lyric poetry as if it were descriptive prose, we might find preposterous absurdity rather than a beautiful and imaginative representation of a profound truth. If we try to read heroic narrative as if it were historical chronicle, we might get an unrealistic or distorted picture of the nature of humankind and our interaction with God. If we try to read a poetic or liturgical story of origins as if it were a primitive scientific report, we might see a chronicle of divine magic rather than an artistic portrait of the Creator–Creation relationship.[4]

The discussion of Intelligent Design being taught in public schools as if it is scientific rather than religious theory reminds us how some would treat the Bible as a science textbook. We also must beware of those who would try to use it as a guide to sexual ethics "whether or not it makes sense." The Bible permits prostitution, polygamy, sex with slaves, concubinage, treatment of women as property, and very early marriage. Consider the practices of levirate marriage or divorce.

> When a married man in Israel died childless, his widow was to have intercourse with his eldest brother. If he died without producing an heir, she turned to the next brother, and, if necessary, the next, and so on. Jesus mentions this custom without criticism (Mark 12:18-27 par.)... I am not aware of any Christians who still obey this unambiguous commandment of Scripture. Why do we ignore this law, and yet preserve the one regarding homosexual behavior? ... The law of Moses allowed for divorce (Deut. 24:1-4); Jesus categorically forbids it (Mark 10:1-12; Matt. 19:9 softens his severity). Yet many Christians, in clear violation of a command of Jesus have been divorced. Why, then, do some of these very people consider themselves eligible for baptism, church membership, communion, and ordination, but not homosexuals? What makes one so much greater a sin than the other, especially considering the fact that Jesus never even mentioned homosexuality but explicitly condemned divorce? Yet we ordain divorcees. Why not homosexuals?[5]

In fundamentalist religions, this sort of critical evaluation is denied to women. It is considered "smarter" for a woman to maintain thoughtlessness about the complexities of the Bible and the mysteries of life than to display a holy curiosity and a Christlike questioning. If she obeys as a good woman should obey, she will survive as a member in this system. But if she disobeys, she will be shunned and her independent thoughts judged as irrelevant — dispersed from the mouth of a rebel, an Eve. Albert Einstein's words are lost to these women: "The important thing is not to stop questioning. Curiosity has its own reason for existing. One cannot help but be in awe when [she] contemplates the mysteries of eternity, of life, of the marvelous structure of reality. It is enough if one tries merely to comprehend a little of this mystery every day. Never lose a holy curiosity."[6]

Jesus' gospel was not about ignoring the mystery, giving up intellectual faculties, evangelizing the traditional family, or reinforcing the political norms of the day. Jesus lived with a social consciousness, caring about and responding to people's real needs, without offering them simple religious answers. He lived his life rooted in the practice of truth, freedom, and welcome, not in manipulation, fear, and dogma.

The unfortunate reality of Christian fundamentalism's domination of women and intolerance of diversity is alive and dangerous. Women sometimes pay a heavy price for expressing their own religious ideas and experiences. The Re-Imagining God Conference in Minneapolis in 1993 was a global theological colloquium, sponsored by several denominations, for women to rethink and reframe the patriarchal nature of Christianity. This conference generated intense debate, with critics alleging that the women had been praying to a pagan goddess — because they had used the ancient name of *Sophia* to describe the wisdom of God — a charge conference organizers denied.

Sophia is a Greek word meaning "wisdom." The name Sophia is used to represent the feminine aspect of God described in Proverbs 8, which later became assimilated with the masculine *Logos* of John 1. This "wisdom," or *Chokmah* (Hebrew), calls herself the "first-fruits of God's fashioning, before the oldest of his works …. I was beside the master craftsman, delighting him day after day, ever at play in his presence, at play everywhere on his earth, delighting to be with the children of men." (Proverbs 8:22,30,31).

Nancy Berneking and Pamela Joern describe some of the repercussions of this legendarily controversial conference: "Within days after the closing ritual of the conference, conservative factions of some denominations mobilized an effort to denounce the conference. Mailings were sent encouraging churches to withhold funds from denominational activities and call for the resignation of church leaders and the censure of future feminist/womanist/mujerista activities."[7]

"The horror stories included tales of hate mail, job losses, death threats, charges of heresy, and more. Backlash, the bane of women throughout history, had surfaced again and was being coordinated by a coterie of the religious right."[8]

Mary Elva Smith, the director of the Women's Ministries Program Area of the Presbyterian Church (U.S.A.), describes how this backlash has been silencing feminist theologians in her denomination ever since. Smith, who attended the conference, says the silence that ensued in its aftermath was terrible. Although she didn't agree with every speaker, she says, the sensationalized coverage of it was erroneous: "I was there, and what was reported was not what I experienced."

Smith, who was then a member of the General Assembly Council (GAC), recalls former General Assembly moderator Freda Gardner's comments to the GAC. In Smith's paraphrase, Gardner said, "I'm sixty-something. I'm a professor at Princeton Theological Seminary. And you still don't believe I can think for myself." That kind of silencing, Smith says, was a slap in every Presbyterian woman's face. "And I don't think we deserve that."

"The result of using your power always carries with it a risk," Smith points out. "We are called to use our power with wisdom ... and to encourage and support one another." She says there is nothing inherently bad in feminist theology, no matter what its critics might believe. "Feminist theology is within the Reformed tradition, which is not [set] in stone," Smith notes. "We're reformed yet always being reformed. Feminist theology falls within the Reformed tradition. ... It brings to it another perspective that needs to be heard."[9]

Such shutting down and interrupting of the expression of women can make us fearful of moving forward. To trust boldly our awareness, we must listen to our inner voice, honor our perspective, and engage actively in our own reformation.

> Commandment: You will not be aware or value your intuition;
> you will believe what you are told.

Jesus, the teacher, spoke his truth. Some of his message was rooted in the sacred teachings of the culture in which he lived and learned, but much was from his own understanding of his experience of life in an agrarian culture. He spoke of farming and shepherding, domestic realities and family relationships. He named what he observed and he spoke with authority, trusting his own intuitive awareness. Consider the story of the Samaritan woman:

> On the way he came to the Samaritan town called Sychar. ... Jacob's well was there, and Jesus, tired by the journey, sat down by the well. ... A Samaritan woman came to draw water. ... "Go and call your husband," Jesus said to her, "and come back here." The woman answered, "I have no husband." Jesus said to her, "You are right to say 'I have no husband'; for although you have had five, the one you have now is not your husband. You spoke the truth there. ... God is spirit, and those who worship must worship in spirit and truth." (John 4:5–24)

Jesus simply reached out to the woman and told her the truth that he realized about her life. He acknowledged her for naming the truth for herself. He expressed no judgment, only awareness and understanding. His message rang louder and truer than any voices of judgment lingering within. She was transformed by this encounter and went on to speak her own truth to her whole town. What might Jesus observe and name if he came to our towns? To our homes? What might Jesus say if he visited our churches? What would he think about our country? What truths must we acknowledge about ourselves? How can we be transformed to speak our truths with confidence?

Although Jesus trusted in his ability to see and name what was true, opportunities for the fundamentalist woman to honor or develop her own intuitive sense are suspect as "New Age" or "occult." Meditation and yoga, ancient practices that emphasize quiet focus and enhance the integration of the body, mind, and spirit, often are warned against or even forbidden in fundamentalist churches. Many of these arts and practices contain age-old wisdom, much of it congruent with the teachings of Jesus. Like feminine expression itself, these practices are shamed and oppressed lest their influence challenge the church into a truer alignment with Jesus' vision.

Case Study: Inner Voice of Truth

People are transformed when they are willing to listen and act with authority in response to what they discover to be true. Sometimes they even hear the quiet, still voice of God speaking louder than the voices of domination and control.

Nancy wondered why she could never comfortably assert herself in the relationships of her life. Why, even with her closest friends and colleagues, did she feel inhibited and afraid to speak, like a fearful little girl? Like her mother before her, Nancy was married to a corporate executive. When her husband received his first promotion, she was in her late twenties, and she attributed the terror she felt at business functions to her lack of experience. Yet even as a woman in midlife, she regarded every corporate dinner party with a dread most of us reserve for lengthy dental procedures.

Nancy was rarely able to eat at these parties, and she spent every moment trying to anticipate the "right thing to say" in conversations with people who were no longer strangers but still barely acquaintances. She felt young and naive with other adults; so she worked out a strategy for these situations. She asked questions, always hoping her conversation partner would fall into a lengthy story or explanation. While she fanned their egos, she hid the fact that she had lost her own voice. After years of avoiding speaking her thoughts and feelings on most topics, she was now usually unaware of them, overshadowed as they were by "the right thing to say."

Nancy had grown up in a male-dominated, fundamentalist family, in which the unspoken yet clear message was women should wear beige; women should be invisible — like children, they should be seen and not heard. In Nancy's family, men were respected. Only men were expected to go into the world, to conquer and excel, to gain status, power, and position within the community. Only their voices and opinions were acknowledged. As a young girl, Nancy saw her father reinforcing such male dominance and superiority at home. She watched her mother submit unquestioningly to these family rules of behavior. In her family, parents paid for a son's education, but a daughter paid her own way. Clearly, a woman's place was in the home, not in the world.

These family dynamics offered Nancy no support for excelling in her world or for developing into a whole and healthy woman. Her family attended a Protestant church where, Sunday after Sunday, she observed that only the men were really visible, only they were in positions of leadership. Women were the blurry background, coming into focus only as they neared their men. Then they could be clearly seen — as support.

Nancy came to therapy because lately an unexpectedly insistent inner voice was calling her to ministry. She was stunned by the intense and endless "gnawing" of this desire. After trying for years to silence that inner voice, she scheduled an appointment to speak with her minister. She recalled that visit with rueful humor.

The pastor's office was large, with mahogany wainscoting and heavy draperies. Just walking in made her feel small and childlike. The pastor, a man old enough to be Nancy's father, sat behind his huge desk. He was in full dress uniform — gray suit, white shirt, and conservative tie — and looked ready to give a sermon at a minute's notice, even though it was only Tuesday. When Nancy revealed the reason for her visit, the minister sighed and began by telling her that he was spending "entirely too much time" counseling women with "notions" of entering the ministry. Finally, he looked at her squarely and demanded to know, "What makes you think you want to be a minister?"

Nancy told him that her feelings were powerful to the point of being overwhelming, that she had prayed for guidance on the matter and, since her feeling had persisted, even strengthened, she took that to be God's way of telling her to act on it.

The minister was unimpressed. "You know perfectly well that scriptures tell us women are not to be given that kind of position in the church. It's scripture you should listen to, not feelings. It seems to me you are forgetting your place."

At this point, Nancy surprised even herself by continuing. She made it clear that she was not talking about ordinary feelings, but "about an inclination so powerful I've never felt anything like it before." She tried to tell him that she was not used to this sort of certainty, that it felt wrong to ignore it.

She must have reached the man at least a little, because he actually gave some thought to her words. "Maybe you're miserable because you're not satisfied with this very difficult time in your life. You've been a wife and mother, and now the children are older. Perhaps you don't feel as necessary in your God-given role as you did even a few years ago. You know, this feminism that's so popular with so many of the women has a way of making a lot of you miserable. You hit a rough patch in your life and decide you need to change everything."

He then offered her the minister's panacea, the all-purpose prescription for female woes: "Perhaps you'd like to teach Sunday school. We badly need a teacher for our fifth graders."

So, for a while, Nancy taught Sunday school classes, reasoning that it was meaningful work, hoping that it might still the voice that called her to theological study and ministry. At the same time, she turned to others in her church — elders, ministers she'd known years before, devout friends. All delivered the same blunt message: "What you want is not possible. Forget it. You're a woman." These loud and limiting voices threatened her resolve.

Before she could respond to her inner voice of truth, Nancy was able to utilize therapy to do the arduous work of uncovering the beliefs so ingrained and internalized that they had become her own. She needed to evaluate what the church was telling her was God's will for her life and to ask: was it truly God's will, or was it something else? Was it simply domination and control disguised as truth? Nancy discovered she needed more than faith in church authority; she needed faith in herself as an intelligent and gifted woman, capable of being the authority of her own life. This eventually led to her move away from fundamentalism. As her journey progressed, she experienced a breakthrough. "I am as powerful now as the voices that used to limit me, if not more so," she reported as she began to make new choices and plans.

Her new insights and maturation paid off. She eventually did go to seminary and became an ordained minister in a progressive denomination that has supported her continued growth as both a woman and a church leader.

Finding the support to trust what we know, and the courage to make it happen, may require radical movement out of our old comfortable patterns and limiting cognitive beliefs. Sometimes what we are told is not to be trusted; we must find our own truth, believing what is true will make us free.

Creation: "I will judge for myself what is true and just."

Recognize Your Authority

Jesus said: "Why not judge for yourselves what is upright?" (Luke 12:57)

This is your indigo chakra of intuition and awareness; honoring your own point of view and opening your mind's eye. It is called the *third eye* or the *brow chakra* and includes the eyes and ears and forehead. The brow chakra relates to being aware: to evaluate information, observe realities, and decide for yourself what is true. Reflect on times in your life when you trusted your intuitive sense as a mother, as a friend, or in a business decision. Honor your ability to integrate new ideas into the context of your own life experience and wisdom. What in the past has interrupted your willingness to trust your own discernment? What darkness obscures your light? Notice light; dim light, candlelight, broad daylight, twilight, moonlight. What does your light look like? Enjoy your brilliance as you learn to rely on your own authority. Radiate the delight of your enlightenment.

Women often feel they are to blame for everything that has gone wrong in their lives and in the world. When we continue to cooperate with and perpetuate a repressive and dominating system, we *are* responsible. We must accept and claim that responsibility and the authority of our own awareness so that we can better understand and move forward in truth. We may be afraid of the consequences that speaking the truth might bring. Speaking truth can be dangerous, especially when the system thrives on silencing its members.

We begin by observing the experiences of our own lives, reflecting on our own journeys, watching the people around us as they change and grow, seeing what contributes to wholeness and what diminishes it. We can look at our families, our churches, and the influence of our habits on the health of the world. We must talk about what is true from our own authoritative point of view, not in line with any particular doctrine, and not necessarily as experts on theological, economic, or political theory — but simply as concerned women insisting on basic human rights for all people, including ourselves. As we develop discernment about our own lives, we can more clearly evaluate what is true and just in our external world.

We can honor our intuitive sense. A woman's intuition is that certain knowing, deeply connected to her emotions, in which an ongoing interactive exchange occurs between the physical world and the spirit world. This inner experience of truth comes from the deepest part of herself, where all dimensions of her soul come together; this is the place where women's intuition is birthed and lives. It includes her feelings, thoughts, and sensory perceptions, but it expands to encompass a knowing beyond words.

Sometimes this knowledge extends beyond the expectations of conventional wisdom. It may encompass ancient truths, generationally transmitted, sent to be quietly cradled within a woman's intuitive womb, perhaps in the way Mary "treasured all these things and pondered them in her heart" (Luke 2:19). Sometimes intuitive knowing is communicated from and within the spirit world; or it is transmitted through nature and animals, or received as part of the collective consciousness of women.

Regardless of what form her intuitive knowing takes, it is essential that a woman connect with this vital aspect of her wise being. Like a tree with strong and verdant branches whose roots travel deep and broad, she is grounded in her body while extending her sensory branches to receive all the higher knowing she needs.

We can find support for alternative ideas. We can make new friends with women who will listen without criticizing. We can become a friend to someone who needs to be heard without judgment. We can practice not being interrupted in our learning, in our intuiting, and in our speaking. We may need to practice attitudes and phrases that will help us to hold onto our own perceptions:

I have my own understanding of this.

I just don't see it the way you do.

That doesn't ring true with my experience.

Apparently we disagree.

I'll make up my own mind.

I'm not sure yet what my position on that would be.

We alone are the experts on our lives, our experiences, our ideas, values, and beliefs. What works for us in family life for resolving conflict and supporting growth will also work in our churches and in our larger circles of influence. Those in positions of power will not do for us the work we are called to do. As the great Hindu activist Mahatma Gandhi said, you must "be the change you wish to see in the world."[10] We can create circles of blessing in which we tell our own stories, and we can inspire others to do the same. Women must take their places in their own homes and in all dimensions of their lives to own and share their voices, their opinions, their influence, their love, and their amazing creative power.

Case Study: I'll Fly Away

As we trust our intuition and honor mystery, we may be surprised in the critical moments of our life experiences. When we allow ourselves to fully live these moments apart from the script of what we are told to believe, we may discover profound understanding and comfort.

Michelle was a warm and loving mother of two grown daughters. She didn't raise her family in the church, but in the woods. She taught her girls to honor the earth and to appreciate their own unique gifts and beauty. She modeled love and care for others. Amy, her older daughter, grew to nurture her spirituality in a quiet way. Her younger daughter, Kari, had a conversion to Christianity during high school and boldly shared with her family through the years the joy of her beliefs and her hopes for their salvation.

When she was in her fifties, Michelle began the journey of her second struggle with breast cancer. She faced each day with courage, receiving love and support from her family. At some point she prayed with Kari to trust in Jesus and claim her eternity in heaven. Amy, with her own views, felt somewhat apart from this new bond of shared belief between her mother and Kari, but they all maintained close and loving relationships with one another. Michelle began to attend a local fellowship church and found a prayer group of women who became an important source of support throughout her illness.

Meanwhile, Amy fostered her own spiritual bond with her mother. She lived close by and nurtured Michelle regularly with her presence and her touch, providing physical therapy and daily massage. Amy's connection to her mom's after-life had already begun. Michelle loved watching birds, and as she became housebound, Amy tried to lure songbirds with feeders outside her mother's window, but without success. For Amy, birds represented the movement between the earth and the heavens, the seen and the unseen, the embodiment of the ethereal, the spirituality of physical presence. She felt the birds could somehow bring her mother comfort. Amy's attunement eventually facilitated a comforting for others she couldn't have imagined.

As the end of Michelle's life drew near, her family encircled her with love, sharing the stories and memories of their lives together. On the morning she passed, at last a bird arrived. It was bold and persistent, joyfully darting and tapping on the window outside the kitchen where Kari and her father were beginning to assimilate their grief. Both were amazed and convinced that somehow, in some mystical way, the tiny bird was a messenger — from God or from Michelle — or perhaps even Michelle's essence itself, bringing them reassurance.

Kari proceeded to plan the memorial service, asking the pastor of Michelle's church to speak. The minister barely knew her, so he didn't speak personally of her life and legacy.

He talked of how Michelle believed she would go to heaven because she had accepted Jesus as her Lord and Savior, and said that those who would like to see her again could do so, too. Michelle's young grandson, disturbed by the pastor's glibness, spoke up to remind people of what a deeply spiritual, loving, and welcoming person his grandmother had been, lest they forget these realities in light of the authoritarian and exclusive message just delivered by the pastor. Some friends and family shared their loving remembrances. Other family members were simply speechless. Some of Michelle's closest friends felt the need to walk away.

Finally, Kari spoke up with the truth of the experience that had most comforted her through her loss. She told the story of the songbird: the mysterious, wonder-filled presence of Michelle, of God, of goodness and assurance. Her experience may not have fit into her religious paradigm, but having had eyes to see, Kari recognized its value for her, her family, and for those who heard her story. Amy's faith in the mystery had unfolded into an unforeseen gift.

Eve, the mother of all living, can inspire our confidence to trust what we know to be true. Sometimes it's hard to sort out what we truly believe. Sometimes something seems right because it is what we have always heard. Sometimes the message is delivered with such persuasive force that we feel powerless to disagree. But in the quiet of our hearts, when we listen to the still, small voice that tells us the truth about ourselves, we will hear the truth about God and about the world.

This part of ourselves may have been entombed for a long time, waiting to be called out, waiting for permission to be reborn, renewed, resurrected, and reconnected to the family of women and to Eve, the embodiment of womanly grace and boldness. But Jesus, love incarnate, who cries when we cry, calls us from the tomb to come out. Eve and Jesus modeled intuitive integrity as they followed their impulses, lived in the moment, shared their food, and valued their relationships. Jesus calls us back to life and calls on our communities to unbind us. Let us go free (John 11:1–44).

We conclude this chapter with feminist theologian Carter Heyward's statement about the authority that can be trusted:

> No person, religion, tradition, profession, rule, or resource should be inherently authoritative for us. We should always ask this question: Does it help us realize more fundamentally our connectedness to one another and hence the shape of our own identities as persons-in-relation?
>
> The authority that can be trusted calls forth something that already is, and if the authority is sacred, the "something" is the possibility of mutuality. When we speak with such authority, or are touched by the authority of others as a resource of blessing, it is because they and we are relating in such a way as to call forth who we are in right relation.
>
> The value and meaning of authority, in the praxis of mutual rela-tion, is to shape justice, the logos of God. As such, authority is the power to elicit among us, between us, and within us, that which already is, to give birth to who we are when we are related rightly. The authority of God is not the power to create out of nothing (the mythos of patriarchal deity), but rather the power to co-create out of the fabric of our daily lives who we are when we are related mutually — with justice and compassion.[11]

Dance: Choose a piece of music that speaks to you of intuition, truth, confidence, and authority. Wear an indigo dress or tie a sheer indigo scarf around your brow. Give yourself permission to embody your third eye chakra through the beauty and clarity of your dance.

Mirror: This sharing of movement, planned for two people, provides a profound opportunity for connection with another, soul to soul. It can be shared in a large group of several pairs. It can be done in silence or with a piece of instrumental music playing. The partners make eye contact and maintain it throughout the exercise. One partner leads by making movements that the second partner can easily follow without looking away from the eyes. You may begin with simple hand and arm movements, then add the legs and body in moving side to side or forward and back as well. After a minute or so, the second person becomes the initiator of the movement, with the first person mirroring. In the third phase, the leadership of the movement goes back and forth between the partners so subtly that perhaps neither knows who is taking the lead in the moment. Be sure to move slowly and carefully, especially at first, so you don't lose or confuse your partner.

Mirror Solo: This same exercise can be done with a real mirror reflecting you. In this case your partner will have no trouble following, but move intentionally, maintaining the constant visual connection. As you gaze steadily at your own reflection, notice the strength and beauty of your movement, the wisdom and confidence in your eyes.

Notes

1 Gary Ezzo and Robert Bucknam, *On Becoming Babywise* (Sisters, OR: Multnomah, 1995), 139.

2 Ronald M. Enroth, *Churches That Abuse* (Grand Rapids, MI: Zondervan, 1992), 105.

3 Rick Warren, *The Purpose Driven Life* (Grand Rapids, MI: Zondervan, 2002), 187.

4 Howard J. Van Till, *The Fourth Day* (Grand Rapids, MI: Eerdsmans, 1986), 11.

5 Walter Wink, "Homosexuality and the Bible," *The Fellowship of Reconciliation*, 5-10. http://www.forusa.org/articlesandresources/wink-homosexuality.html.

6 WorldofQuotes.com, "Browse the Authors: Albert Einstein," www.worldofquotes.com/author/Albert-Einstein/1/index.html.

7 Pamela Carter Joern, "Introduction," in *Re-Membering and Re-Imagining*, eds. Nancy J. Berneking and Pamela Carter Joern, xv (Cleveland: The Pilgrim Press, 1995).

8 Nancy J. Berneking, "Preface," in *Re-Membering and Re-Imagining*, eds. Nancy J. Berneking and Pamela Carter Joern, xi (Cleveland: The Pilgrim Press, 1995).

9 Alexa Smith and Jerry L. Van Marter, "Women's Ministries Director Calls

for New Global Women's Conference." *Presbyterian Outlook*, www.pres-outlook.com/HTML/women822.html (accessed August 22, 2001).

10 WorldofQuotes.com, "Browse the Authors: Gandhi," www.worldofquotes.com/author/Mahatma-Gandhi/1/.

11 Carter Heyward, *Touching Our Strength: The Erotic as Power and the Love of God* (San Francisco: HarperSanFrancisco, 1989), 58.

6

Exploring Self-Expression
Throat Chakra: Speaking and Being Heard

Burn

Some mother wants to burn a flag
Her own spark almost extinguished
By the patriarchy and patriotism
Of her "Christian" culture

But now, her own fire is burning
After all these smoldering years
She has no problem with Jesus
Or with God whose love she knows

But she is incensed with the system
Waging unholy war
On women and children at home and abroad
In the name of God and country

Now, she enlightens every conversation
Shining brightly at last
She welcomes the spectrum of fullness
And is not overcome by the dark

Her countenance radiates courage
Her wisdom elucidates truth
I pledge allegiance to that mother
And to the igniting for which she stands

Characteristic: Women's voices are silenced,
then co-opted for promotion of the system.

Fundamentalist women sense acutely the potential judgment that ensues if the ideas they offer do not fit in. The system supports a narrowly defined body of beliefs. Women speaking up in any way are subject to harsh scrutiny. So, many don't. Furthermore, some opportunities previously available to women have disappeared. Consider the crisis several years ago at Southern Baptist Theological Seminary, a conservative seminary in Louisville, Kentucky. The seminary had announced that Diana Garland, the dean of the seminary's Carver School of Social Work, had resigned in a dispute over faculty hiring. Later, she corrected their commentary, noting, "I have not resigned — I was terminated."[1] Her departure as dean was precipitated by President Albert Mohler's withdrawal of support for a social work faculty candidate, David Sherwood, because of the candidate's views on women's role as ministers. At the president's request, the candidate had written about his view of women in ministry. Sherwood said in part, "In my understanding of Scripture, God's Spirit blows where it wills and certain (but not all) women may be called to any role in the ministry of the church, just as certain (but not all) men may be."[2] As a result of this statement, an uproar began and President Mohler issued this statement: "This institution has always said there are certain issues on which no diversity of opinions can be tolerated."[3]

Ironically, a commentary in *The Christian Century* noted that "one week after the trustees of the Southern Baptist Theological Seminary voted to hire only professors who believe that women are not called to preach, three women students won top awards in April in the school's annual preaching competition. ... The Clyde T. Francisco Preaching Awards are made by a committee of students and faculty, all male, who reviewed sermons in manuscript form without identification of each preacher's gender."[4]

Soon after these incidents, the official squelching of women's voices in this tradition was accomplished. In 2000, the "Baptist Faith and Message," a summary of faith of the Southern Baptist Convention, was revised from an earlier statement of 1963 to completely withdraw the office of pastor from women.

The 1963 document stated: "In such a congregation, members are equally responsible. Its Scriptural officers are pastors and deacons." In the replacement document of 2000, material was added: "In such a congregation each member is responsible and accountable to Christ as

Lord. Its Scriptural officers are pastors and deacons. While both men and women are gifted for service in the church, the office of pastor is limited to men as qualified by Scripture."[5]

The quieting of women's voices also comes from within. Some women believe their voices are not their own. They do not know they can, nor do they know how to, use their voices to assert themselves or to make their message known. They may experience a split between the body and the voice, in which the two become so disconnected that one no longer supports the other. In fact, the voice and the body can work against each other at times, with the body offering cues and signals that the voice is incapable of acknowledging.

During therapy, women sometimes struggle to speak their truth. Their necks become blotchy and red. Veins protrude. Some report a lump or a tightening in their throats when they even think of expressing themselves verbally. Sometimes women become spokespeople for the very systems that limit and silence them.

Paula

As a high school senior, I discovered the speech team. I wrote a speech about how young people are drawn to religious cults because of the extreme sense of belonging they experience in such cults. I began to compete as part of my team. I must have been very convincing with my opening lines: "Dear mom and dad, don't be concerned and don't try to find me. I am fine and happier than I've ever been." I qualified for the national tournament.

With this new awareness of myself as a public speaker, I auditioned for the opportunity to speak at our school's graduation. I wrote a speech about how "we find ourselves through experience." It was an invitation to explore, to try on life, to learn about self through hands-on exposure to the world. I would endorse that advice today. I have raised my children to discover themselves in that way, tempered by the restraints of safety, responsibility, and respect for themselves and others. I was selected to deliver the speech at graduation on June 6, 1977.

Before the day came, however, someone "got to me." My Christian youth leader reminded me what a wonderful opportunity I had to speak up for the Lord and make my speech into an evangelistic message. It would be just the opportunity, I reasoned, to "be not ashamed" of the gospel. So I tweaked the speech to say I had found myself through an experience with Jesus Christ and that they all could, too. Really, I didn't mind. I had plenty of support. The youth leader, my parents, my

Christian friends, my church — we all believed in Jesus. No one suggested that my speech, in my own voice, was just fine the way it had been. I was convinced I could further "the Kingdom" with this message. Only my "non-believing" grandmother, who heard the speech discussed on local talk radio, wrestled with the ethics of the situation.

As I am involved with raising my own children now, I realize what a shame that was. I feel ashamed that I so easily gave up my message and my voice to comply with the will of people in power positions. Today, I wouldn't give up my story — and I would vigorously support my children's resistance to such pressure themselves. What they have to say from their own hearts and perspectives is marvelous. Now I know the same is true for me. I just didn't know it then.

I went on to the national speech tournament, and while sitting on a bench at the Seattle Center, I encountered a young person collecting money for youth programs. "Sure, I'd like to contribute." Just as he left, I realized he was part of the Unification Church, one of the very cults I discussed in my speech. I might have recognized a Krishna saffron robe, but I couldn't spot a plainclothes "Moonie." I became tearful and upset that I had just given financial support to what I described in my speech as a religious cult. Perhaps I was mostly confused and shaken by my own inability to discern who was part of a cult, after all. Today, Reverend Sun Myung Moon of the Unification church is the owner of *The Washington Times* and a major donor to conservative interests — it's still confusing.

I had little success at that tournament and have struggled ever since to reclaim the confidence of my own voice.

Commandment: You will fit in and not express your uniqueness.

Fundamentalist religious institutions require a commitment to agreement and sameness. Rules for behavior, usually unspoken, communicate the primary message of the system: we will not tolerate any member, especially a female, who expresses her uniqueness apart from the system's determination of what is permissible. If one chooses to differ or disagree with the foundational teachings, one is labeled a "rebellious, trouble-making backslider." The unspoken statement in this system is that submission equals goodness. This closed system thrives on silence.

The individual must surrender her mind to that of the system, which programs her not to cause discord by thinking independently. Members are never sure exactly what would happen if they chose to disagree; they just know instinctivey. Members know instinctively that if they step out of line, there will be a price to pay. Thus, their minds reinforce that they'd better not even think it, much less try it. The *it* could be anything from thinking freely to speaking freely to being free. Unspoken consequences for these independent behaviors might involve loss of status, ostracism, or physical or emotional estrangement.

Case Study: If the Shoe Doesn't Fit ...

The pressure to conform to the expectations of the system can be quite subtle. Once a woman can recognize and name the ways such coercion is exercised, she can make choices about how to respond.

When Tiffany first began regular participation in group therapy she was forty-five. Her preferred style of dress, she says, was "a holdover from my days as a hippie." She wears long, full skirts, loose cotton tops, sandals in summer, and boots in winter. She laughs as she notes, "the guy who invented pantyhose — I'm sure it wasn't a woman — should be tarred and feathered." Her long brown hair, streaked with gray, is always worn in a clip at the nape of her neck. She wears little makeup.

Raised in a "moderately religious" household, Tiffany married into a large family of fundamentalist Christians. She feels awkward and uncomfortable when she's around them because she senses their judgment, and that makes her angry. The women in the family make her particularly furious. "They seem like nice enough people," she explains. "They've never criticized me directly. But they clearly do not approve of the woman I am today. I have been told that behind my back I'm talked about as a backslider, a non-Christian — you know, one of those radical feminists who might seduce the younger women with my modern philosophies!"

Tiffany knows how her in-laws feel about her hippie-like appearance, but not because they've actually said anything to her. Instead, they give her gifts — lots of gifts. "I get presents of little cardigan sweater sets in pastel colors," she says. "My ears are pierced — twice on each lobe, in fact. But they insist on buying me clip-on earrings, little fake pearls, with a little fake pearl necklace to match. I carry a backpack instead of a traditional handbag, but that doesn't stop them from buying me purses, lots of them — in patent leather, no less."

But the final absurdity was when Tiffany's mother-in-law showed up one day with a Bloomingdale's shopping bag containing three pairs of "classic pumps" with two-inch heels. Her mother-in-law innocently claimed, "They were having a sale and I thought you might like these to wear to church. ... Pumps are such a womanly, sophisticated look, you know."

Tiffany shared with the group, "I have never worn heels during my entire married life. Why does she think I want to start now? Besides, she knows I've recently taken a break from church."

Tiffany felt this "gift" was her mother-in-law's indirect way of expressing her disapproval of Tiffany's lack of conformity with the family values. Clearly, in this family system, living to please others and behaving by the rules of "we-ness" are requirements for acceptability and continuing membership. Tiffany felt the pressure to yield to the family's subversive tactics, not only within herself but from her husband as well. As a boy, he had internalized his family's fundamentalist rules, knowing the right way to respond in this system. Her husband knew that if they, as a couple, did not obediently respond to his parent's controlling wishes, they would be labeled as black sheep. He had been taught to fear that threat.

With the group's support, Tiffany learned she had choices about how she would respond to her in-laws' actions. Some gifts, she decided to graciously receive without feeling controlled or intimidated. Others she chose not to accept and instead returned them, explaining her reasons. Some, she simply passed on to a charitable organization. Now abiding by her own guidelines, she continues to dress as she pleases, think for herself, and develop her own creativity in a variety of ways.

Despite the pressure she feels to agree and comply with her in-laws' values, today she chooses to worship at a Unitarian church and participates in full-moon circles. She socializes with people who more accurately reflect her own open-minded beliefs and who value diversity. Sometimes she chooses to share her ideas with her in-laws, but for the most part, she has learned that within this family, there is little tolerance not only for how one dresses, but for different ideas and opinions. She has learned not to allow their approval, or lack of it, to control her or inhibit her. She now realizes that the best gift she can offer her family is expressing her uniqueness with integrity and boldness, speaking her truth in love. Through this offering, she gives them an opportunity to expand their world.

Tiffany and her husband have benefited from couples therapy. Through hard work and a commitment to love each other practically and daily, they are learning to respect each other's different needs with respect to their in-laws. Tiffany remains more detached, purposely not making contact that is too engaging or too draining for her. She supports her husband in being more in the foreground with them, since they are his family. Her husband supports Tiffany's position completely and has carefully learned how to "leave his father and mother while cleaving to his wife." Tiffany appreciates the tension of this challenging position and loves him more for his willingness to balance his love for her with his love for his family. She respects his need to choose both, and he loves Tiffany more deeply for this beautifully supportive and compassionately understanding position.

The fundamentalist intolerance for human differences manifested in the failure of her Christian in-laws' to testify, in practical terms, of God's great love for human diversity, saddens Tiffany. Instead of promoting tolerance, this belief system stifles the wealth and breadth of God's creative genius. In the earth's expansive color, the great variety of species, and the wonder of each individual, Tiffany sees God's rich and varied expression. Within the closed system of fundamentalism, diversity is perceived as a threatening, practically sinful reality. Often, those drawn to fundamentalist Christianity as a framework for living are those who like things to remain predictable. Sameness equals security. Differences represent a threat to what is known, the ultimate threat to one's illusion of a secure position in the world.

Only through recognizing and honoring human diversity and respecting our differences will we change and grow into full maturity as individuals and as larger communities. Then, paradoxically, we can discover and celebrate our connectedness as well as our individuality, the commonality of our uniqueness.

Creation: "I will speak up fearlessly; tell my own stories;
develop my art; and own my voice."

Open to Creative Expression

"Pray for me to be given an opportunity to open my mouth and fearlessly make known the mystery of the gospel of which I am an ambassador in chains; pray that in proclaiming it I may speak as fearlessly as I ought to." (Ephesians 6:19–20)

"Words flow out of what fills the heart." (Matthew 12:35)

For the blue chakra, we focus on the throat area, where the voice is generated, to give voice to what lives inside — the true-blue self. Perhaps you feel tension associated with this chakra expanding through your neck and shoulders. It is your heritage to speak your truth and to be heard. Listen to the internal voice that only you know. Imagine yourself speaking to the people who never heard what you wanted to say. Reflect on all the ways you express yourself — perhaps through music, handwork, poetry, sculpting, or cooking. All of these examples are just some opportunities for creative artistic expression. Through what medium does the clearest sense of you find voice? How can you find support for your audible voice in speaking your opinions, sharing your insights, and bringing the depth within you into the breadth of your community? Whether you profess, confess, or digress, fully express yourself in your own resonant voice.

Many capable and competent women describe themselves secretly as

- experiencing a lack of confidence,
- knowing they fail to show up in the important moments of their lives, and
- disbelieving they have the tools to live at ease in their world.

Owning our voices as women confirms

- that we trust our ability to talk back;
- that we are involved interactively;
- that we rely on ourselves in each moment;
- that we believe and know we will not miscommunicate; or
- that, if we do, we can clean it up.

Sometimes we need to practice speaking up, getting used to the sound of our own voice when it's not particularly polite or submissive or agreeable. We might practice saying phrases like these:

- I don't agree with your opinion.
- I'd like to say how I feel about this issue.
- I'm not finished speaking yet.
- I would like to finish without being interrupted.
- I guess we will have to disagree on this one.

Many women also report blocks in their creative expression. Several factors contribute to the limitations a woman might experience in developing her artistry. She may have

- no time for her "selfish pursuits,"
- no permission to take time,
- expectations of perfection rather than honoring "good enough,"
- a lack of connection to her feelings and creative center,
- no personal sense of power or authority for putting forth an idea,

- no support for her unique expression,
- lack of necessary training at developmentally appropriate times,
- fear of judgment.

There are many ways to nurture creative expression, and success in one venue may facilitate another. Dancing may free the poet in you. Drawing may unlock the storyteller. Singing may awaken the songwriter. Painting may empower you to speak out. Creative expression itself is a powerful tool for transformation.

For the healing of the church, women can offer their creativity as lay-people as well as clergy. Their capacity for integration can nurture new forms of liturgy, enhancing the fullness and inclusiveness of religious experience. Each gathering of people in church can be infused with elements of surprise and newness, with opportunities for the deepening of genuine human relations and spiritual insights. Women can offer their creative expression in powerful and effective ways to bring their individual churches, and the Christian church as a whole, to a closer cooperation with Jesus' liberating and life-giving message.

Our internal reality is articulated through the voice, a place where the private meets the public and the world hears. Whether speaking to a group, a colleague, a friend, a partner, or our children, our thoughts and beliefs shows up the second we open our mouths. The truth of what we say is then confirmed or denied by our behavior. What we speak or do not speak has a profound effect on how we interact with our environment and on how we experience belonging. Our voices are central to our emergence in the world. As we own the power in our voices internally, we claim the power to speak externally in our communities.

Each of us creates ever-expanding circles of influence simply by living each day. We constantly affect one another with our smiles, our attitudes, our words, and our support. Speaking up confirms and strengthens what we believe every time we do it. Social activism provides opportunities to join with others in exercising our voices and our values. While our internal process nurtures our commitment to action and our concern for the world outside us, our work in the public sphere (political, communal, or religious) strengthens our efforts with our private psychological and emotional core issues.

When we allow our voices to be conscripted to promote a dogma, we collaborate with the intentions of that system. When we dare to allow our authentic inner voices to be exposed, we begin to reverse the domination and silencing of the fundamentalist system. When we rise up to radiate and articulate our genuine and unique gifts from our Creator, we collaborate with the intentions of the divine. When we tell our own story, we are truly witnessing to God's presence and power in our lives. When we tell the old, old story, we must tell it in our own voices, in our own ways, from our own experiences of its truth for us.

Dance: Choose a piece of music that speaks to you of self-expression, speaking up, boldness, and creativity. Wear a blue dress or tie a blue scarf loosely around your neck. Give yourself permission to embody your throat chakra through the beauty and resonance of your dance.

Yes/No #1: This exercise creates an opportunity to more fully own our yes and no statements, by supporting the fluid movement of the owner-ship of our bodies and our voices in making our choices. Yes statements relate to our dreams, our creative expression, our moving forward in birthing our ideas. No statements relate to our boundaries, our limits, our values, our stopping places, our personal spaces.

This exercise is for two people: the sender and the receiver. They sit facing one another, a few feet apart. The sender imagines what she would like to say yes to, and as these ideas pass through her mind's eye, she audibly says "yes," or "YES!" or "yeah," in whatever manner captures her intention. She can own her yes statements (in all of their nuances) with awareness of the participation of her whole flesh in her responses. This activity continues for two to three minutes. The receiver sits quietly neutral, making no response, simply holding the space in support of the ownership of the sender's yes statements. Then the roles are reversed, so the receiver becomes the sender.

Now repeat the exercise using no statements. The first sender should imagine the things she wants to say no to. Some nos may be assertive, even aggressive; others are matter of fact. Again, this exercise is a whole body experience. Repeat the process of expressing no statements with the receiver as the sender.

Discuss the experience. Take a moment to write about what you have discovered. (One could also work with this exercise in a mirror if necessary.)

Yes/No #2: In this exercise, the idea is to build confidence in vocal expression and in setting personal limits. It is designed for two people participating together. Partners stand about ten feet apart, facing each other. The first partner may begin by saying "yes," and the other may respond by moving forward toward her. When she says "no," the partner must stop. She continues these requests/commands with varying degrees of intensity, to which the partner will respond accordingly. A strong "no" should elicit a sudden stop; a hearty "yes," a robust forward. Switch roles; talk about it. Try it again if you like. Write about it.

Resurrection/Egeiró

Walking and leaping and praising
To stand up is to rise up
To overcome fear
To speak up

To rebuke the wind he *arose*
Stand up, do not be afraid
Your sins are forgiven, *get up*
A touch on her hand and she *arose*
He took her by the hand and she *stood up*
They *woke up* and trimmed their lamps

He is risen
She is risen
We are risen indeed
Walking and leaping and praising

Notes

1 Mark E. McCormick, "Dean Says Seminary Fired Her from Post," *The Courier-Journal*, March 22, 1995.

2 Bob Terry, "A Crisis at Southern Seminary." *Word & Way: Journal of the Missouri Baptist Convention*, (March 30, 1995): 2.

3 Leslie Scanlon, "Dean of Baptist Seminary Forced to Quit." *The Courier-Jour nal*, March 21, 1995.

4 Elizabeth Anderson and Cathleen Falsani, "News of Churches," *Daughters of Sarah* (Fall 1995): 76.

5 SBC-Net Official Website of the Southern Baptist Convention "Comparison of 1925, 1963, and 2000 Baptist Faith and Message," SBC-Net, www.sbc.net/bfm/bfmcomparison.asp.www.sbc.net/bfm/bfmcomparison.as.

7

Unveiling Authenticity
Heart Chakra: Love for Self and Others

The Veil

She put on the veil to hide her discomfort
With the watching and judging, from fear,
So much that she dreamed was deemed not in alignment
With the values and rules, it was clear,
Of the ones who had influence, those with the power,
Who talked of God's love, but were scary.
So she covered her countenance, never to seem
Too confrontative or contrary.

Forgotten, the trust in what she had once loved,
In her own sense of beauty and truth
She now tried to be what she thought she should be:
Submissive, supportive, subdued.

A bird flapping her wings in the face of a wind
With never the courage to dive,
Helping others achieve while she struggled to breathe,
'Til her soul was just barely alive.
The veil was a comfort, a place she could hide,
In her pain with her grief as her art
But she still longed to soar with precision and drive,
To nurture her passion of heart.

Characteristic: Role is valued over authenticity.

As we watch young children developing, we see some girls drawn to dolls, some boys to sticks and wheels, and others not. Clearly each individual comes with their own blend of traits, which we might label with our own biases of what is classically feminine or masculine. To clarify and examine your own bias and assumptions, take a moment to make a list of qualities as you imagine them:

Feminine Characteristics   **Masculine Characteristics**

_____   _____

_____   _____

_____   _____

_____   _____

_____   _____

_____   _____

_____   _____

Do you find yourself crossing over in some ways, or do you fully embody your own gender specifics? Are there characteristics you have denied in yourself because of external judgments? Do you wish you had more characteristics from either one list or the other? How does society value these particular traits? What is lost when we deny parts of ourselves in order to relieve our anxiety about not fitting the mold? When you look honestly at your true self, can you welcome all the parts of you?

During a young woman's development, she may become overwhelmed by the ambiguities, choices, and pressures she faces. She may drape her discomfort in the Good Woman role, because she feels safer projecting an image than to be the self she has had little permission to explore. She may long for the acceptance and belonging that compliance promises. When it becomes too difficult to be with what is deeply human about herself, she might find in fundamentalism a means to cloak the parts of her that don't neatly fit the role. Fundamentalism at its core is an avoidance of one's humanity.

In the fundamentalist system, gender roles are strictly defined. The young woman is instructed to be submissive and modest, with "a quiet and gentle spirit," so she will attract a spiritual leader/godly man. If she plays the role well, she may do just that — and the man she attracts may be playing a role equally well. If either or both of them begin to express more of their authentic selves, they may find themselves poorly matched in temperament, in love with a role rather than a real person. Once she has married, a young woman may find the expectations of the Good Woman role suffocating but not recognize any option to ignore them, especially once children are involved.

Roberta

I recall a conversation with an older woman who was a member of my conservative Protestant church. As we talked about ourselves as women, she told me how lucky I was that I had been born a generation after her. She marveled at the freedom she believed the women in my generation had, in comparison to the severe lack of choices her generation faced growing up. As she talked, she revealed unfulfilled dreams — the missed opportunities for her self-expression apart from the roles of wife and mother, the book she could have written, the career she could have had. Even though she had found happiness and fulfillment in her domestic, homemaker role, she hoped I would not be engulfed in the same way she had been. Quietly, she whispered to me, "Don't let anybody tell you how to live your life. Be a woman on your own terms!"

As I looked around at church the next week, I noted that nearly every woman of my generation was married, with at least one or two children. Each had abandoned her education or her career, outwardly personifying the Good Woman role, looking remarkably like the preceeding generation. Many of these women, however, were at home full-time by choice. As I spoke with them, I discovered that some were very happy and found raising a family fulfilling. Others, however, were not happy. Some admitted to feeling stifled, depressed, and trapped, yet they were committed to doing what others expected, believing they had no other options. Still others looked sad and depressed but professed feelings of contentment and fulfillment. While I was taking this informal poll, one woman accused me of being selfish because I loved my career, demanding: "When are you going to have a family?

Remember, children are a sign of God's good favor." In her eyes, I had fallen from grace.

Clearly, some progress has been made in support of women's choices, but the Good Woman role is still alive and well. These women were experiencing enormous pressure to live their lives in accordance with the Christian female stereotype. One day soon after, much to my own surprise, I realized how strongly I was resisting motherhood. I did not want to feel trapped like so many women my age. On the surface, I thought I had chosen merely to put off having children so that I could develop my career. I believed my career would help me avoid feeling trapped. But I was unaware that, in defining myself as different from my mother and from my church peers, I was limiting myself. My life choices were not really my own, but a reaction to my family and church experiences.

My dad and I enjoyed many midnight chats, as he liked to call them. During our conversations, he often told me what I needed was to "find a man, get married, and have some babies." Looking back, I think he was frustrated and pained by my periods of confusion and depression, as I was trying to figure out what I was going to do with my life. Rather than simply *being* with me in my struggle, he sought to provide the answer for my life. I was not aware how much I was reacting against his simple solution for my unhappiness. I was going to prove to Dad that I was not the kind of female he expected me to be … even at a high cost to my authentic self.

Only after becoming aware of these influences on my life decisions — and admitting to myself that I wanted more than a career — did I feel free to want children, not because I was expected to, but because I genuinely wanted children. As I look back, I see that I, too, had been locked in a role, only I was expressing this role through a rigid commitment to my career as an avowed independent. I viewed my career as a primary aspect of self-identity, while other aspects of my feminine self-expression remained dormant. I reached the place of true liberation and authentic choice when I acknowledged that a woman who is truly free from the role can express herself *in response to her own desires and dreams*, not in reaction to another's desires for her life. Women who are truly free live their lives as fully integrated women in any location, whether at home, in the workplace, out having coffee with a friend, or in the church. A woman needs to be free to be herself, to have her own voice, to make her own choices, and to live her own life wherever she is. That is real freedom and authentic soul expression.

Such fullness of opportunity is hardly championed by conservative Christian spokespeople. In fact, Janice Shaw Crouse, of the Beverly LaHaye Institute (Concerned Women for America), not only acknowledges, but validates the continuing expectation society places on women to fall into a prescribed role. She describes "sexual competition" as the playing field for women.

> Sadly, the data tells us that contemporary cultural trends are not any more female-friendly than they have been for millennia. Sexual competition is still a young woman's playing field. But apparently many of today's young women, playing around with Mr. Big, aren't aware that they should be competing to find "Mr. Right" before their fertility runs out. Most of them don't realize that, after college, their marital options greatly shrink at the same time that their window of opportunity for children is closing.
>
> Young women need to hear the whole truth: by focusing on career over marriage and family in their 20s and 30s, they strengthen the likelihood that career is all that they will have left in their 40s.[1]

Or as Dobson puts it, "a woman typically has deep longings that can only be satisfied through a romantic long-term relationship with a man. Her self-esteem, contentment, and fulfillment are typically derived from intimacy, heart-to-heart, in marriage,"[2] and "the natural sex appeal of girls serves as their primary source of bargaining power in the game of life."[3]

Herein lie the core fundamentalist assumptions about women's needs, roles, and opportunities: for a woman to be satisfied she must find a husband early (before the pickings get slim) using her sex appeal as her basis for exchange. Is the prescription for fulfillment really so universal and simplistic? Do we really all want the same thing? Is sex appeal all women have to work with? Why do some, like Crouse and Dobson, continue to insist on such conformity rather than challenging misguided assumptions and inequities and offering support for each woman's individuality?

The high-intensity management of children and home life is a rich and valuable segment of parents' and children's lives, but it doesn't usually extend to retirement. Mothering isn't the only thing women can contribute and achieve. It is difficult for a woman to begin wondering about her marketable gifts and talents just as she is adjusting to an empty nest. Our childhood and young adulthood should be about this type of discovery. Instead, fundamentalists would simply have all women assume the role, play by the rules to catch Mr. Right before their fertility runs out, and then embrace motherhood as career.

Case Study: My Heart Is Racing

Parents are powerful players in keeping women in role. With the backing of their religious tradition, they can exercise a formidable influence.

Maggie entered therapy as a result of her fundamentalist parents' increased disapproval with her lifestyle: She didn't have a husband, and she didn't have children. She had been experiencing a lot of self-doubt and insecurity, questioning her life path, which at one time, she felt very secure about. In her younger years, she often said that she thought she would like to get married, but now she felt something blocking her. She had no conscious idea what or who this block might be.

When Maggie was in high school she wore her brown hair in a pageboy and used a lot of hairspray to keep it perfect. Now in her early forties, she still wore the same hair-sprayed pageboy. Like her hair, her clothes echoed an earlier era. In madras skirts, penny loafers, and broadcloth shirts with button-down collars, she pulled off the neat appearance that was obviously important to her.

When asked to describe herself, she listed the important elements of her identity in the following order: "I'm an only child. My parents are very religious people … they're fundamentalist Christians. They're very conservative and they think I'm too liberal." She paused, then added, "I'm a kindergarten teacher. Well, I'm trained as a teacher, but I'm actually working as a principal. I'm an elementary school principal!"

The order in which she gave these details reflected her beliefs about her roles and provided a concise outline of Maggie's problems. Though a woman in middle age, she still thought of herself as a child. Though she was a responsible adult, doing work that by any rational standard could be seen as contributing to society, she perceived herself through the eyes of a dependent and minimized her accomplishments.

Maggie explained, "My parents encouraged me to go into elementary education because that was a sensible career for a woman — the old line about how you can always 'go back to it' after you've raised your family. For the first few years after I started to work, they were supportive. But then they got kind of funny about my job, sort of distant. Whenever I'd talk about one of my students, my mom would say something about how I shouldn't have to take care of other people's children. The implication was that I should be having some of my own. I wasn't working on getting married as hard as I was working on my teaching career, and that worried them."

One evening Maggie came to therapy straight from her parents' home, where she'd had dinner. She was agitated when she arrived. The dinner conversation had revolved around mothers who work outside the home. Her mother had been quite critical, saying that such women sacrifice their children to their own selfish ambitions. Maggie, many of whose colleagues were working mothers, spoke in support of career moms, telling her mother, "They seem to me to take mothering very seriously, and they suffer a lot from the criticism people level at them for not being home all the time. Not all women can be home *all* the time, Mom. In fact, many women believe they are *better* mothers when they spend some time outside the home, developing other aspects of themselves. Not all women fit the domestic mold."

After a long silence, Maggie's mother reopened the subject from a new angle, asking, "When did you start becoming a liberal?" Maggie pinpointed this moment as the time her anxiety began rising. She spoke up again in defense of her colleagues, and in defense of herself, but her voice shook as she spoke. "It's not that I'm liberal, Mom. Things were different when you raised me. Now a lot of women have to work just to get by. And many women find fulfillment working outside the home. I think that's great. It's about time."

It wasn't much of a fight. In fact, as Maggie had correctly pointed out, it wasn't a fight at all. Yet as she told the story, Maggie became even more agitated. She reported, "My heart is racing, and I'm dizzy. I feel nauseous, and I can't catch my breath…. It's like they've taken away something good from me. I grew into something that I would not have been." Maggie couldn't diagnose her own panic attack. She was unaware that her symptoms were related to the difficult task of growing into adulthood and breaking her patterns of dependency on her mother and on the church.

Much of what Maggie had to work out in therapy centered around the perceived discrepancy between the way her fundamentalist parents appeared — nice people, loving parents, with good, upstanding moral character — and the judgment, disappointment, and disapproval emanating from them. Over months of painful work, Maggie came to see that her parent's love, which they professed to be abundant and free, was in fact a means of control and quite conditional upon her fulfilling their demands. "Sometimes I feel if I don't please my parents I'll just die," she commented. "And other times I feel if I don't stop caring about what they think of me, I'll die, too."

Whenever she asserted herself independently, expressing opinions and feelings opposed to her parents and their values, Maggie felt their withdrawal. Their expressed concern for her masked their desire to manipulate her, to keep her the dependent child, to form her into the woman they wanted her to be.

Years later, as Maggie proceeded in therapy and developed confidence that she could survive without her parents' approval, she was able to acknowledge her sexual feelings toward women. Maggie knew she had accomplished much work when she was able to invite her parents over for dinner and ask her lesbian lover to join them. Maggie said, "Mom, remember when you thought I was a liberal? Well, I want you to know that I am liberated ... a liberated lesbian, and this is my lover."

To challenge the beliefs one has inherited and to discover one's self requires openness, courage, and support. This encouragement may come from a therapist, a partner, friends, children, or a spiritual community. Too often, however, churches provide only reinforcement for the veil, supporting dependency and complacency, valuing the Good Woman role over authenticity.

Commandment: You will be forced to be what others need you to be; you will not be selfish.

Churches all over the country have organized study groups to apply the indoctrination program of *The Purpose Driven Life*. Many of the book's messages urging community and commitment are positive, but this book is undergirded with pure fundamentalist intentions. The author uses only male imagery for God, normalizes hierarchical domination, and subtly blames and shames women (Bathsheba, Tamar, etc., p. 196). Messages supporting every fundamentalist characteristic and commandment are embedded in the text. Readers are told that "self-denial is the core of servanthood" (p. 266); "It is your job to protect the unity of the church" (p. 160); You must "learn unselfishness" (p. 167); "Real servants don't complain of unfairness, don't have pity-parties. ... They just trust God and keep serving. ... It is also not our job to defend against criticism" (p. 268).[4] These admonitions are at the heart of the very issues women need help in overcoming; they don't need to be reinforced. Really, these messages are designed to keep women in their place.

Our uniqueness as women and our varied dreams do not always fit nicely into the role religious institutions would have us play. But when our individual perceptions and desires are denied, we all sacrifice something precious — our vitality. A woman who continues to live in a system of victimization, who continues to receive corrective messages that define who she should be and how she should act, eventually solidifies her limited self into the Good Woman role, embodying what is expected of a proper woman. She internalizes these messages as truth and enters a stage of emotional stagnation. These insults, affecting the totality of her being, cause a split in the physical, intellectual, emotional, sexual, and spiritual aspects of her soul, contributing to a disintegration of the self. Damage in any one area affects the others. As her wholeness is interrupted, the expression and integration of the whole woman is impaired.

By adulthood, any dimensions of the fundamentalist woman that are inconsistent with the stereotypic Good Woman are extinguished. Because each consecutive stage of growth is dependent on the successful mastery of the earlier stages, the woman becomes arrested in her development. Often she does not even know this is the case; she has become adept at compensating for internal vacancies. She may have learned to look like she has confidence and skills — displaying "the strong, together, empowered role" — but deep inside she often experiences a deficit. The rigid adherence to role requires her to make precarious adjustments. Emotionally and psychologically far younger than the body she inhabits, she does not yet possess all the internal resources she needs to move beyond a superficial competence.

Case Study: Shrinking Away

The fundamentalist female is both directly and indirectly discouraged from having a life apart from the expectations and needs of the system and the family. Life is not about her choices. The system's interests are placed above her own. When she yields to systemic control and domination, she has no opportunity for her own organic needs to emerge and find fulfillment. This stagnation leaves her, as well as the system, incomplete and fragmented. Individuals mature and grow, not by adherence to law, but through the individual response to, and fulfillment of, personal needs and interests. In Hailey's case, personal needs and interests were completely submerged for the sake of others, until at last she literally began to shrink away.

Hailey was the second of her family's two daughters. Her older sister, Sharon, was the "problem child." She ignored family rules, experimented with alcohol, and seemed always on the verge of trouble with the law. Sharon was hard to handle, a rebellious teen. To her strict religious parents, she was also a rebuke and a humiliation. They attended a support group at their church, looking for reassurance that Sharon's behavior was not their fault. There they openly revealed the struggles they were having, asking for help and prayer, subtly shaming and stereotyping their oldest daughter as a "problem," a "bad girl," the one with the "strong spirit that needed to be broken."

None of this got past Hailey. Perceptive and hyper-vigilant, she determined never to add stress to her family's already taxed system. She became a Good Girl, sacrificing herself to the needs of her parents, dutifully obeying all the rules without being told. "Hailey takes care of herself," her mother proudly told the support group.

In reality, no one was taking care of Hailey. She was isolated, not only within her family, where Sharon consumed everyone's energies, but also at school. Hailey quickly learned how to make her involuntary isolation appear as if it was working for her. Her aversion to any sort of adolescent rebellion — from dancing to defying parental curfews — set her apart from the other kids. Of course, her behavior had its rewards with the adults: it gave her a lot of time to accrue accomplishments and to achieve goals. These goals, however, were those chosen for her by her parents. They were not her own. While she concentrated all her efforts on coloring inside the lines, no one was attending to her; no one could see the larger picture; no one encouraged and guided her in the pursuit of her own heartfelt dreams and desires.

Hailey's parents praised her at home, and church members marveled over her as the gift God had given her parents. The implication that Sharon was something less than God's gift deepened the rift between the sisters that had already been carved by the parents. So in early adolescence, Hailey's needs were minimized, first by her family, then by herself. Her parents and church lauded her goodness, her sacrificial selflessness. Hailey and the Good Girl became one.

As a result, she became depressed and developed the beginnings of an eating disorder. Blaming herself for her plight, Hailey lacked insight into what was causing her pain. Although she had trouble admitting it to herself, the daily grind of self-sacrifice was taking its toll on her. Her internal self-talk echoed what her parents had always told her was true: "I have parents who love me. I'm second in my class at school. The people at church think I'm practically a saint. I can make other people happy. Why am I so unhappy?"

Hailey's journey to taking up less and less space, becoming smaller and quieter, is a common experience for girls and women in fundamentalist systems. Fortunately, her unhappiness and her weight loss brought her to the attention of her favorite teacher, and she eventually received the support she needed.

The school counselor referred her for a psychological assessment and private psychotherapy. Her parents were thrilled that their medical insurance covered the cost of her years of treatment.

With the help of her observant therapist, Hailey was able to acknowledge, "There's no voice in me telling me what I want."

"What happened to that voice?" her therapist asked.

"I stopped listening to it, so it stopped talking."

Hailey became aware of how even her physiology was revealing the truth of her Good Girl role. As she learned to breathe into the tight spaces of her rigid body she began to access her emotional self. Awakening to the excitement of embracing her own truth, and quieting the messages of others' perceptions, she began to reconnect with the truth of her own soul. She began to eat more freely and learned to make good choices about which foods she allowed into her "temple." She learned that pleasure and feeling good were things that she could enjoy and welcome into her life.

Through years of devotion to herself and perseverance, she was able to unveil her Good Girl role and realize that there were some aspects of the role she wanted to hold onto because they were congruent with the authentic parts of herself. Other aspects of this role she happily discarded, celebrating the newfound lightness and joy that she encountered in simply being herself.

Fundamentalist systems characteristically employ attitudinal stones of judgment and shame to control women, keeping them silenced and in role. Consider the story of the woman brought to Jesus by the Pharisees. The Pharisees asked Jesus whether she should be stoned for adultery. (Notice that we never hear about her male partner.) The Pharisees had already judged her and were calling on Jesus to pronounce her death sentence. Instead, Jesus encouraged the group to judge themselves instead of the woman: "Let the one among you who is guiltless be the first to throw a stone at her" (John 8:7). The members of the crowd, convicted by their own consciences, dispersed. Then Jesus said to the woman, "'Woman, where are they? Has no one condemned you?' She said, 'No one, sir.' And Jesus said, 'neither do I condemn you. Go, and sin no more'" (John 8:10–11). This story illustrates how Jesus felt about hypocritical judgment and condemnation.

Some churches openly shame and judge those who defy their role; others are more covert. Usually the control is disguised as something else: love, protection, or guidance. Regardless of the sugarcoating, the judgments are poisonous to the soul, eliminating in the woman a willingness to take risks. Judgment, shame, and control breed distrust and fear. Relationships with any degree of genuine authenticity and intimacy become difficult.

The fundamentalist woman who cooperates with the system cultivates a vacuum while she should be developing a strong and integrated sense of her self. The system is quick to fill up her emptiness with the Good Girl/Good Woman role. The role provides a semblance of self for the woman, but it is not her authentic self.

The script for the fundamentalist woman is particularly rigid; there is only one path carved out for her: obedience, domesticity, and motherhood. This is the Good Woman role. If the woman realizes she has needs that cannot be filled through domesticity, she must repress and deny them. The script says that she should be completely content fulfilling other's needs and ignoring her own. According to the script, only selfish, unspiritual women attempt to meet their own needs, whether physical, sexual, intellectual, or emotional.

If she is an independent woman, one who met her career interests and identity needs prior to marriage and family, she may be expected to leave her career altogether for the sake of her husband and children. The professional part of herself, carefully nurtured and developed, as well as her position within the culture, which she worked hard to achieve, will be discounted and minimized. The unspoken expectation among many fundamentalists is that it is only barely acceptable for a woman to invest herself in a career — provided she has no children. Once she has a family, she should find her fulfillment and satisfaction at home. This prescription makes the woman feel there is little choice for her in the matter.

Often a woman who does not choose to sacrifice her soul and live her life expressed through the role of Good Woman is ostracized, criticized, and not supported for her involvement in activities apart from family life. This isolation creates an intrapsychic conflict. If she has personal interests and desires apart from her husband and children, she is faced with the dilemma of choosing to deny her inner voice and full expression in the world or to follow her internal truth and experience isolation and criticism from her family and church. This reality — as it is presented to the fundamentalist woman — is polarized: good or bad, for or against. If she breaks the rules and pursues personal interests, she may be judged selfish and willful. She may even face excommunication from the inner sanctum of the community.

Women who choose to take control of their own lives and opt for a path other than the established Good Woman route often are treated like second-class citizens. Single women are interrogated as to when they will get married. Married women are asked when they will have babies. Young girls are squeezed into molds to meet other people's needs at the expense of their own wholeness.

Creation: "I will discover authenticity; love others; also love myself; believe in the power of compassion to transform."

Find Your Heart

"Do whatever is in your heart, for God is with you." (1 Chronicles 17:2)
"You must love your neighbor as yourself." (Mark 12:31)

"In love there is no room for fear; but perfect love drives out fear."
(1 John 4:18)

Green is the color for the heart chakra, which includes the arms and hands, together with the heart — wonderful body parts for hugging. The heritage of the heart is to love and be loved. As you pay attention to your heart center, remember not only whom but what you love. What reflects a true expression of yourself? Appreciate the beauty and grace your heart and hands express. What people are you drawn to? What activities? When do you feel like you are most yourself? How do you love yourself? How has the authentic you been concealed by the roles you take on? By the roles expected of you? How is your heart closed with judgment of self and others? In what ways has your heart been broken, denied, or manipulated? How has it grown cold? Breathe deeply, filling your chest fully. Whose love do you receive? With whom do you share your love? Feel your heart reborn and refreshed, as if it were brand new and never jaded — a fleshy, messy, woundable, renewable heart.

Case Study: A Dream of Vitality

To open our hearts to others, we must welcome the fullness within. Then we can share from that fullness, rather than from a stunted, resentful, dutiful self.

Vanessa had two life dreams: she wanted to be an artist and she wanted to be a mother. Her parents approved of motherhood, but they were merely patient with Vanessa's craving for art. It was, they reasoned, a hobby, but nothing more. Her parents worked hard to convince her that the dream of motherhood was enough to satisfy her completely. Vanessa's father reasoned that her husband would be the one to financially support her, so she wouldn't need a career to support herself. Besides, he warned, "The art world is so unpredictable." When her art dreams persisted into her teens, her father had a long talk with her.

What Vanessa remembers best about that evening is her father's loving, protective voice. He believed he knew what was right for her, and he believed he knew what would make her happy. What Vanessa's father didn't know was that he was killing the truth of his daughter's dreams. "You can always paint in your spare time," he assured her. He also told her that the happiest day of his life would be the day he walked her down the aisle.

From that day forward, Vanessa stopped dreaming, and though she had hoped this would keep her close to her father, the death of her dream killed a part of their relationship, creating a chasm between them. When she stopped talking about being an artist, she stopped talking to him about everything important to her. She still loved her father, but she didn't want to spend time with him. When she was near him, she felt her energy drain away.

A few years later, Vanessa's father got his dearest wish: at a lovely, costly wedding, he gave her away to John, a "good religious man and husband." By the time she married John, Vanessa's relationship with her father had become all form, no content, although he never suspected it. He had been pleased that his talk with her had been so effective.

Vanessa's relationship with her father set the pattern for her relationship with her husband. John shared Vanessa's father's concern for her and worked hard as a lawyer to give her material things. Children, beautiful and healthy, came quickly, and they deflected Vanessa's dream for a while. Maybe, she thought, her dad was right, after all. And who could get up for three nighttime feedings and paint the next day, anyway? Vanessa also learned the universal lesson of young mothers: there is no spare time. At times, however, she was resentful toward John, feeling that he, too, had somehow robbed her of her life, in assuming, like her father, that he knew and wanted what was best for her. She then felt guilty. John worked hard to provide a nice life for his wife and family.

So Vanessa looked forward to the time when her kids were old enough to create art with her. She was shocked, however, when she found such activity to be tense and stressful. At the first sign of crayons and paper, Vanessa felt anxious. As she painted or drew with her children, she was overwhelmed by feelings of loss and sadness. When her children said, "Mommy, I hope I can draw like you someday. You could have been an artist," Vanessa cried.

She became short-tempered. She told herself, "Toughen up, it's not that bad. You have so much to be thankful for — your loving husband, your beautiful children. That should be enough. You probably wouldn't have made it as an artist anyway."

This internal conflict is what brought Vanessa into therapy. She rebuked herself — for her inadequacy as a mother, for her inappropriate longings, and for her sorrow. In an early session she cried, "I have these lovely children. How could I possibly be dissatisfied?" Because she felt resentful of her husband and cut off from her children, her family was robbed of receiving Vanessa in all her beauty as a whole person. When she was able to see and admit to herself how vital her artistic expression was to her whole being, she began to make changes. She decided to set aside an hour each night to paint. Vanessa was fortunate that John was willing to make the necessary adjustments to offer support for her endeavors. He gave a few more baths and developed into quite a bedtime storyteller. Just a year later, a local gallery displayed Vanessa's work; shortly thereafter, she was commissioned by the library to paint a mural in the children's section.

Now that she has chosen to become an artist as well as a wife and mother — and, in so doing, has developed the artistic, creative part of herself — Vanessa offers a more authentic and alive self to her husband and children. Her family experiences her more energetic presence. Because she has given herself the freedom to be herself, Vanessa can give John the same freedom and support to develop more of the creative aspects of his own authentic self. As a mother, she fully supports her children's self-expression so that they, in turn, will be able to stand up for themselves and their own fulfillment, living creatively and fully expressed in the world.

To pursue a path of authenticity and open-heartedness is, in essence, to throw off the veil of role. This concept has been called, variously, following your bliss, discovering what is alive in you, focusing your passion, hearing your call, being your authentic self, or simply exploring whatever it is you love to do. Authenticity involves connecting to the deep and unique part of yourself that is particularly gifted and life-giving.

Karen Armstrong, in her memoir *The Spiral Staircase*, calls this journey bringing out one's own heroic potential, living as intensely possible here and now, or discovering how to be fully human. This heroic quest begins when a woman sets out on her own path, acknowledging her own pain and feeling it fully. Also, Armstrong describes her realization:

[Faith is] not about belief, but about practice. Religion is not about accepting twenty impossible propositions before breakfast, but about doing things that change you. Faith is a moral aesthetic, an ethical alchemy. If you behave in a certain way, you will be transformed. The myths and laws of religion are not true because they conform to some metaphysical, scientific, or historic reality, but because they are life enhancing. They tell you how human nature functions, but you will not discover their truth unless you apply these myths and doctrines to your own life and put them into practice.[5]

As in the symbol of the cross, the heart is where our connection to the divine meets our connection to others. Here we find the intersection between our personal spiritual practice and our social activism as we become agents of change. We receive a blessing to be a blessing, and in sharing that blessing, we are blessed.

When our hearts are tight with repression and interruption, we promote rigidity and judgment throughout our families, our communities, and our earth. When our personal expression and work in the world flows from an open heart, we move through the world with love. It seems almost magical that the power of love can truly be stronger than fear and hatred, but as we claim and practice this power of acting in love we will see unbelievable effects on every level from the personal to the political. When our influence emanates from authentic open hearts, we participate with God's intention for healing and wholeness, even as we live our own daily resurrections.

Dance: Choose a piece of music that speaks to you of authenticity, love, reaching out, and growing. Wear a green dress or tie a green scarf around your chest, or wear it as a veil. Give yourself permission to embody your heart chakra through the beauty and expansiveness of your dance.

Cocoon: Rediscovering one's authentic self might be imagined as peeling layers off an onion, shedding the skin of a snake, death and rebirth, or the metamorphosis of a butterfly. For this movement experience, choose two pieces of music, the first brooding and meditative, the second light and enlivening. Set up the music selections to play one after the other. Curl into a child's pose or fetal position and cover yourself with a veil (you can use a sarong, a throw, a sheet, or a blanket). Spend the entire first song in the cocoon in stillness. You may find yourself swaying gently or twitching as you wait to emerge. Do not plan your unfolding, simply prepare to be surrendered to it. As the second piece of music begins, allow your body to respond in the full expression of your self. Move into your resurrection. You may enjoy this alone or with a partner, or it can be facilitated in a group experience. Write or share your thoughts about the experience if you like.

Hand Dance: This exercise is an opportunity to experience the exquisite beauty of your own movement, to enhance your sensitivity to another, and to create a work of art to share with a partner. This exercise is for two individuals or for a group, working in pairs. You can play a piece of soothing and soulful instrumental music. Partners can sit or stand facing each other. One person begins using her hand as if it were a dancer on the stage of the space between the partners. She moves her hand as an extension of her heart in creative expression. After a few moments, she stops and holds her hand in a shape in the space. The second person begins to move a hand, having listened carefully to the first expression. The movement may be contrasting or complementary, but it is a sensitive response to the first. Then hold, and back to the first. This movement is passed back and forth for a few minutes.

Next, the first person brings in her second hand, moving both hands together in and around the space and the shape of the partner's hand. When she brings it to a hold, it is the second person's turn to move both hands. Again the movement is passed back and forth. Finally, the partners begin to move all four hands together, maintaining the sensitivity and attitude of listening developed through the initial moments.

This experience can be adapted to movement of the whole body, following the same process of moving, shaping, responding, and then moving both bodies together.

a seed

longing to grow

stretching down roots

wriggling in the rich soil

unstealable, unchokable

turning toward the light

basking in the light

transforming light

reflecting light

bearing fruit

sheltering

branches

eyes to see

ears to hear

heart to understand

the mysteries unfolding

treasure hidden in a field

new things as well as old

— Matthew 13—

Notes

1 Janice Shaw Crouse, "Free Love: Boulevard or Cul-de-Sac," Concerned Women for America, www.beverlylahayeinstitute.org/articledisplay.asp?id=6016&department=BLI&categoryid=femfacts.

2 James Dobson, *Marriage Under Fire* (Sisters, OR: Multnomah, 2004), 12.

3 James Dobson, *Dare to Discipline* (Wheaton, IL: Tyndale, 1970), 183.

4 Rick Warren, *The Purpose Driven Life* (Grand Rapids, MI: Zondervan, 2002), 160, 167, 196, 266, 268.

5 Karen Armstrong, *The Spiral Staircase* (New York: Anchor Books, 2004), 270-272.

8

The Dance of Balance
Solar Plexus Chakra: Power to Act

The Dance of Balance

In symbolic expression
of masculine and feminine,
a woman and a man lock hands
in a dance of balance.
She raises one leg in a graceful arabesque and he supports her weight.
He creates a shape he could not hold without her support.
They lean apart and come together.
Unscripted, simply improvised,
they move in response one to the other.
Together the two fill one space
A spectacular union
of exquisitely diverse individuals,
attached by invisible elastic,
they move expressively in silence:
close, then distant,
tense, then relaxed
ever connected
by hearts and hands
in this dance
of interdependence
and harmony.

Characteristic: Exclusive language is used; women are not permitted to act
powerfully or be ordained in the church; injustice is legitimized.

Turn on almost any Christian music radio station and you will be assured within five minutes that God is male; that Jesus is Lord in a hierarchical system; and that shame, self-denial, and sacrifice are the defining elements of Christian faith. You will hear very little about Jesus as servant, liberator, or challenger of hierarchies, but the music is captivating, almost hypnotic. It's also terribly gender-biased, the messages of patriarchy settling easily into the unconscious.

Language is a powerful force for transmitting dogma. We tend to frame our understanding of things with the tools language provides. Much of the processing of language occurs on an unconscious level. In his bestseller *Blink*, Malcolm Gladwell, reports on some very interesting research using "priming experiments" in which the language that subjects are exposed to preconditions their behavior to play out in fairly predictable ways: some subjects behaved more or less assertively depending on which group of words they had been subliminally exposed to. Another experiment involved black college students and twenty questions taken from the Graduate Record Examination, the standardized test used for entry into graduate school. The students were asked to identify their race on a pretest questionnaire; this simple act was sufficient to prime them with all the negative stereotypes associated with African Americans and academic achievement — and the number of items they got right was cut *in half*.

Gladwell concludes, "The results from these experiments are, obviously, quite disturbing. They suggest that what we think of as free will is largely an illusion: much of the time, we are simply operating on automatic pilot, and the way we think and act — how well we think and act on the spur of the moment — are a lot more susceptible to outside influences than we realize."[1]

Traditional Christian language is steeped in patriarchy. When all we have ever been exposed to is male language to describe God, it's hard to imagine God as anything but male. The same is true in the language we use to describe humanity. When we use *mankind* to refer to all people, more than half the population is disregarded. What if we were to refer to *white people* when we really mean all people, and simply expected our listeners to edit for themselves? What if the Declaration of Independence stated "that all *white men* are created equal"? Of course, that was the founders' initial assumption regarding both gender and race. Preference for men is still the fundamentalist assumption regarding gender, until we consistently choose to use language that is intentionally inclusive.

The portrayal of God as a male deity has a profound effect on the church. Girls are taught early on that *man* is created in God's image. Woman, created as an afterthought from Adam's rib — from man's image — is something less than godly. Consider Mary Daly's analysis:

> Since God is male, the male is God. ... [The] symbol of the Father God [which is the only image allowed in Christian fundamentalist interpretation], spawned in the human imagination and sustained as plausible by patriarchy, has in turn rendered service to this type of society by making its mechanisms for the oppression of women appear right and fitting. If God in "his" heaven is a father ruling "his" people, then it is in the "nature" of things and according to divine plan and the order of the universe that society be male-dominated.[2]

According to this logic, domination of the woman by the man represents God's design. The Bible, however, offers many images of God that are not at all rooted in domination or masculinity. In his article "El Shaddai: A Feminine Aspect of God," Brother Daniel Stramara explores one dimension of God's feminine expression:

> The name El Shaddai is used only 48 times in the Bible. What does it mean? Traditionally this name is translated as "the Almighty," or even more exactly "God of the mountain." This is based on the Akkadian word shadu meaning mountain. But shad is a perfectly normal Hebrew word meaning "breast." In symbolic language a mountain is breast-shaped. The ending -ai on Shaddai is an old Ugaric feminine ending, such as found on the name of Sarai, Abraham's wife. Hence the most probable ancient meaning of El Shaddai is "God, the Breasted One."

Stramara goes on to explore passages in which this naming engenders "the feminine, relational side of God that creates intimacy through Covenant ... blessings of the breasts and womb ... inspiration ... intuition ... spirit ... breath ... a whirring of wings ... a mother bird with her young." He quotes Ezekiel: "I heard the noise of their wings; when they moved, it was like the noise of flood waters, like the voice of Shaddai" (Ezekiel 1:24).[3] We also have the concept of Shekinah, a Hebrew word descriptive of the radiant glory and presence of God.

We must not limit our understanding of God to only masculine metaphors. Mary Potter Engel says, "Those who claim Father as the title or the divinely revealed name of God, according it a special status beyond that of all 'humanly constructed' images, would do well to remember the warning of the fiery bush that God is the Unnamable One, the Uncontrollable One. Unless one keeps this in mind, the use of Father as the name for God is blasphemy." Similarly, Sister Sandra M. Schneiders affirms that not only is it permissible to imagine God as a woman, but also "it's necessary if we wish to have a healthy, balanced image of God operating in our spirituality. God is spirit, neither male nor female." Schneiders believes that we need to keep many metaphors of God active simultaneously to keep ourselves aware that "none of them is adequate to the Holy Mystery who is God," and so to avoid idolatry.[4]

Some women, however, like Crouse (Concerned Women for America), would surely deny the danger of such idolatry, instead maintaining vehemently the exclusively masculine revelation of God. She says,

> It is important to note that while sexuality is not ascribed to God, His self-revelation in Scripture is masculine in gender. Likewise, the Son and Holy Spirit are referred to by masculine designations. Therefore, the Christian community embraces this disclosure of God as Father, Son and Holy Spirit… There are almost none, if any, feminine metaphors for God in Scripture.[5]

Al Mohler (Baptist Seminary), on his website, corroborates this single-gendered image of God: "God has named Himself as Father, and the linguistic framework God has revealed about Himself, including His names, is grounded in masculine, and not feminine, language or images. Our triune God is not a compassionate mother, a womb, or a rainbow."[6]

Such framing serves only to separate us from the possibilities of growing in our understanding and experience of divine presence. Christin Lore Weber in her Woman's Rosary Book, Circle of Mysteries, offers a more helpful perspective on how we image God:

> All images of God are, of course, metaphorical communications of unknowable mystery fashioned in a language we creatures can take in and accept. God transcends gender, but we do not. In our sexuality we experience what is deepest in life: love, conception, birth, lactation, and the wise blood of menopause, which initiates the passage to death. We seek to understand the mystery of God in the only way we can, through the deepest experiences

we have. Images of God which include both men's and women's experience of the mystery are the only images that are whole.[7]

By insisting on a male God, the church continues to feed women's oppression. Women's genuine, heartfelt concerns and authentic needs are easily dismissed as "radical forms of feminism." As in other closed systems, the individual's concerns are invalidated, her needs judged and rejected as unimportant. In addition to the external messages, the internalized male bias, which women have unknowingly accepted, causes difficulty as well.

Sexist interpretations of the scriptures are hurled through smiling teeth as church leaders use outdated religious traditions to remind women of their inferior status and demeanor. Because of their theological interest in maintaining the historic patriarchal orientation of Christianity, many fundamentalists and conservative scholars do not draw out the implications of historical interpretation for understanding the biblical teachings on women. Karen Jo Torjesen remembers our history of Christian injustices:

> It is crucial to acknowledge at long last that women were and can be Christian leaders, that there is nothing debased about being female or sexual. The contemporary controversy over women's ordination has striking similarities with the conflict over slavery. In the nineteenth century Christianity was involved in a profound moral struggle that pitted Christian tradition against the essential message of the Christian gospel. Slavery was a recognized and legitimate social institution in the societies that produced the Old and New Testaments. At the end of this struggle the "good news" of Jesus' authentic Christian message that salvation is extended to all and therefore that all are equal prevailed; the social institution of slavery was not only not essential for the ordering of Christian society, but contrary to true Christian values. Contemporary Christian theologians need to undertake the same task of extricating the essential teachings of the Christian gospel from the patriarchal gender system in which it is embedded.[8]

These essential teachings often are clouded by words that reinforce the status quo. People are loath to give up the language with which they feel comfortable and which confirms their bias, particularly in religious communities. They remain attached to hymns and prayers that are familiar or traditional, even when the language or content is limiting or even offensive. This degrading usage is a great challenge in churches when women begin to realize how they are invalidated and made invisible by an insistence on language that is exclusive and gender-biased.

Many Protestant denominations and the Roman Catholic Church still do not allow women to be ministers. In the Christian Reformed Church, in June of 2006, "186 male delegates declared that women may not be delegated to synod, the church's broadest assembly, or serve as synodical deputies (synod's representatives) at classis meetings." They also recommended not addressing the issue again for seven years. Some shamefully assigned this agreement to the work of the Holy Spirit while others acknowledged that in this denomination "women are tolerated but not embraced."[9] Women present in the audience wept as the decision was being made. At the same meeting, for the first time, the same body voted to remove the word "male" from the list of stated requirements for ordination. Slowly, they move backwards and forwards, continuing to give mixed messages about the value and qualifications of women to all.

The dearth of women in church leadership limits the experience of women in worship while undermining their spiritual calling and ambitions. Women lack female role models who effectively exercise their leadership overtly and responsibly — and in ways that are feminine.

Evangelical leader, sociology professor, and Baptist minister, Tony Campolo, in an interview in July 2004, takes issue with Christians who would bar women from church leadership.

> They point to certain passages in the Book of Timothy to make their case, but tend to ignore that there are other passages in the Bible that would raise very serious questions about that position and which, in fact, would legitimate women being in leadership positions in the church. In Galatians, it says that in Christ there's neither Jew nor Greek, bond nor free, male nor female, all are one in Christ Jesus. In the Book of Acts, the Bible is very clear that when the Holy Spirit comes upon the Church that both men and women begin to prophesy, that preaching now belongs to both men and women. Phillip had four daughters, all of whom prophesied, which we know means preaching in biblical language. I'd like to point out that in the 16th chapter of Romans, the seventh verse, we have reference to Junia. Junia was a woman and she held the high office of apostle in the early Church. What is frightening to me is that in the New International Translation of the Scriptures, the word Junia was deliberately changed to Junius to make it male.[10]

Influenced by male language, excluded from leadership, and trained to submit, women lack role models and even opportunities to practice exercising personal power effectively. These are the mechanisms through which the fundamentalist culture creates conflicts in women. Why we as women give up our power to act on our own behalf and in our own wisdom is hard to understand and even harder to forgive. It happens so gradually and so subtly that by the time we have given it away, we may hardly notice it is gone. We must wonder how this extinguishing of women's power is accomplished and understand how forgiving ourselves can re-ignite us.

Case Study: Julia "Bears" Her Soul

In the following account, Julia Van Renssalear, a young mother, tries to find the courage to be powerful for the sake of her child.

Julia

In the deep recesses of my mind, it is socially unacceptable to be a powerful woman. That's because my mother is a powerful woman in her tiny universe. She was when I was a child, and I hated her for it. She abused that power a million times over and didn't use it to save me from my father. My brother called her WitchBitchAsshole for years to honor that power. My father is crumbling (by his choice) from her power. I tried to fight it during adolescence and eventually gave up to create my own empire. But now, to step into my power in my role as mother, I am paralyzed. I tentatively do the actions suggested to me, but I am not firm in my steps. I am not consistent when it comes to standing up for my rights and my son's rights. I have learned and come to believe that it is a bad thing to be powerful because:

No man likes a powerful woman, so if I am powerful:

- My husband won't want me back.
- No other man will ever want me.
- I'll be seen as unattractive and unfeminine.
- Power is associated with anger, and I don't want to be an angry bitch.

I don't want to be my mother. I know that starting from a vantage point of not wanting to be like Ma is setting myself up for being like her. ...I can't be a real woman and be powerful at the same time. (I can only be my mother.)

What about marlins? The one in *The Old Man and the Sea* was eighteen feet long and tremendously powerful. Powerful and graceful and big and beautiful — the old man admired and respected her power. Why can't I be powerful like a female marlin? Or what about bears? A female polar bear would kill in a minute for her cub without stopping to be sorry about her femininity or her attractiveness to male bears. It's ridiculous even to think about it. Why can't I be a big white bear, stunning enough to take one's breath away but strong enough to kill with one single swipe of the paw? Touch my cub and you die. No matter how many times we mated, no matter how many seals we shared. Touch my cub and you die. I wish I could react swiftly and surely to my son's predicament, in order to take care of my own cub, and rest assured that once he's okay I will choose when to be agitated and when to relax.

The polar bear goes about her business: she is not an angry bitch of a polar bear, she is not perpetually swiping at other polar bears; she simply reacts when she needs to. It's her cub. Otherwise, she's a perfectly nice polar bear in Arctic society.

In a system in which a woman is not comfortable being powerful, the fundamentalist paradigm allows her to remain alienated from the expression of her own power. This system allows her to get what she wants without the risk of speaking her own voice. In claiming to be a submissive wife, a woman is provided a "ticket out": she does not have to openly express her power and can legitimately remain dependent on her man to express the power for the couple. The woman vicariously experiences power through her husband, accepting the secondary position as good enough. After all, the position has its benefits — it allows her to be held unaccountable, not really responsible for the choices that are made. This technique is especially disingenuous in a marriage when the wife acts as if the husband is in charge while she is really managing all the important decisions behind the scenes, sometimes even deliberately manipulating him to accomplish her desired outcome.

Instead of initiating responsible action, women may find themselves helplessly immobile or prone to respond to demands with a flurry of unfocused reactivity. When women are not acknowledged as part of the power structure, nor permitted to act in their own name, they may easily collaborate with the dominant power structure in the name of the power and for the sake of the power alone. Consider the biblical story of Queen

Jezebel and King Ahab. Ahab was unhappy because Naboth of Jezreel would not sell or trade his vineyard. Jezebel told Ahab she would take care of the situation. "So she wrote a letter *in Ahab's name* and sealed it with *his seal*" to arrange for Naboth to be accused of heresy and unpatriotic behavior and eventually to be stoned to death (1 Kings 21:1–16).

Because she did not have her own authority or her own experiences of developing wise judgment, Jezebel simply acted in the name of her husband on behalf of what she perceived to be his agenda. In expressing this pseudo-power, her ability to access her true power was thwarted. Like Jezebel, fundamentalist women are cut off from the life experiences that support their competency in acting with clarity and integrity. When decisions are made for them, they miss the opportunities to develop decision-making skill and confidence. Lacking permission to wield their own power in their own name, they become disconnected from their responsibility to exercise power judiciously and are willing to go along unquestioningly with external authorities, sometimes facilitating injustice.

People are more accountable for their behaviors when they know their name will be attached to the outcome. When power and responsibility are merged, a higher level of ethical behavior can be expected. If we don't have to take credit or responsibility for the outcome of our decisions, it's easy to behave carelessly. Relational integrity and improved outcomes result when each partner owns her or his own feelings, needs, and creative ideas, and when women and men work together to find mutually agreeable solutions. Women must claim their ability to share power responsibly.

In Iroquois society in the 1700s, women were equal partners with their men and played a profound role in political life. An Iroquois husband left his own family's hearth to live with his wife's family — part of a clan headed by a clan mother. These women determined who would become a chief and when a chief should be removed.

> Through matrilineal descent the Iroquois formed cohesive political groups that had little to do with where people lived or from what villages the hearths originated.... Iroquois children were trained to think for themselves and yet provide for others... The Iroquois did not respect submissive behavior.... [They] governed behavior by instilling a sense of pride and connectedness to the group through common rituals... The esteemed women of a clan gather together when a title is vacant and nominate a male member to be chief. Next, the men of the clan give their

approval, and the nomination is then forwarded to the council, where the new chief is installed.[11]

A society structured in this manner seemed to create a different climate than what colonial women were experiencing at the time. In 1784, James Madison visited Iroquois country and discovered a white woman living amongst the Oneidas (one of the nations of the Iroquois). She told how she had escaped her life as a servant in New York and of her happiness living among the Oneidas. She reported, "Here I have no master, I am the equal of all the women in the tribe, I do what I please without anyone's saying anything about it; I work only for myself — I shall marry if I wish and be unmarried again when I wish. Is there a single woman as independent as I in your cities?"[12]

The representative form of democracy practiced successfully by the League of the Iroquois, both predated and profoundly influenced the evolution and development of the United States Constitution. Unfortunately, it seems that this very critical factor, the equality and valued involvement of women in governance and society, was lost with little notice by the constitutional framers. It was not until 1920 that U.S. women were finally able to vote. Sadly, the Equal Rights Amendment has still not become a part of our constitution. The ERA was first proposed in 1923, and was subsequently ratified by thirty-five states. In 1982, the time limit for its ratification expired with three states still needed for it to become an amendment to the constitution. By this time well-organized religious resistance had become vocal and effective. Tim LaHaye frames the argument:

> Who needs the ERA? Not women as a sex but lesbians and homosexuals need the ERA; and believe me that's really what it's all about! Homosexuals and lesbians who number maybe 6 percent of the population, recognize their unpopular status. They decided early that the feminist movement and the ERA provided them with a handy vehicle to ride piggyback upon "women's rights" and achieve homosexual rights. Fortunately citizens who suddenly realized how close we were to the city limits of Sodom and Gomorrah successfully resisted the ERA[13]

In reality this simple amendment written in 1923 by Alice Paul was meant to guarantee "equal justice under law" for all citizens. The text of it merely states:

Section 1. Equality of rights under the law shall not be denied or abridged by the United States or by any state on account of sex.

Section 2. The Congress shall have the power to enforce, by appropriate legislation, the provisions of this article.

Section 3. This amendment shall take effect two years after the date of ratification.

In addition to this political insult, the United States is the only industrialized country that has not ratified CEDAW (Convention on the Elimination of All Forms of Discrimination against Women). It is a United Nation international treaty, which intends to comprehensively address fundamental rights for women in politics, health care, education, economics, employment, law, property, and marriage and family relations.[14] The ongoing reality of women's status as "less-than" continues to contribute to their "exploitability."

Case Study: Irresponsible Power

The church as well as the state exercises great power in establishing the treatment of women, setting the example for the smaller system of the family. When a girl is programmed to please others, mindlessly obey authority, and allow others to dominate her, she comes to believe she has no right to her own power and no right to express her power in her world. Silenced and shamed, she loses touch with her own authentic expression. The following story highlights a chilling experience of growing up female in the fundamentalist tradition.

Jessie was a beautiful twelve-year-old with long, shining hair and big eyes. She was also a desperate child who cried a lot and for no apparent reason. She ate little and slept less. Even her mother and her best friend were unable to reach her. Fearing Jessie was suicidal, a school counselor sent her for a psychiatric evaluation. Fragment by fragment, as she slowly revealed her story, the cause of her depression was exposed.

Jessie's Uncle Henry, her father's brother and the pastor of their fundamentalist church, had sexually abused her for six years, until she was eleven. Jessie had never told her story before, and with each whispered word she shook with fear. Her uncle had persuaded Jessie that their inappropriate intimacy was God's will. He had warned her that God would strike her dead if she told anyone. He had assured her that their "games" together helped him to be a better pastor, and that God was happy about that. After all, didn't she want God to be happy? Imagine what God might do if He was not happy. Uncle Henry had also quoted Bible verses to her while he helped himself to her innocent and vulnerable body, sexually molesting her to support his madness. He promised her she would be rewarded in the afterlife — if only she could endure until then.

Sunday after Sunday, Jessie sat in the same church pew with her mother, her father, and her younger brother, forced to look upward toward heaven, receiving her uncle's penetration from the pulpit. She was filled with hatred and disrespect for the man her family and friends called a powerful Christian leader, a man of God. She felt ashamed and judged herself for her feelings. Sunday after Sunday Jessie sat in her own home, penetrated again by his glance across the dinner table. Jessie's mother had decided it was her womanly duty to invite her brother-in-law and "his lovely family" to Sunday dinner. After all, she said, "Henry is such a good and decent man. It's the least we can do to serve him in his ministry for God. He needs us. He does so much for others. I'm glad we can help him."

So every Sunday Jessie's stomach churned as she endured a double dose of her uncle's hypocrisy, first in his sermon at the church, then in his sermonizing at the table. Sunday after Sunday, as her Uncle Henry sat directly across from her at her family's dining room table, he communicated silently, using his eyes to play power with her. Every week she grew sick and sicker with anxiety as Sunday approached. She sat through dinner after dinner, unable to eat the pot roasts, the chickens, and the glazed hams her mother meticulously prepared to please Uncle Henry. Jessie's eating habits angered her father, who saw his own piety called into question by his inability to make Jessie behave. "What's the matter with you?" he demanded weekly. "Your mother made a delicious meal. Can't you eat better than that? Shame on you! You're embarrassing us in front of your Uncle Henry!"

So Jessie sat, Sunday after Sunday, afraid and shamed into silence, knowing that she could never challenge the power that dripped from Uncle Henry's lips, believing that everyone else — even Uncle Henry — was right and good, and that she was wrong and bad, very, very bad. This secret, she must hold inside.

We have heard many similar stories from fundamentalist women who were told by the women in their lives, "If you think the pastor did something to harm you, you must be misinterpreting his actions. He's a man of God, called to service; he would never try to hurt you. Are you sure your imagination isn't just running wild?" Because everyone in her environment questions her truth, the girl or woman may come to question herself. She has been taught that no matter what, the man is right. He is innately right, innately good, innately more powerful. If he is perceived in her church as a "godly man," yet at the same time abuses his power with a little girl, it must be the girl's fault. In the fundamentalist system, there is no one she can blame but herself. She must be like Eve, a temptress, the one who caused the man to sin against his own will. The man is the authority on what is right and what is wrong, and the woman — or, in this case, the little girl — is subordinate, the one who must obey, only later to judge herself for her mindless obedience. Man was ordained by God to hold the position of power, according to the fundamentalist church, and woman was created by this same God to submit to this power while renouncing her own.

In this system, like Eve, because we are women, we are considered inferior. Because we are women, we are mute. Because we are women, we are powerless. Because we are women, we are at fault. These are the immobilizing beliefs women carry. If only religion were about mutuality and love and not about domination, control, and hierarchy. But instead we see inequity and injustice normalized.

The Division of Youth and Family Services was called in to assess Jessie's case. She received help in the form of individual psychotherapy and professional workers educated and counseled her family through this painful dilemma. Her family initially did not believe her, but with time, they began to accept the reality and truth of Jessie's story. She chose never to prosecute her uncle. He died in middle age of a brain aneurism.

Jessie struggled for many years through weekly psychotherapy, determined to recover and release the emotional trauma of her memories. Through supporting herself in voicing her truth, loving herself, and exercising her own power, she was able to gather the fragments of her body's memories and integrate this experience into her emerging self. Forgiving herself became a daily practice as she continued to develop the skills necessary to act powerfully in the circumstances of her life.

The brutal injustice described here in the life and body of a little girl elucidates in an extreme way the horror perpetrated by those who would protect the privilege of their power and position at the expense of others less powerful.

Commandment: You will not act independently or become a mature woman.

Many Christian churches have "parented" women in rigid, overprotective, abusive, and suffocating ways, at the same time blocking women's souls from reaching spiritual maturity. Ironically, just as an abused child forms a traumatic bond with the abusive parent, so does the woman attach herself to the religious institution and its destructive behavior.

Like an abusive parent, the church offers her a home, a safe haven — *as long as she remains the obedient daughter,* passively accepting the abuse, afraid to speak out, unconsciously protecting the system.

Within the system, rigid characteristics function to maintain the status quo. The normalized status quo then functions, on a covert level, to validate the craziness within, denying members an understanding of the madness occurring right before their eyes. While the status quo is vehemently maintained, there is no allowance for necessary confrontations, changes, or challenges; the system remains in a constant state of internal breakdown. Members experience the reverberations of this breakdown but often are unaware or unable to name what they are experiencing. As good Christians, they work harder to prove to the external world that there is no systemic breakdown occurring and no personal upset, thus denying the truth of the necessity for change.

In the well defined "chain-of-command," men are under God's authority and women are under men's. Patriarchy in fundamentalism is called *divine headship.* Practically, this means that women should defer to their husbands while husbands are to listen to religious leaders for guidance. As women cooperate within this design, they abdicate their own responsibility.

Responsibility is the ability to respond truthfully in one's humanness. Self-ownership inherently demands response as a woman takes dominion over her speaking, her attitudes, her behaviors, and her self. Without claiming ownership and authority for herself, she has no power to respond to situations in an appropriate and constructive manner, conducive to her continued expansion and autonomy. Exercising responsibility for self is a catalyst for maturation and growth as a human being.

A fundamentalist interpretation of difficult circumstances may involve explanations such as, "The devil made me do it," or the more familiar, "It must be God's will." Self-ownership is absent in these statements. In fact, they show a complete avoidance of the self-responsibility necessary for taking action. In Christian fundamentalism, the power to respond lies outside of the individual, in the hands either of the devil or of God, rendering the individual paralyzed, powerless to respond to the situation.

In fundamentalist systems, avoidant, irresponsible behavior may be framed as "waiting on God." Given this characteristic, we can better understand why sexism within the Christian church has not been eradicated (or even barely confronted). If God wanted it to be different, the reasoning goes, God would change it. Certainly, church members are not to be held responsible.

> I shall start, then, with the church, into whose bosom God is pleased to gather his sons, not only that they may be nourished by her help and ministry as long as they are infants and children, but also that they may be guided by her motherly care until they mature and at last reach the goal of faith ... so that, for those to whom he is Father the church may also be Mother.[15]

In many of his writings, John Calvin, reflecting on the opinions of the early church fathers, refers to the church as "Mother." Why is it that within Christianity, God is portrayed as "Father," the ultimate male deity, while the church is named as the ultimate female institution? Together, are they supposed to model the ideal traditional marriage?

Perhaps the early church fathers felt that by naming the institution of the church as female, it would be easier to dominate and control her and her female members. Although the church is labeled as a female entity, in many churches, men allow only men to hold public positions of power. In reality, the church is an institution hiding behind the mask of a female identity, which insists on male leadership and worships a singularly male God. This gives the subtle but powerful message to women in the church that the male gender is superior. The experiences they have in the church will be defined by males.

When members are encouraged to respond to the religious authority of the church as mother and God as father, a childlike state of helpless and irresponsible over-dependency is fostered. With such authoritarian parents, the autonomy of becoming mother and father to one's self, is difficult. This language of the church as a feminine entity also feeds the childhood fantasy, that Mama will always be there to take care of her children. The members believe that the church is and will remain the ultimate Good Mother. She will be there to be the giver, to meet needs, to give guidance, to divinely direct lives — as long as members remain obedient, good children. If not, this same Mother becomes a taker, and their life, as they have known it, will be eradicated.

If the fundamentalist woman remains with Mother Church, she retains membership even as her soul is deadened. If, in order to save her soul, she moves away from Mother Church, she will be dismembered and cut adrift. The church is acting irresponsibly when she shows herself to be a mother who can support only women's dependency and obedience, not their independence and wildness.

While the fundamentalist church refers to itself as Mother, it is desperately lacking in mothering ability. Its treatment of women is anything but motherly — not gentle, not nurturing, but wounding. Mother typically refers to "a creative or environmental source; to give birth to; to care for; to nourish and protect."[16] The expectation is that a mother creates a safe haven for her child; that she will be there to love, to care for the child in a healthy manner, to support and be dependable. Mother is that ultimate one expected to provide the security and comfort found only at the breast.

Any truly good mother wants her children to reach their full potential in adulthood and will go to great lengths to support their development. But the daughters of the fundamentalist church do not receive this kind of mothering. Rather than being supported, women's full maturation is stunted. The fundamentalist church has mothered women poorly. Just as the church has maligned Eve, so this same mother continues to suppress and destroy women.

Jesus did not refer to his followers (the institutionalized church to come) as Mother. In fact, he often called himself the bridegroom, inferring that his followers, the earliest Christian community, were more like a bride. Possibly the early church fathers could not tolerate the thought of the church being the bride of Christ. Perhaps this image was too sexual for them. Perhaps it was too far from the figure of mother — the virginal Mother Mary (the image they wanted to promote). Did the bride metaphor conjure up sensual images of the first sexual female, the first bride, Eve? Somehow by naming the body of the church Mother, the early church fathers could safely neutralize, desexualize, domesticate, and strip away her sexual nature, just as they could her daughters. The church, like all good religious women, would exist in Good Woman role.

A bride, on the other hand, might connote a sexual woman, full of unrealized passion and potential. In referring to the church as bride, Jesus metaphorically created an image of a woman who is present and available on her wedding night, a woman who allows and welcomes penetration and aggressively opens in return, experiencing erotic spirituality because she understands true intercourse with her groom. Is it any wonder that Jesus has had difficulty getting inside the impenetrable virgin Mother Church?

The mother–child relationship is very different from a bride–bridegroom relationship. Unfortunately, when the church is described as mother instead of a bride, it is rigidly locked in the role of co-parent with Father God. In this family arrangement, where does Jesus fit?

Is he the infantilized child of the church, not allowed to be fully grown-up? Interestingly, the church, historically and still today, gives its greatest energy to celebrating the birth of Jesus the baby, the infant son.

Consider other American holidays, when we celebrate past presidents and great leaders such as Martin Luther King, Jr. Although it's their birthday we commemorate, we think of them as adults, not as babies in cradles. We honor the person's contributions in life as an adult, not as a child, not as the baby Jesus, confined to his manger, rendered impotent through a distorted portrayal of the church as his virginal Mother. How does it affect the church when we think of Jesus only as son and not as bridegroom? Given this perspective, the denial of passion and the suppression of mature human sexuality, both female and male, is no surprise.

Once Christian churches restore women to equal partnership with and full participation in the leadership of the church, and in every aspect of life, we will experience more fully the gifts women bring.

This transformation can begin in the individual woman as she opens to her responsibility for full participation, but it also requires a more visible presence of women in leadership. Women gain the confidence to support their own concerns in the presence of other women. Helen Caldecott, the founding president of Physicians for Social Responsibility, has dedicated her life to ridding the world of the threat of nuclear war. She has noticed that when women are underrepresented in governments the values of the feminine are overlooked and the entrenched male-dominated mode of thinking is perpetuated. Women must break their silence.

> When the atom was split, Einstein said, "The splitting of the atom changed everything except man's mode of thinking. Thus we drift towards unparalleled catastrophe." ... With the world laced with nuclear weapons (2,500 on hair-trigger alert in Russia, and 2,500 H-bombs on hair-trigger alert in America) ... with six other legitimate nuclear nations (France, Britain, China, Israel, Pakistan, and India), and with many others chomping at the bit to emulate the nuclear superpowers, the world is entering into a strangely volatile and destabilizing era. ... Violence and killing is condoned by societies dominated by male values, while the 53 percent of the population made up by women also condones this psychotic behavior by their silence.[17]
>
> The magic number is 30 percent [according to a UN report]. Below 30 percent representation [in government], women tend to please the men and vote for missiles. Above 30 percent, they say, "No, you're not getting your missiles — we're voting for milk for children." So women need to support each other in order to

do what they know is correct behavior, and express their nurturing instincts. It's got nothing to do with politics.[18]

As of January 2005 the U.S. ranked 63rd world wide in the percentage of women occupying parliamentary seats with only 15.2% in the House and 14% in the senate. This is lower than the world average of 15.8%. Nordic countries have 39.9% representation and Arab states have 8.8%.[19]

In her Mother's Day Proclamation of 1870, Julia Ward Howe also invites women to take up the responsibility to promote the general interests of peace:

Mother's Day Proclamation
by Julia Ward Howe

Arise then ... women of this day!
Arise, all women who have hearts!
Whether your baptism be of water or of tears!
Say firmly:
"We will not have questions answered by irrelevant agencies,
Our husbands will not come to us, reeking with carnage,
For caresses and applause.
Our sons shall not be taken from us to unlearn
All that we have been able to teach them of charity, mercy, and patience.
We, the women of one country,
Will be too tender of those of another country
To allow our sons to be trained to injure theirs."

From the voice of a devastated Earth a voice goes up with
Our own. It says: "Disarm! Disarm!
The sword of murder is not the balance of justice."
Blood does not wipe our dishonor,
Nor violence indicate possession.
As men have often forsaken the plough and the anvil
At the summons of war,
Let women now leave all that may be left of home
For a great and earnest day of counsel.
Let them meet first, as women, to bewail and commemorate the dead.

Let them solemnly take counsel with each other as to the means
Whereby the great human family can live in peace. ...
Each bearing after his own time the sacred impress, not of Caesar,
But of God —
In the name of womanhood and humanity, I earnestly ask
That a general congress of women without limit of nationality,
May be appointed and held at someplace deemed most convenient
And at the earliest period consistent with its objects,
To promote the alliance of the different nationalities,
The amicable settlement of international questions,
The great and general interests of peace.

Creation: "I will exercise the power to act; realize female and male in partner-ship; honor the poor and disempowered; move in God's domination-free order."

Support and Balance

"It was those who were poor according to the world that God chose,
to be rich in faith and to be the heirs to God's domination-free order,
which God promised to those who love God. You, on the other hand,
have dishonored the poor. Is it not the rich who lord it over you? Are
not they the ones who drag you into court? ... You will love your
neighbor as yourself. ... Talk and behave like people who are going
to be judged by the law of freedom. Whoever acts without mercy will
be judged without mercy, but mercy can afford to laugh at judgment."
(James 2:5–9, 12–13)

Now we will pay attention to the solar plexus chakra. We find it right in
our gut. The color is yellow, and this chakra radiates with the power to
act — fire in the belly. Light a candle today. Look at the flame and take
inspiration from its dance. From this chakra we move forward for justice,
for others as well as for ourselves. Here we give and receive support and
strive for balance. Here we exercise our own equilibrium of male and
female energy, accessing the appropriate strengths needed to address
our current concerns.

Imagine purposefulness in thinking about what you want to accomplish in this moment, in this day, in your life. What holds you back from
completing your goals and how can you mobilize today to act towards
completing one of your goals? What experiences have disempowered
you or left you feeling incompetent? How can you enact competence?

When have you offered judgment instead of mercy? How can you transform that judgment into acts of mercy? How have you cooperated with systems of domination even at your own expense and how can you change that today? What might you need to forgive in yourself in order to move forward effectively?

What is it like to imagine God as your breasted mother or Jesus as bridegroom? What do you feel in your tummy? Do you have butterflies? A knot? A burning passion? Imagine within yourself a balance of feminine and masculine energies. What support do you need from others to move forward? What support can you offer to yourself? How can you balance your needs with those of the people you support? Imagine your own energy and power working in balance with that of others in your life. How can you enhance partnerships of power? Recognize and delight in your power to act today in your own effective way; effectiveness defined by your own standards.

Freedom is the antithesis of life for women buried in fundamentalism. They have been socialized, in part because of the story of Eve, to blame and shame themselves. This learned habit creates constant and nagging self-doubt and self-sabotage. The woman's power to act is immobilized as she struggles with a vacuous loss of confidence. Instead of receiving grace and mercy, she drags herself into the unrelenting court of her mind, holding fast to her mistakes, finally accepting even further shame for treating herself in this way. In therapy sessions, she expresses embarrassment to be caught perpetuating this cycle of judgment upon herself.

Faith in God and commitment to God's domination-free order calls us to forgiveness, compassion, and action. How can we care for our neighbors without learning to support and care for ourselves? When we honor the law of freedom, we learn to laugh at the judgment we heap upon ourselves and upon others. In accessing and choosing our compassion for self and others, we ignite our passion for action, for balance, and for support.

We are reminded of Jesus' story of the rich man and Lazarus (Luke 16:19-31). The rich man had it in his power to ameliorate the suffering of Lazarus but chose not to do so. In maintaining his privileged entitlement, he missed the opportunity to balance power and redistribute resources so that Lazarus could simply live. The current state of the global economy reflects the greatest disparity of wealth we have ever known. Ulrich Duchrow, a German theologian and economist, reports that "four hundred and ninety-seven billionaires hold as much wealth as 57 percent of the world's population. If those 497 people would share 5 percent of their wealth, all the basic needs of the world could be covered."[20] In contrast, Janice Shaw Crouse (Concerned Women for America), appears unconcerned about any responsibility the rich may bear for the situation of the poor. She holds that "it is incomprehensible that supposedly intelligent and well-educated people would make a statement that 'human greed and hard heartedness' is the cause of human suffering and material desperation — thus blaming the rich for the situation of the poor." In fact she states that "[t]he basic assumption is that the wealthy have become wealthy at the expense of the poor — a very incomplete and erroneous view of economics and the role of entrepreneurship."[21]

We have all colluded in supporting those in positions of power, often propping up the very systems of domination that Jesus opposed. Men have often made great accomplishments (as well as great mistakes) with the unquestioning support of mothers, wives, and daughters. Women need to claim that same support for themselves — from themselves, from other women, from their families, from the church, and from Jesus — to accomplish what they are called to do. We can welcome what lives and moves in men that is feminine, as well as what is masculine in ourselves. We need not be bound by rigid roles that limit our freedom and our fullness.

With such support we can live out our giftedness, offering the blessings that we as women have to bring, our pieces of wisdom to the puzzles of life. With the full complement of male and female energies and characteristics working together on all levels — in the individual, in the family, in the church, and in the culture — we can do and be our best. Women and men working together in true partnerships of power and service will value what each has to bring. The honoring of women's experiences, insights, and gifts will make our communities more whole.

We also courageously must withdraw our support from that which is damaging. The distribution of the dollars, votes, and attention of women can demonstrate clearly what we believe in and what we don't. If the products we are buying do not promote sustainable practices and a living wage for workers, we can buy different ones. If the politicians who represent us are not voicing our concerns with integrity, we can vote for others who will. If the church we attend is oppressive to women, we can make a new beginning in a new spiritual community that isn't. Jesus would do no less.

What would happen if the church listened to Jesus' message as if she were listening to her bridegroom and lover — hanging on his every word; not wanting to miss the smallest inflection of his voice; seeking to understand his actions on earth; reaching out to touch and stroke his face; searching his eyes to catch a glimpse of his naked, human soul? Have we, as bride and body, missed a deep and passionate intimacy in our relationship with our bridegroom? We join with the prophet Joel, who in the Old Testament proclaims, "Call the people together, summon the community, assemble the elders, gather the children, even infants at the breast! Call the bridegroom from his bedroom and the bride from her bower!" (Joel 2:16). Let us celebrate in this reunion!

As the church embraces her identity as a bride, may she remain on that threshold of transformation, ever growing and changing, continually unfolding. Maybe then, true oneness will result as the bride and bridegroom merge fully in body and soul. Our prayer is that the church will become a wild and ready bride, allowing herself to fully penetrate and be penetrated by her bridegroom.

If the church allows herself to move beyond the limiting role of Mother, allowing her female members also to move beyond the limiting role of Good Women, maybe the true seed of Jesus and his love will grow in her, and Christianity's mission in the world will be reborn. In moving beyond virginal Mother, perhaps she will vulnerably open herself to the varied dimensions of soul living within her own body, experiencing renewed passion and spiritual pleasure.

If the church takes on the responsibility to move herself, including all of her denominational branches, beyond role, maybe women will find true healing and transformation in her embrace, inspired to integrate their many diverse selves — those of bride, mother, lover, sister, friend, and soul supporter. Maybe then, the church can model for her female members a holy, integrated self, living as a genuinely inspired community and acting as a responsible institution, liberated to creatively revision God beyond gender, church beyond mother, and woman beyond role.

Dance: Choose a piece of music that speaks to you of balance, support, action, and strength. Wear a yellow dress or tie a yellow scarf around your middle. Give yourself permission to embody your solar plexus chakra through the beauty and intensity of your dance.

Forgiveness: Perhaps you hold a secret shame — abuse, an abortion, a divorce, disappointment in not acting powerfully, an indiscretion of some kind — that keeps you from accepting and blessing your goodness. Perhaps it causes you to shame or control others in search of your own absolution. If you feel the need to loosen its hold on you, you might benefit from this ritual of forgiveness.

Select an instrumental piece of music that is melancholy but strong. Take a few moments to make a mental or written list of all the reasons and decisions that went into the making of the circumstance you regret. In silence, pay attention to where in your body you most notice the tightening or pain or residue of what it is you hold.

In your memory, go all the way back to when you might have contributed to a different outcome if you had had the support you needed. Access your compassion for yourself. Rock yourself gently. Imagine one or two gifts you would have offered to yourself if you could have. Begin to play your selection of music. Allow the place in your body that you have identified to be still and receptive. Let it be tenderly nurtured through this dance of forgiveness. Allow your whole being to embody and receive the gifts of support and healing that you have imagined. Let the words of Jesus wash over you: "Neither do I condemn you, neither do I condemn you." Claim your forgiveness.

As painful as your past may be, it is a part of you — your story, your wisdom, your prelude to the present. Take a moment to acknowledge your experience and write down what you would like to remember.

Expansion and Contraction: This dance is for experiencing the tension between polarities and finding a balance of support. Partners stand facing one another, locking right hands securely. The left hand is free to move. This exercise can be done in silence or with music. One will contract and offer support while the other stretches into as full an extension as possible. With the next breath, the roles are switched. The movement continues with the expansions and contractions passed back and forth. The contracting partner should be securely grounded (no slippery socks) to safely bear the expanding partner's weight. Notice if breathing can be coordinated with the movement, exhaling on a contraction, inhaling on an expansion. Discuss and write about this balancing act if you like.

Work Out: Engage in regular rigorous physical exercise in the interest of building body confidence, an appreciation for the competence of your physical strength and your ability to engage it. Give thanks to your body for the energy it generates and the action it supports. Enjoy the physical experience of feeling fit and powerful.

Core Concerns

I wake up early
stomach churning
worms seething, tumbling, in terrifying flux

do I really want to tell this story?
to be called a heretic, an apostate, or worse?
I long for the pepto bismol days
so sure of my message
the simple version of what my beliefs were about:

how it was better for the poor to know they were going to heaven
than to have food or economic justice
how sending money and praying for their salvation
would relieve my concerns
how there was never a reason to terminate a pregnancy
and we must prosecute any doctor or woman
who would dare an abortion
how no sex outside marriage
between one man and one woman
was the perfect prescription for societal bliss
how submission to my father and later my husband
would keep me safe in God's chain of command
how my religion was the only one true
the rest of the world on its way to Hell

but I traveled a little outside of my box
raised children and self all over again
befriended women in crisis
discovered the real challenges of social harmony
began questioning the practical breakdown
of just who might belong in heaven and hell anyway
I started to listen to my own gut

I believe in Jesus, the human one, more than ever
his compassion my comfort
his words my food
the mystical presence of his Spirit always with me
but the evil done and doing in the name of Christianity
turns my stomach sour
and sorry for pledging and promoting

blind obedience to a dogma
so easily co-opted
for domination and destruction
of political process
for international interference

did the friends I once evangelized
end up in churches
where the power and gifts
of girls and women
were methodically neutralized like mine?

my fear of speaking up
about what I now know to be true
percolates in my stomach

this courage for acting my convictions:
atrophied abdominals to exercise
physio-spiritual rehab
for my own responsible
agitated
core

Notes

1 Malcolm Gladwell, *Blink* (New York: Little, Brown, and Company, 2005), 54-56.

2 Mary Daly, *Beyond God the Father: Toward a Philosophy of Women's Liberation* (Boston: Beacon Press, 1973), 13.

3 Bro. Daniel F. Stramara, "El Shaddai: A Feminine Aspect of God," *The Pecos Benedictine* (Pecos, NM: November 1985), 2.

4 Mary Stewart VanLeeuwen, *After Eden: Facing the Challenge of Gender Reconciliation* (Grand Rapids, MI: Eerdmans, 1993), 149.

5 Janice Shaw Crouse, "Critique and Analysis by the Good News/RENEW Network of the United Methodist Women's Division 2004 General Conference Petitions," Renew Network for Christian Women, www.renewnetwork. org/Archived%20Files/Critique_and_analysis_2004%20GC_petitions.htm.

6 Albert Mohler, "The God Who Names Himself," June 21, 2006, www.albert-mohler.com/commentary_read.php?cdate=2006-06-21.

8 Karen Jo Torjesen, *When Women Were Priests* (San Francisco: HarperSanFranscisco, 1993), 268-269.

9 Gayla R. Postma, "Synod 2006: One Step Forward, One Step Back for Women," *Banner* (July 2006), www.thebanner.org/magazine/article.cfm?article_id=568

10 Laura Sheahen "'Evangelical Christianity has been Hijacked': An interview with Tony Campolo," *Beliefnet* (July 2004), www.beliefnet.com/story/150/story_15052_1.html.

11 Donald A. Grinde, Jr., "Iroquois Political Theory and the Roots of American Democracy," in *Exiled in the Land of the Free*, 230-239 (Santa Fe: Clear Light Publishers, 1992).

12 Ibid., 259.

13 Tim LaHaye, *The Battle for the Family* (Grand Rapids, MI: Revell, 1982), 139.

14 Human Rights Watch, "Cedaw: The Women's Treaty," October 26, 2005, http://hrw.org/campaigns/cedaw/.

15 John Calvin, *Institutes of the Christian Religion* (Louisville, KY: Westminster John Knox, 1559/1977), 74-75.

16 The American Heritage Dictionary of the English Language (Boston: Houghton Mifflin, 1973), s.v. "Mother."

17 Dr. Helen Caldicott, "Men: Natural Born Killers," Frontpagemag.com, www.frontpagemag.com/Articles/ReadArticle.asp?ID=6682.

18 Gregory Dicum, "No Nukes is Good Nukes: An interview with longtime anti-nuclear activist Helen Caldicott," www.grist.org/news/maindish/2005/05/03/dicum-caldicott/index.html.

19 International Women's Democracy Center, "Fact Sheet: Women's Political Participation," www.iwdc.org/resources/fact_sheet.htm International Women's Democracy Center.

20 Rose Marie Berger, "The Miracle at Accra." *Sojourners* (July 2005): 36.

21 Janice Shaw Crouse, "Critique and Analysis by the Good News/RENEW," Network of The United Methodist Women's Division 2004 General Conference Petitions, www.renewnetwork.org/Archived%20Files/Critique_and_analysis_2004%20GC_petitions.htm.

9

Domination and Female Sexuality
Sacral Chakra: Sexuality

Fullamalarchy

My mother grew up in a matriarchy
And she didn't really like it

So she married into a patriarchy
And I really didn't like it
I gave my best to help it work
But it cost me an awful lot

Still recovering, reclaiming,
Regaining, reframing,
My dignity, my voice,
My confidence, my art

So I'm creating something different
And I like it very much

We're developing an equalarchy, a mutuarchy perhaps
It's a partnerarchy, familarchy,
Fullamalarchy adventure

With love, and justice, and liberty for all

Characteristics: Relationships are hierarchical; traditional marriage;
devaluation of the feminine; anti-gay; anti-choice.

Idolatry of Hierarchy

When the Israelites were in the desert, before they reached the Promised Land, Moses went to the top of Mount Sinai to receive the Ten Commandments from God. When he had been gone for a long time and they feared he would never return, the people built an idol, a calf made of gold, before which they sacrificed burnt offerings. Fundamentalist Christianity, with its exaltation of the Good Woman role, upholds the traditional family as a kind of golden calf. The real woman is sacrificed as the traditional family is worshiped and idolized as sacrosanct. The distinguishing feature of the traditional family is hierarchy.

Many Christians hold fast to a belief in traditional marriage that is really a quite recent phenomena. As Meredith McGuire explains in *Religion: The Social Context,*

> [T]he Christian ideal of the institution of marriage is often represented as being exactly the ideal held during the whole history of Christianity. Actually, however, both the ideals and practices of marriage have changed considerably, and current religiously legitimated arrangements, such as the practice of church weddings, are relatively recent. The effectiveness of legitimations of present-day marriage practices depends on treating these practices as traditional and on forgetting or de-emphasizing those parts of history that are inconsistent with present norms and practices.[1]

The idea of equality and mutual submission is considered heresy in many religious circles. Men must be on top, women on the bottom. Psychologist Dr. Teresa Whitehurst offers this description of sermons preached in support of this paradigm.

> Conservative preachers have been teaching with great fervor these last few years that obedience to men, not to Christ, is a Christian woman's highest calling; thinking for herself or disagreeing with men is thus her greatest sin. ... Conservative Christian men have come to believe, at the urging of preachers with their own authoritarian agendas, that they can and should condemn (punish) their wives whenever they use their pretty little heads to disagree on serious matters such as politics, religion, or war. Husbands are

ego-stroked every Sunday by male preachers as "family leaders" or as "the head of the household."[2]

Many fundamentalist religions today treat the woman as inferior, defining her role as that of a "helpmate," rather than as an equal partner. This doctrine of unequal male/female relationships creates an imbalance of power within the relationship and paves the way for increased domination, control, abuse, and lack of appreciation on a daily basis. Because of these religious attachments to hierarchical structures, Christianity has a religious and social history replete with power imbalance and gender prejudice. According to Walter Wink,

> [T]he family in dominator societies is so deeply imbedded in patriarchy, and serves as the citadel of male supremacy, the chief inculcator of gender roles, and a major inhibitor of change. It is in families where most women and children are battered and abused, and where the majority of women are murdered. In a great many cultures, men are endowed with the inalienable right to beat, rape, and verbally abuse their wives. The patriarchal family is thus the foundation on which the larger units of patriarchal dominance are based.[3]

The apparent hierarchical relationship within the Christian doctrine of the Trinity subtly reinforces the fundamentalist teaching on headship. What is inferred is that God, the Father, maintains the respected position of the senior male. Second in command is the Son, dutifully and obediently fulfilling the commands of the primary male deity. Lowest on the totem pole is the Holy Spirit, that amorphous, almost genderless being, who is the only candidate capable of being mistakenly merged with the feminine. This member of the Trinity is at the bottom of the heap, vulnerable to every order of the two males on top. Of course, even the Holy Spirit is rarely endowed with a feminine pronoun. This view of God, modeling patriarchal hierarchy, may be misconstrued as the divine plan for gender relationships. Clearly, Jesus' work on this earth was not rooted in hierarchical power, nor his gender ever discussed in his teachings. Some, however, might see in Jesus' maleness more divine evidence for the justification of patriarchy.

Much of America's social history is rooted in Christianity's ideas and perceptions of gender relations. Men have seen their fathers and grandfathers treat their wives as subordinates and their mothers and grandmothers silently submit, in the name of religion, no questions asked.

This tradition has become the normal and right way for a fundamentalist man to treat his wife.

In fundamentalist homes, this chain of command theology is a primary destroyer of effective and mutually empowering interpersonal behavior patterns. When tasks and responsibilities are not shared, the community of the couple and the family suffers. Harmony breaks down precisely because individuals are not working together equally, and resentments build. Women are expected to pick up the pieces. After all, when you're on the bottom, it's your job to do what is delegated to you by those at the top. A loving and fulfilling relationship rooted in mutual respect is difficult, if not impossible, to maintain when you're saddled with a master/slave mentality.

According to family systems theory, when a member in any system (family or social) changes, all members of the system must also shift and change. This truth becomes particularly evident when women take action toward change. As we have seen in the past decade, with more women choosing or needing to work outside the home, many couples have divorced. One of the factors leading to this marital breakdown is the inability of the couple to accept and move through the necessary life transitions from traditional male/female stereotypic roles to greater flexibility.

Couples who grew up in families in which the parents were rigidly attached to fixed roles often find it difficult to adapt to role reversals when necessary or desirable usually for one spouse more than another. In fundamentalist systems, the woman who has gone outside the home in search of a career is quickly blamed for the challenges the family faces. However, couples that stay together through this cultural transition, flexing and adapting with the changes, often reap positive results.

Many report they have more deeply experienced the joys and lessons of shared parenting. Men have developed their nurturing capacities, while women have enjoyed their professional growth. Many women who contribute to their family income through their work report a heightened sense of self-esteem and fulfillment.

For an article titled "The Stay-at-Home Dad" in *Christianity Today*, Suzanne Woods Fisher interviewed several role-reversed families. The challenges for these fathers were not unlike those facing stay-at-home mothers. One father reported, "There's an adjustment period — no paycheck, no affirmation, and you're facing the hardest job you'll ever have." Another admitted, "Loneliness, isolation, and recreating an identity not based on achievement are the main drawbacks." Nevertheless,

Fisher writes, "All of these families insist their kids have profited by the arrangement," and the dads "report an amazing powerful bond with their children."[4]

In their book *Raising Cain: Protecting the Emotional Life of Boys*, Dan Kindlon and Michael Thompson write:

> We have to teach boys that there are many ways to become a man; that there are many ways to be brave, to be a good father, to be loving and strong and successful. We need to celebrate the natural creativity and risk-taking of boys, their energy, their boldness. We need to praise the artist and the entertainer, the missionary and the athlete, the soldier and the male nurse, the storeowner and the round-the-world sailor, the teacher and the CEO. There are many ways ... to make a contribution in this life.[5]

There are as many ways for women to contribute, as well, and many ways to structure family life so that the fullness of each individual is able to blossom.

Promise Keepers of Women in Their Place

An organization of Evangelical Christian men who call themselves Promise Keepers (PK) is perhaps the most visible proponent of men's leadership in the home and women's subjugation to that leadership.

The Promise Keepers are a Pentecostal revival movement that uses culture to attract new political recruits to the Christian right. The organizers have updated the venue from tents to sports arenas for what they hope will be the greatest mobilization of evangelicals in history — nothing less than a twentieth century-scale Great Awakening.[6]

Observers find Promise Keepers unapologetic in asserting fixed gender roles in marriage, highlighting man's role as head of the family. Understandably, feminist women fear the sexism and the power of this movement, founded in 1990 by Bill McCartney, former head football coach at the University of Colorado. Perhaps one of the most threatening messages that has come from this group is found in this quote from one of the movement's books, *Seven Promises of a Promise Keeper*. Under the heading, "Reclaiming Your Manhood," the author tells the reader to inform his wife: "Honey, I've made a terrible mistake. I've given you my role. I gave up leading this family, and I forced you to take my place. Now I must reclaim that role." Don't misunderstand what I'm saying here. I'm not suggesting that you *ask* for your role back. I'm urging you to *take* it back" (emphases in the original).[7]

In a period when the traditional family is undergoing dramatic changes — an increase in divorce and blended families, gay people partnering and raising children, and single women choosing to conceive and raise children without the partnership of a man — the Promise Keepers provides security and stability to those who feel threatened by these alternative families. But is it actually the family these men are scrambling to preserve, or is it men's power and position within both the family and the culture?

The Promise Keepers enable fundamentalist men to maintain their traditional masculine status by masking their own fears of displacement beneath this seemingly noble cause. Do alternative families cause fundamentalist men and women to bring into question the rigid gender roles and life choices prescribed to them by the church? Do alternative families, with their flexibility toward issues of gender expression and role, undermine the fundamentalist blueprint for male and female behavior within marriage and family? The clear political agenda is the rigid adherence to the traditional family, with women remaining domesticated and subservient to men. Is this traditional fundamentalist family really worth saving if it truly encompasses the deadening of women's souls?

Under superficial analysis, the goals of the Promise Keepers appear to be worthwhile and supportive of women and children. They favor fathers taking a more active role in the raising of their children and being more faithful to and supportive of their wives. Often, wives actually coerce their husbands to attend the rallies (90 percent of attendees are married men). Fundamentalism teaches that a good Christian woman is not overly demanding of her husband; therefore, women are relieved to allow the Promise Keepers to become their vicarious demanding voice.

Mary Stewart Van Leeuwen offers this analysis:

> PK is actually appropriating the feminist critique of the stereotype that keeps men from expressing their emotions, nurturing their children, and showing other qualities that are often mislabeled as exclusively feminine. PK enjoins followers to reject the image of the friendless American male and instead adopt biblical virtues like encouragement, forgiveness, mutual confession, and mutual aid. Don't be fooled by the stadium trappings; the sports symbols are there to make men feel safe about crying and confessing their sexual addictions and other self-centered ways.
>
> Now the bad news: Promise Keepers equivocates about the nature of gender reconciliation in a way not paralleled by its consistent message on racial reconciliation. PK has made racial

reconciliation a non-negotiable promise. No such clear and strong message exists when it comes to the relation between men and women.

When questioned, for example, about the fact that some speakers advocate full equality between marriage partners while others endorse a husband's benevolent paternalism, PK representatives claim the organization has no formal position on male headship. It is, they note, an issue on which Evangelicals with equally high views of the Bible disagree. But when PK founder Bill McCartney publicly announces, as he did on National Public Radio, that God almighty has proclaimed husbands to be the spiritual leaders at home, why should anyone not assume that this is PK's official position? On such a core issue, PK should make a choice. Mutuality should be the message.[8]

Critics express fear that a call for men to be Promise Keepers is a call for women to "keep their place." Dr. Carolyn Holderread Heggen, in her book, *Sexual Abuse in Christian Homes and Churches*, reports a disturbing fact surfacing in sex abuse research. After alcohol or drug addiction in the father, the best predictor of sexual abuse "is conservative religiosity, accompanied by parental belief in traditional female-male roles." Furthermore, in a survey of clergy from conservative churches, which she conducted with V.O. Long, Heggen reports that respondents described a spiritually healthy woman as:

> 'submissive in the home,' 'gentle and soft spoken,' 'lets spouse make decisions,' 'dependent,' 'passive,' 'finds identity through spouse,' and 'withholds criticism.' These qualities were not used by conservative pastors to describe a spiritually healthy male or adult of unspecified gender.
>
> Because conservative churches teach that such qualities are important for a Christian woman, she may feel pressured to adopt attitudes and behaviors which detract from her ability to protect herself and her children from an abusive man.[9]

Case Study: Monica Vows Her Life Away

The following story highlights the incongruence of a woman choosing a traditional marriage, where she ultimately could not fit.

Monica was raised in a very religious, very conservative Protestant family, a family in which men ruled and women submitted. At twenty-five she married Gary, a man in her father's mold.

All brides are beautiful, but Monica was stunning. She's a natural beauty — dark, glossy hair and deep blue eyes set off by a peaches-and-cream complexion. A wedding gown of flowing silk and lace accentuated her Southern belle femininity. As Monica says, "I was in love with ruffles, flowing skirts, and high heels."

Although Monica and her parents planned the physical details of the wedding meticulously — filling the church with fragrant white flowers, hiring a string quartet to play carefully chosen selections — Monica didn't lose sight of the ceremony's real purpose, and she worked hard on writing her vows. On the day of their marriage, Monica promised Gary, "With confidence, I will submit myself to your headship as unto the Lord … as your helpmeet, I will be your partner in the service of God." She promised, "[I will] continue my walk with God, developing the inward beauty of a gentle and quiet spirit, committing myself to helping you grow to become a man who seeks after God's heart." Gary promised Monica, "[I vow] to be your leader and spiritual head of our family, to nurture and cherish you as my own self, to look only for your good, to protect you and provide for you."

The people from Monica's conservative church who attended the wedding ceremony greeted her with affirmation and praise for her vows. "Those are the most beautiful vows I have ever heard … and so sound! … Those vows said it all." The senior pastor of her church, a man world-re-nowned in the conservative Christian community, also approached Monica, praising the "right doctrine" to which she had attested. He said he was pleased to hear the promises of a "solid, upstanding Christian woman," and that he was "sure you have pleased God as well." Monica felt honored and proud as her pastor, the senior authority figure in her life, acknowledged her.

But over the next ten years of her marriage to Gary, Monica began to see that in those carefully worded vows she had made deadly promises — promises that were killing off any chance she and Gary had for a mutually satisfying relationship. In therapy, Monica began to see the ramifications of these vows for her own life. They didn't make sense any longer. She felt as if she was losing her mind. She was tired of feeling that her opinion was less important than Gary's. She knew she was capable and competent, and it seemed silly to play small in order to appear submissive in deference to him. Now she was a respected marketing director for a large corporation and a powerful community leader. Even her style of dress had changed over the years. Monica now favored tailored clothes, set off by pieces of bold jewelry. Though still a beauty, she was no longer mistaken for an old-fashioned, traditional Christian woman.

What Monica called the turning point came at a wedding that occurred almost ten years after her own. Both the bride and groom were marrying for the second time. The bride wore a simple ivory suit and Monica was surprised by the couple's vows: "I will respect and trust you. I will be your equal partner, giving and receiving, speaking and listening, inspiring and responding."

At the reception, one of the teenage girls who had been at the wedding said to the bride, "You two promised to talk mutually with each other and to listen to each other. That's so cool! I'm going to remember that when I get married."

In the hours following the wedding, Monica found herself mulling over those vows, jealous of her friend and angry with her husband. She thought of all the times she had submitted without really wanting to. Even an issue like the color of the living room — Monica had agreed to paint it beige, Gary's choice, rather than the fuchsia she liked — took on significance as a symbol of a power relationship that was out of balance. "I decided that day that my living room would be different, that my marriage would be different, that my life would be different!"

Since that time, Monica and Gary have worked out many of the issues that stemmed from their "religiously correct" wedding vows and have written new ones. They each promised to love, to listen openly and speak honestly, to support each other's continued growth, and to respect each other as equal partners and companions.

Today Monica says, "My husband doesn't fully understand why things had to change. I guess he liked being in control. Still, there are times when he confesses that he really likes the changes in me, that he feels he has a partner now. Truth be told, he even likes the living room painted fuchsia — the room is alive."

Domination in the Family

Relationships rooted in inequality fuel confusion and distortions of power. Misunderstood concepts of power progress toward power actively misused, otherwise known as abusive relationships. An object is far easier to abuse than a human being; hence, the victimization and role stereotyping of girls and women in Christian fundamentalism serve a utilitarian purpose. They dehumanize the woman, normalizing her inferior status, causing her to objectify and perpetuate such behavior herself with little, if any, awareness of what she is doing. She loses sight of the sacredness of her own life and her right to freedom. When a woman no longer believes she has the right to be fully alive and autonomous, she is more apt to silence herself, her dreams, and her desires. She will treat herself as her role. This mistreatment of herself mimics others' silencing and victimizing of her. Her soul's deep needs and desires gradually become obscure and unimportant to her. This systematic repression of women is characterized by three actions:

1. the victimization of girls and women through domination and control;

2. the rigid stereotyping of a woman's role in all domains of her life; and

3. the physical, intellectual, emotional, sexual, and spiritual abuse that results.

We broadly define abuse as that which kills one's aliveness, denying one the freedom to be authentic. Abuse destroys a woman's vitality, silences the expression of her soul, and prevents her from becoming a complete and integrated female. As a victim of abuse, a woman loses appreciation for and connection with her intuitive, instinctual, and authentic self. Split off from her deepest yearnings, she is unable to express her creative power.

James and Phyllis Alsdurf, in their book *Battered into Submission*, examine how women are even blamed for the abuse. Consider a Focus on the Family radio program recorded in 1984 that was broadcast several times, in which James Dobson paints his picture of "one of the most common causes of wife abuse":

> Here's the situation. The husband is not a very verbal person and is rather passive. He's not meeting his wife's needs. She is deeply angry about this and her approach is to bludgeon the tar out of him. She's not pulling him toward her, she is hammering him verbally. He can't handle that verbally. He cannot hold his own with her in words because she's a far more verbal person than he. ... And she is tearing him and she is attacking him and she is just giving him what with all the time. And finally he gets so frustrated that the only thing he knows to do is to respond with power and he turns around and beats her up.[10]

In contrast, the Alsdurfs find that men who batter their wives often are articulate, successful, and competent in their roles outside of marriage. They come from all walks of life and many hold positions of leadership. In fact, one study found that more highly educated batterers typically inflicted more serious injuries. It is alarming that Dobson, a man whose ideas are widely distributed, would publicly present such a distorted picture of an abusive marriage in which he minimizes, even justifies, the man's violent behavior. He actually suggested that battered women get their husbands to beat them so that they can leave the marriage without guilt:

> I've seen situations where the wife, I think, wanted most to be beaten up. There is a certain moral advantage that comes from having been hit by this man. Then you're in charge, you're self-righteous, you can leave, you have your exit. You want out, you can't find a moral way out because the Bible says marriage is forever, and if you can just push that guy until he turns around and blacks your eye, then boy the whole world, God included, can see that you were the one that's right and you were the one that was taken advantage of, and all of a sudden you're a martyr.[11]

In his book *Love must be Tough*, Dobson continues his justification of wife abuse:

> I have seen marital relationships where the woman deliberately "baited" her husband until he hit her... I have seen women belittle and berate their husbands until they set them aflame with rage. Some wives are more verbal than their husbands and win a war of words any day of the week. Finally, the men reach a point of such frustration that they explode, doing precisely what their wives were begging them to do in the first place.[12]

With this distorted psychology behind their therapeutic interventions, Christian women predictably remain in the battering situation, believing they deserve abuse. In expressing these views, Dobson joins with the male client, sympathetically favoring the husband's experience, even colluding with the male's position of power, at the wife's expense. This idea is a violation of sound marriage and family therapeutic practice. To present such a distorted picture of a typically abusive marriage is misleading and appalling; it minimizes, even justifies, the man's pathologically violent behavior.

It is time for the church to examine to what degree its chain of command theology supports abusive behavior. From her contextual analysis of marital equality and violence against wives, sociologist Kersti Yllo found that the rate of wife beating in couples in which the husband dominated was 300 percent greater than for egalitarian couples. Yllo concluded:

> [R]egardless of context, violence against wives is lower among couples where there is a relative equality in decision-making. In

general, domination of decision-making by husbands is associated with the highest levels of violence against wives. This violence is not just physical. It is emotional as well. More importantly, it is attitudinal, which is often acted out through behaviors and attitudes that are undermining to the woman.[13]

Even subtle attitudes have powerful effects. Psychologist John Gottman has studied partners in marriages to observe factors that indicate whether they will still be married in fifteen years. He has determined that the single most important sign that a marriage is in trouble is when one partner shows contempt for the other. He explains how contempt is worse than criticism. "[I]f I speak from a superior plane, that's far more damaging, and contempt is any statement made from a higher level. A lot of the time it's an insult. ...It's trying to put that person on a lower plane than you. It's hierarchical."[14]

Hostility to Homosexuality

There is a common and disturbing theme in boys' locker room banter. Coaches dismissively call players "ladies," and the taunting among players frequently maintains how unlike women the athletes must be in order to be proved adequate. Boys who develop later than others are teased about their size, the high pitch of their voices, or their lack of body hair. Slurs such as sissy, pussy, bitch, fairy, and faggot all challenge one's masculinity while implicitly maligning the feminine.

With all this dominating, shaming, and minimizing of the feminine, it's easy to imagine why a man might be filled with agonizing conflict when he notices tender stirrings within himself or an attraction to another man. When all things associated with the feminine are deemed inferior and to be dominated, the very real feminine part of him must also be pushed aside. God forbid that any fiber in him tends toward homosexuality! To prove his manhood, a man might join any possible campaign to stamp out tolerance for alternate sexual expression. Such hostile homophobia is rooted in the will to dominate and diminish the feminine.

Fundamentalist theology, not surprisingly, opposes the sanctioning of homosexual marriage. In Dobson's recent book, *Marriage Under Fire: Why we Must Win this Battle*, he attempts to build an alarmist case against gay marriage. The Arlington Group, which he chairs, poured $2 million into 2004 campaigns in states with "one man, one woman" marriage amendments on their ballots. Many suspect that the resultant turnout of conservative voters significantly influenced the presidential outcome.

Fundamentalists argue that gay marriage must be prevented because children need both a father and a mother. Our concern is for the children who, for whatever reason, develop into homosexual adults themselves. When we disallow same-sex marriage, we fail to offer these children and young people positive role models of fidelity and family life.

Strident voices smugly preach, "We don't have to debate about what we should think about homosexual activity, it's written in the Bible."[15] Such narrow rhetoric amplifies the lack of compassion for self and others. Are such men fearful of their own unique sexual orientation, which may not be exclusively heterosexual? Do they fear gay marriages wherein a man may freely express feminine as well as masculine dimensions of himself? Are they fearful of lesbian marriages, in which women are happily self-sufficient without the presence of a man? Is the defense of the "traditional family" and the fervent desire to deny benefits, privileges, and legal status to other types of families fueled by the interest in preserving established male authority?

From a positive perspective, what do heterosexuals struggling for egalitarian relationships stand to learn from same-sex partners? How much of our relational role-playing is deeply rooted in our heterosexually normative socialization? When gay or lesbian partners dance, who leads? Does it depend on the dance? The day? The mood? The ability? Or can they pass the leading back and forth in such a manner that no one can tell?

Add to all these questions the reality of those who are born with anatomy that has been determined not standard for male or female, those who are "intersexed." Consider this letter to the editor of *Time Magazine* on March 5, 2004, from "Jane Doe," Bloomington, Indiana:

> We can all debate whether marriage for gays and lesbians should or should not happen, but those of us in the intersex community dread someone defining marriage. I have Androgen Insensitivity Syndrome (AIS) and never knew until I was 35. Though I look female, I have XY chromosomes and was born with testes. It would be incorrect to describe me as biologically male or female — I am biologically intersexed. As an intersexed person, who do my politicians think I am supposed to marry? How can they define for me marriage as one man–one woman?
>
> I believe it will be impossible for the courts to achieve any functioning definition of "man" and "woman." Some estimates today show that 1 baby out of 100 is born intersexed in some

manner. What combination of factors will our legislators or courts use to determine whether I am male or female to defend marriage? Chromosomes? Gonads? Appearance of genitals? Gender identity? Something else?

Those who support the gay marriage ban argue that the rights of gays and lesbians are not abridged because they are permitted to marry, just not to the partner of their choice. The same right exists for intersex individuals, yet without any explanation of how their sex is to be determined. I would submit that my biological reality wins over any fixed definition.

Marriage is, of course, a fundamental right. As such, every individual should be entitled to enter into marriage. Any legislation introduced seeking to bar marriage for gays and lesbians will hurt those of us who are intersexed.[16]

The Intersex Society of North America has learned "from listening to individuals and families dealing with intersex that:

- Intersexuality is primarily a problem of stigma and trauma, not gender.
- Parents' distress must not be treated by surgery on the child.
- Professional mental health care is essential.
- Honest, complete disclosure is good medicine.
- All children should be assigned as boy or girl, without early surgery."[17]

The recent standard of medical practice is to assign gender and surgically alter the child's genitals, if atypical, in the interest of creating the capacity for heterosexual, penetrative sex. As adults, many intersexed people report extreme dissatisfaction with the results of these interventions.

The more we learn about human sexuality, the more we understand how complex and nonstandard each individual's sexual makeup is, due to variability in chromosomes, hormones, morphology, brain development, and socialization. As a society, we must move toward embracing the diversity of each of God's creations rather than insisting on homogeneity, exclusion, and judgment.

Case Study: A Secret

What happens when a fundamentalist woman explores and makes public her authentic sexual expression apart from a man? The following journal entry was written by a fundamentalist Christian struggling to understand her sexuality. Is she homosexual? Is she bisexual? Is she heterosexual? She's not sure. What she is sure about is that there is no one to talk to about this; she knows if she speaks to anyone, she will be disqualified and banished from the circle of women deemed respectable. Her church is especially conservative and harshly judgmental, even of people who smoke cigarettes. In this fundamentalist institution, sex is understood in the context of heterosexual marriage. A woman's sexuality is certainly not free to express itself apart from a man. Her fear of discovery (within herself and within her fundamentalist system) is so great that even in her personal journal she refers to her sexual quest as an "it."

Julia

A secret. Scared. Wondering, is "it" okay? What is it? What does it mean? Who am I? Is this a phase? Excited. Passionate even. An alive part of me.

And that's the important thing. It's alive and I won't let anyone squash it until I've lived it a bit. Looked at it a bit. Decided alone what I want to do with it. I know life when I see it. I know uninhibited, unhindered, spontaneous, surprising life when I see it. Maybe strands to take from it and leave the rest? As long as what I leave is chaff; I will not simply dismiss or ignore what is true and good.

What if it's true but not good? Or true but I choose not to act upon it? That's within my realm of choice. But is it good? Are some natural, spontaneous feelings, the first stirrings of life after many years of oppression, bad? I can understand not wanting to act upon stirrings, but are the stirrings themselves bad?

Might they be a stepping-stone to other feelings, other stirrings? Might I accept them now (as I secretly do) as one stone upon a very long path? If I pray and ask God to guide me on that path, ask to breathe into me deeply the intuition whether this particular stone is a good stopping place for now (versus my ever present guilt), do I proceed as I feel led within?

I am just tired of saying no to everything inside. The default "no" switch has been deactivated, and what I'm doing now is letting all the "yeses" spring up one by one, just to watch them grow. This is good. I like this. It smells nice. This one will lead me to no good. I will trim this one down, or even pull it out by its roots. I don't wish for hedonism, some selfish life devoid of discipline. I just want plenty of "yeses" and the necessary "nos," but no more than necessary.

She concluded with a poem:

I found my license to breathe recently.
Strangely enough, it was in my back pocket all the time,
damp from the sweat of my trying to find the answer.
My lungs straining for one, no, many, good deep gulps
of fresh, cool, clean spring air. The oxygen
exuded by ferns clinging to a rock by a waterfall.

Crisp autumn air, with hints of copper and maroon
rushing down my throat to greet me.
All this time, I had permission. My mother
must have forgotten to tell me as a child. I know
I used to shy away from those who inhaled too deeply:
Not safe. Shallow breathing brings less exposure to the
elements. Exactly.

Shallow breathing brings less exposure to the elements.
Deep breathing can bring a sharp surprise on a cold
winter morning when my mind is still wrapped in flannel,
but when the snowy air hits my lungs, I am suddenly
alive enough to see the hints of blue in the brilliantly
white snowbanks, and the trees stand against a pale sky
with their arms held high to God.

Julia compares her sexual exploration to breathing, ... the act that gives life to us all. Without this exploration, she might suffocate and die. She finds her license to breathe in her back pocket. She does not need a town hall or any other institution of authority to give her permission to live or to express her sexual self freely.

For a soul to thrive, it must be able to manifest itself authentically. The judgments hurled against homosexuals by many fundamentalist churches are but one example of the devaluation of a soul's search for truth. When expression is stifled, deadness and fragmentation result, within the woman and within the system.

In fundamentalist churches and families, a woman's genuine search for her authentic sexual expression — especially if it is discovered to be ho-mosexual — is equated with evil, evaluated as sinful, desperately in need of salvation. It's easy to see why, in these systems, women go underground with the truth about their sexuality; the fear of damnation, both in this life and the life hereafter, is burned into their souls.

A woman must be free to define the expression of her own sexuality apart from a man; when she is not, a part of her soul dies. If she is required to live her life sexually imprisoned, she must find a way to compensate for her soul's extinction. She must learn to construct walls to hide behind, distancing herself from herself and her innate sexuality. She has difficulty admitting to herself that she is not sexually alive or free; therefore, she lives her life encased in role, detached from her own authentic passions, believing this is living. Apart from her own awareness, she expresses her sexuality as others expect her to, accepting their domination and control of her soul's rightful path, believing this is the Christian way. She lives always anxious and fearful of what awaits her if she does not subordinate herself to their commands.

Within fundamentalism, a woman's sexual expression is restricted. She is required to live her life sexually objectified, losing touch with her own unique female expression of her sexuality. Detaching from her sensual and earthy feminine powers, she is expected to act out a girlish virginity. This metaphoric clitorectomy effectively and figuratively amputates the free expression of her sexual and sensual passions.

Commandment: Your sexuality is not your own and will be appropriated by men; your emotions are not important.

The Abortion Controversy

Women have been subjected to a variety of social controls through the ages. The anti-choice movement in the United States arises from a much broader context in which, among other signals of misogyny, public power and authority have been denied to women for centuries. Although framed as a theological/moral argument, at its core, the abortion debate masks a political and social agenda focused on women's oppression. Women have been easy targets for unconscious fears, denied and projected outward, raised by anything and everything that seems uncontrollable and unpredictable. The degree to which control is exercised over women often is an indicator of the profundity of stress felt by fundamentalist persons and groups, as fundamentalism itself is a product of extreme social stress. The anti-abortion preoccupation reflects that same stress as women move steadily toward change.

When the fundamentalist church supports conservative candidates and movements, a primary goal is to control and dominate not only fundamentalist women but all women, both those "in the fold" and those outside. With the merging of fundamentalist religion and politics, this goal becomes a possible reality. In the book *Fundamentalism & Gender*, Karen McCarthy Brown warns, "We should be suspicious of any religion that claims too much certainty or draws social boundaries too firmly."[18]

How can a woman live her own life if she is not permitted to manage her own body? This complex controversy has been reduced to oppressive simplicity. A woman's body belongs to God. She may not presume to assume responsibility for her own reproductive choices. God will decide how many children she will have and when she will have them. Life begins indisputably at conception, and the resultant embryo is equal in status to the woman whose body contains it. The church will be God's mouthpiece on this subject ... not just for Christian women, but for every woman.

Fundamentalist dogma speaks only of the life and death of the fetus, but not of the life, losses, and struggles of the woman involved. Rather than valuing both the woman and the fetus and giving both a "reverent consideration," the church turns to the fetus with boundless compassion, while turning against the woman with pitiless contempt. As Randall Balmer writes,

> Given their own history, however, their identification with the fetus is not surprising. For fundamentalists, the fetus serves as a marvelous symbol, not only because of its Freudian or psycho-analytic connotations of crawling back into the womb to escape the buffetings of the world, but because they see it in their own image. [He quotes Randall Terry, head of Operation Rescue] "Abortion is the symbol of our decline, the slaughter of the most innocent." ... Fundamentalists for decades have seen themselves as vulnerable.[19]

This fear-based perception creates an intense need from within the confines of the culture to control with a tighter rein. These "wild women," with their outlandish, humanistic values, must be tamed! The abortion issue is critical to the fundamentalist church's continued existence; — a necessary political agenda they must win. This competitive attitude reveals their militarism around this subject. After all, if the womb of a woman is allowed to be invaded, and if these same women are allowed to determine their own destiny, what might happen when the womb of Mother Church is invaded by the outside world? The tightly closed system of the fundamentalist church is experiencing a threat. It is in danger of having its most favorite doctrine aborted — the control of women. What kind of changes will this bring? God only knows!

While the fundamentalist church emphasizes the infantile position of the child within the womb, there is a parallel investment in keeping the woman in a childlike, dependent state as well. The attempt to overturn abortion rights laws leads to the logical next step of the fundamentalist mission: a world that guarantees and ensures the woman's place in the home. After all, the more babies a woman has, the greater the guarantee of her domesticity. When a woman's sole place of employment is in the home, a full-time job for which she receives no pay and little recognition, she remains financially dependent on the husband while his emotional needs remain the top priority. Powerlessness, self-doubt, and insecurity are not uncommon struggles for women isolated at home with children. Although the reality of the family that can live on one income alone in this day is a rarity, the idealized insistence on the woman remaining in the home persists.

Anna Quinlan brings light to this reality in her discussion of Plan B emergency contraception, which works by inhibiting ovulation, fertilization, or implantation and could possibly cut the number of abortions in half. Many in the anti-choice movement have vigorously opposed women's access to this drug.

> If easy access to a pill that has been shown to significantly decrease the number of abortions is not a welcome development, what is the real point of the anti-abortion exercise? Is it to safeguard life, or to safeguard an outdated status quo in which biology was destiny and motherhood was an obligation, not an avocation?[20]

In September 2007, 250 people gathered for a Pro-Life Action League event to condemn *all* forms of artificial birth control. The league's director, Joseph Sheidler, said, "Contraception is more the root cause of abortion than anything else." Experts at the gathering assailed contraception on the grounds that it devalues children, harms relationships between men and women, promotes sexual promiscuity and leads to falling birth rates, among other social ills.[21]

Our point is not to argue the morality of abortion, but to argue the immorality of denying a woman the right to control her body's most intimate and sacred functions. Fundamentalist religious institutions have chosen to frame this complex issue with narrow simplicity. They have no compassion for the many women who view pregnancy as a serious crisis. We must investigate some of the socioeconomic reasons a pregnancy may be considered a crisis situation.

In the United States, abortions had been steadily decreasing through the 1990s. Since 2001, this trend has reversed. Glen Stassen, a Christian ethicist at Fuller Theological Seminary, reported in conversation that the Center for Disease Control's "Morbidity and Mortality Report" had recently come out for 2002. It says that abortions increased (slightly) in 2002. They decreased by approximately 60,000 per year in the 1990s. 2002 is a significant change. 2002 is also the first year *ever* in the record when the infant mortality rate increased. The records go back to 1940. Every year it decreased until 2002, another evidence of the undermining of mothers and infants.

Stassen wrote in an op-ed for the *Houston Chronicle* on October 17, 2004, that low wages and the loss of jobs and health care have contributed to the rise in abortion rates. Stassen, the father of a severely handicapped child, expressed his personal awareness of the crucial importance of public and family support for parenting, especially of a special child. He concluded his report: "Economic policy and abortion are not separate issues; they form one moral imperative. Rhetoric is hollow, mere tinkling brass, without health care, insurance, jobs, childcare and a living wage. Pro-life in deed, not merely in word, means we need a president who will do something about jobs, health insurance and support for mothers."[22]

For any life form to complete its journey to whole emergence, several environmental conditions must be perfect. We find in nature a preponderance of seed produced so that those who find fertile soil and the appropriate conditions for nurture, will survive and even thrive. One of those conditions must be a ready and welcoming womb. Our concern as a society must be that we offer each child a womblike community in which to grow. The concern of the individual must be that she responsibly and tenderly manage her own womb.

Repressive attitudes are not the sole property of the anti-choice fundamentalists. While those who oppose abortion have reduced the issue to "murder," those who support a woman's right to choose too often have reduced abortion to "an office procedure," something a woman can recover from in much the same way that she recovers from the anesthetic. In fact, the issue is vastly more complicated than either side has been willing to admit. Both sides are guilty of minimizing the sanctity of a woman's choice.

Imagine society if our guiding belief emphasized the right of a woman to freely choose, as well as her obligation to choose thoughtfully and responsibly. Imagine if the church were a safe haven, in which women and men could discuss sexuality and abortion openly and respectfully.

Imagine a society that honestly discussed and supported responsible sexuality. Imagine women making choices with integrity and love, guided by God and supported by compassionate women and men. Imagine if a woman's sexuality were a domain left to her own regulation, apart from the domination and control of others.

Sex (Protection) Education

We help our children learn to feed themselves. We support them in their toilet training in hopes they will manage this bodily function independently. We expose them to many fields of knowledge in their education. We even teach them and allow them to drive. But when it comes to helping them understand, enjoy, and manage the most powerful, life-giving, and complicated dimension of their humanity — their sexuality — some choose silence or offer simple dictates from a fundamentalist orientation. Dobson's advice is for parents to end their sex education program immediately before their child enters puberty and not discuss it anymore. "Once they enter this developmental period, they are typically embarrassed by discussions of sex with their parents. Adolescents usually resent adult intrusion during this time, preferring to have the subject of sex ignored in the home. We should respect their wish."[23]

Developing teens do continue to need support and conversation about issues of sexuality, especially as the information becomes more relevant to their experience. As parents are willing to keep this dialog going, they will discover the wisdom they need to proceed in truth, refining their own values as they do.

⌒

The Silver Ring Thing, a teen program that supports abstinence only, was created by Denny Pattyn in 1995 and uses a high-tech entertainment venue to urge teens to buy and wear a twelve-dollar ring as a symbol of their pledge to remain abstinent until marriage.[24] The program purports to offer teens "protection from the destructive effects of America's sex-obsessed culture." Education about abstinence for teens — in the context of broad-based information about sexuality, health, responsibility, and self-respect — is vital. On the other hand, being frightened by sensationalized stories of sexually transmitted infections, while receiving moralistic pressure for abstinence compliance only, leaves young people ill-prepared for the real challenges of navigating sexuality and intimacy.

In a recent longitudinal study of adolescent health known as Add

Health, it was noted that virginity pledges were only effective when pledging constituted minority group behavior — in effect, as a counter-cultural choice. The report also noted the strong influence mothers have on their adolescent children's sexual choices. Finally, the researchers pointed out that when the teens that had made an abstinence pledge broke it, they were one-third less likely to use condoms.[25]

Paula

We are bundled in snow gear with eye protection and riding gloves, on a crisp and drizzly Saturday morning. The instructor tells me we are a first. He has seen dads with their daughters or sons, but not moms. I am surprised. Not that I think every mother takes her daughters to motorcycle training, but surely some others do. My daughters and I have come for training in riding our family's European-style scooter, but my older daughter does fantasize about being a "biker girl." The younger one is only reluctantly willing to take the class but certainly wants to ride the scooter. We all pick up the gear shifting and safe braking gracefully, and I start to feel the call of the road.

I begin to wonder about my friend who so wanted a motorcycle when he was a teenager, and his parents strictly forbade it. I know that as soon as he moved to another town, he got himself a bike. Just saying no wasn't enough. His interest remained a shameful secret that he thought he had to keep from his parents. I am doubtful he was ever properly trained in safe cycling, and I suspect he pursued fairly risky behaviors on his motorcyle. I wonder if he encountered some STIs (scary traffic incidents) he might have avoided had he had comprehensive education. I am glad he survived without major injury, but I'm sorry that his particular passion had to be hidden, and that he never got the support to pursue it as safely and successfully as possible. To my knowledge, he never did integrate this interest and pleasure into the whole of his life in an open and shameless way. Some parents treat their child's sexuality in a similar fashion.

On our second day of training, I grab the front brake too quickly and take a painful spill. Fortunately, we are in the training lot and not out on the street, but now I'm shaken up a bit. My experience teaches me to be more cautious. Our bodies are so vulnerable when speed, pavement, and heavy vehicles are part of the picture — even more so when alcohol is involved, as the excellent and hilarious training film points out. The instructor reassures me that he has been safely cycling for twenty-two years without an accident or fall, but that proper training and experience has been invaluable.

I am grateful for this opportunity we have to actually learn and try out these new skills while evaluating our abilities. I now know a lot more about motorcycling and whether, when, and how I really want to do it. So do my daughters. Thanks to my fall, I feel even more certain that I will not be the one to buy a motorcycle for my biker girl. But if it is something she still wants when she is self-supporting, and she continues to assess her own abilities and desires through her training and experiences, I will not shame her for it. I trust that she will choose wisely and operate with care. These principles of training, risk assessment, experiential learning, careful navigation, and honoring one's passion have application in the realm of sex education.

~

As a young Christian woman I believed the clear dictate that "no sex outside of marriage" was God's plan for my life, but I could find little help with the specifics from my church community. So I felt guilty about any rules I might be breaking. Doing "everything but" seemed to be a working model for some. No hand holding or kissing at all was the rule for others. While the "double standard" continues to hold a higher requirement for female chastity, I often wonder how girls who have been trained to obey and submit can be expected to "just say no." Of course, they often don't or can't. I said "no" by shutting off to my sexuality and exercising a fairly rigid adherence to legalistic limits. I wish I had said, "yes" to my emerging sexuality while honoring my own intuitive limits, informed choices, and divine guidance. I was fortunate to survive my early years of marriage while recovering, since sexuality isn't something we can just turn on and off. It is integral to all of our being.

At times I have worried about what definitive messages to give my children about sex, yet I have been giving them messages all along as I positively acknowledge their sexual development and grow in embracing my own sexuality. I have realized that, with plenty of access to knowledge and loving support for their created goodness and wise responsibililty, they will do a great job of deciding how to nurture and express their own sexuality. They developed mastery and confidence with those other life skills (feeding, toileting, driving) in much the same way. They, and not I, will ultimately make these important and personal decisions.

My job is to honor rather than shame their sexuality. I can be sure they have the information they need to make decisions that support their safety, their life plans, and their wholeness. I can be a part of promoting their self-confidence and self-respect so that they are empowered to choose well. I can help them understand the importance of nurturing intimate relationships rooted in "equality, authenticity, and appropriate vulnerability."[26]

So we talk about options and wonder together about outcomes. I caution them about the role alcohol plays in unplanned sexual behavior. They observe people's lives and how the sexual choices they make affect them. We grieve together the tragedy of unwanted pregnancies and unwanted babies. We hope for a world in which girls and all persons are given respect and support for their rights and their responsibilities.

What I hope for them is that they will make choices about their sexual expression from an integrated sense of themselves, using sound and sober judgment. I hope they will honor and experience the sacredness of sex. I hope they will enjoy mature relationships of mutual respect. I hope they will listen to their own inner voices and maintain their openness to divine guidance, rather than fearfully following the dictates of external authorities. I don't expect their personal sexual morality to be dictated by their respect for their parents or their fear of God's wrath as Dobson does:

> I discussed the importance of the child's respect for his parents. His attitude toward their leadership is critical to his acceptance of their values and philosophy, including their concept of premarital sexual behavior... We should make it clear that the merciful God of love whom we serve is also a God of wrath. If we choose to defy His moral laws we will suffer certain consequences ... "for the wages of sin is death."[27]

Much sounder parental resources exist. Advocates for Youth provides education to support young people, parents, and educators. The following is from their website:

> "There is no scientific evidence that abstinence-only-until-marriage programs — those that censor information about contraception — are effective."
>
> On the other hand, research continues to show that comprehensive sex education, which teaches both abstinence and contraception, is most effective for young people. Youth who receive this kind of education are more likely to initiate sexual activity later in life and use protection correctly and consistently when they do become sexually active. Evaluations of comprehensive sex education programs show that these programs delay the onset of sexual activity, reduce the frequency of sexual activity, reduce the number of sexual partners, and increase condom and

contraceptive use. Importantly, the evidence shows that these programs do not encourage teens to become sexually active. In short, responsible sex education programs work!

Despite their proven effectiveness, none of the sex education programs are eligible for funding through the federal government's multi-year, multi-million dollar abstinence initiative because, even though they encourage abstinence, these programs include information about condoms and contraception. Rights. Respect. Responsibility.® is a campaign to help society get over its discomfort with talking about sex. The Campaign is a call to get real about teens and sex so that young people can more effectively prevent pregnancy, STIs [sexually transmitted infections], and HIV/AIDS.

It promotes honest, accurate sex education, helps parents talk openly to their children, and encourages policy makers to craft policies based on the research highlighting effective programs. It is grounded in lessons learned by studying countries that do a much better job at protecting their youth from pregnancy and disease.

1) In the Netherlands, the teen birth rate is over eight times lower than in the United States.

2) In Germany, the teen abortion rate is nearly eight times lower than in the United States.

3) In France, the teen gonorrhea rate is over 74 times lower than in the United States.[28]

It seems that all people could agree that fewer abortions and improved health and wellness for young people are worthy goals. Comprehensive sex education has more to offer toward approaching these goals than abstinence-only programs.

The Value of Breasts

The emphasis on sexual containment — and the control of women's bodies and their intimate life choices — is still rampant in American culture. A fundamentalist man is free to possess his own body; a woman is not. The distorted imaging of her female body constitutes one of the earliest imprints a fundamentalist girl receives. When the female body is imaged as a sewer rather than a sanctuary, any possibility for a healthy and loving attitude toward her body is seriously challenged. She learns to view her own body as others do.

Case Study: Whose Hooters?

In the fundamentalist system, a woman's bodily organs, which are biologically her own and are critical to her child's survival and nurture, are treated as if they are the possessions of men. Her rights and needs are not valued as much as a man's, nor are a child's needs considered important. As seen in Shelley's story, even the biological and psychological needs of a breastfed newborn, are seen as trivial.

Shelley should have guessed what would be in store for her as she and her family traveled to the home of her brother, a fundamentalist Christian. Along the highway, they passed a Hooters billboard. Yes, Hooters, a restaurant her brother and his family frequented, did apparently stand for breasts: the billboard featured a huge picture of a big-breasted female lying across the sign in a skimpy top.

As Shelley, her husband, and their ten-week-old baby sat at the table after the delicious lunch her sister-in-law had provided, Shelley began to discreetly nurse her daughter. "Put that thing away!" shouted her eleven-year-old nephew, jokingly referring to her breast. Shelley found it hard to believe that her nephew was genuinely shocked; she had seen a huge pin-up poster of Pamela Anderson (the Baywatch bombshell) in a bikini with shapely breast implants displayed prominently on his bedroom wall.

Her adult brother chimed in, "That's your breast, and breasts turn me on, and you're my sister!"

Her sister-in-law warned her that their friends, who were coming for dinner that night expressly to meet Shelley and her family, would be offended if they were to see her nursing in public. "Could you please nurse in private?" her sister-in-law asked, "Possibly upstairs?"

"They won't see much of me," Shelley commented. "The baby nurses frequently." Her sister-in-law shrugged and smiled weakly. So Shelley spent a good part of the evening in her room, alone with her child, nursing.

The following morning, Shelley sat on the beach, nursing her baby, feeling relaxed and recuperating from the hurt and shaming of the previous night's episode. Another young mother came along with an infant the same age as hers and sat down near her. As Shelley glanced over at the mother, she noticed that the woman's breasts had the unnaturally round, firm curve of "plastic" breasts. Shelley wondered briefly if this woman could still nurse with breast implants? She wondered if she had received a partial answer when the woman pulled out a bottle and began feeding her infant. "What's wrong with this picture?" she asked herself.

According to the La Leche League, if breast augmentation surgery is done carefully, it should be possible for a mother to nurse with implants. It just seems unfortunate that in a culture so fixated on firm, round breasts, many women are still shamed in their families and in the culture for breastfeeding, the very life- and health-supporting function that breasts are perfectly designed for in almost any shape and size. Why do women take on these judgments of what is big enough or good enough, in evaluating their own unique bodies? Why is it legal to show pictures of flashing breasts on billboards, while real women have been prevented from discreetly breastfeeding their real babies in Wal-Mart stores? (A sign restricting breastfeeding in a Colorado store was recently removed.) Why are women's breasts treated as if they belong to the general public?

Although many other cultures in the world recognize and honor both the sexual and biological value of breasts, Americans seem to view breasts solely as "man-pleasers," in the same way that fundamentalist Christians regard women as "man-pleasers." Within both Christian fundamentalism and American patriarchal culture, breasts are emphasized more as titillations for men than as sustenance, health, and nurture for babies and young children.

In this culture, a woman's value is still proportionate to what she has to offer a man. Consequently, using her breasts to meet the biological and emotional needs of her young is insignificant in comparison to the pressure of dealing with men's sexual appetite. Shelley decided to follow her maternal instincts and make her own informed choice regarding what to do with her breasts. That decision relegated her to a dark room, where her breasts and her baby would remain hidden.

Permission for Abuse

Certainly, when a female denies her emotions and realizes she has no rights and no voice, she becomes a primary target for abuse. In fundamentalist systems, regulations cover the way a woman should dress and the way she should speak. Women are to be muted, wear soft colors, speak softly, not stand out, not speak up. What seems trivial on the surface, a dress code, has its roots in the deeply felt belief that women do not own their bodies. Inherent in this belief is the permission for abuse.

Case Study: Slipping Away

Many women have grown up in churches and family systems that teach them to believe their bodies and their lustful desires are sinful, and therefore must be controlled and tamed. Tracy grew up believing it was her bad body that caused her trouble.

Tracy is a twenty-seven-year-old fundamentalist Christian. She is blond and blue-eyed, with the "map of Ireland" on her face. She came to therapy because she recently got married and was having difficulty having sex with her husband. She repeatedly said, with a pained look on her face, "I just go numb. I just lie there and wait until it's over and go somewhere else in my mind. My husband is so upset with me. He calls it a lack of passion, but I don't believe that's what it is. ... I just don't know what to do. I really love my husband, and I'm afraid I might lose him. I just know there is something wrong with me. It's all my fault. I'm the one to blame, not him."

Although there were many forms of domination and abuse in Tracy's childhood home, the one that greatly impacted her was sexual abuse. It all started innocently. When her mother was hospitalized for a bad gallbladder, her father — a leader in their church — took over the job of tucking Tracy in at night. Tracy was eleven years old at the time and had just started puberty. Her body was changing, but she still had the mindset of a little girl who implicitly trusted her daddy.

During these times, her father began to fondle her, his large hairy hands reaching underneath her pink eyelet bedspread. Tracy did everything she could to leave her body. She focused on that one daisy in her flowered wallpaper, imagining she was by herself in the middle of a deserted daisy field, enjoying a beautiful, sunny summer day. If she focused really hard, she discovered she could completely detach herself from her body. "The only problem," Tracy said, "is that when I go away, I can't come back ... and now, my husband feels it when I go away ... he feels my body freeze and so he stops. He tells me he will not do to me what my father did. I feel so horrible! Even now as I talk about this I can feel myself slipping away."

Tracy did everything she could to silence her own truth and ignore her body's signals. If only she could detach herself from her body, as if it were not her own, like a dress that could be unzipped and stepped out of. There are many ways women unzip in order to cope. Some women hide their flesh in baggy clothes, others detach from their sexuality. Some punish their "bad bodies" through self-mutilation, addiction, or eating disorders.

But emotions cannot be denied forever. A woman's story will eventually seek ears to hear. After years of therapeutic help, Tracy still struggles to feel her reality, speak her truth, and remain connected to her body.

Unfortunately, this kind of abuse is all too common within the Christian fundamentalist culture. Clearly, women, even girls, are more susceptible to passively receiving abuse, unable to claim the power to say, "My body is my own; my body is good; and NO, you have no right to freely access my body."

While the Bible refers to the body as the "temple of God with the Spirit of God living in you" (1 Corinthians 3:16), in Christian fundamentalism the female body is perceived more as a waste dump, possessing the earthy and destructive passions of the flesh. Consider again Tertullian, who defined woman as a "temple built over a sewer."[29] These words graphically depict the pathological polarizations fundamentalists hold in their perceptions of women's bodies: Madonna or whore, chaste or carnal, never a blend of the two.

Soul Death by Pageantry

Contemporary American culture, penetrated by fundamentalist religious dogma throughout, is replete with examples of social and institutional degradation of women. Surprisingly, one of the most potent symbols has survived the changes brought about by feminism in the past twenty-five years: the beauty pageant. The Miss America "Scholarship" Pageant fits neatly with fundamentalists' requirements for a woman to be covertly seductive but chaste, smiling, happy, and compliant. Many of the values for feminine expression learned by fundamentalist girls are reinforced in such pageants. At their core, both systems objectify and sexualize women while denying that they do so.

In addition, the Miss America Pageant offers a concentrated, metaphoric view of how many women in our culture live their daily lives. Required to be contestants in the Pageant of Womanhood, we experience societal pressure to prove our competency. Quietly, we determine our womanly worth through our domestic displays of entertainment abilities, careful to keep a tidy house and not be judged too messy, too imperfect, or just plain inadequate. Additionally, our intellectual, social, and political accomplishments, as well as our womanly curves, are there for all to critique. We secretly compete while feeling compelled to do it all with a smile worthy of Miss Congeniality, as if we are vying for the title of Worthy Woman. And so we strut our stuff, hoping to be declared a winner by all those critiquing — those who hold the power to disqualify us at whim.

Women who compete viciously in the corporate world and strive to move up the hierarchical ladder of success sometimes unknowingly reinforce the patriarchy. They compete for the crown, the promotion, the title — but at what cost? And what about women who try afresh everyday to be the epitome of Motherhood, competing with the Super-mom ideal, hoping to win the elusive prize, some approval or external confirmation of their womanly worthiness — the Best Mom on the Planet. And if we don't get it all just right, points are deducted by the predetermined judges of our lives — the bosses, the husbands, the fe-male friends, and (worst of all) ourselves.

Roberta

In 1982, I was a senior at Calvin College, a small, academically rigorous college affiliated with the Christian Reformed Church. I was studying psychology, sociology, and theology. After graduation I decided I would go on to get a master's degree in Theological Studies at Calvin Seminary. This program was the one graduate degree approved by both my Dad and my church. I had considered being a social worker, but Dad thought church education was the best thing for me. He worked hard to convince me that it would be a safer path, and that's what I believed. Ironically, I now realize how dangerous my experience in the church really was. The church, I was told, was the place where I could change the world for God. In reality it was a womb for a false self, a protective cocoon, which acted as an interruptive buffer between me and the reality of life's experiences.

What I really wanted to do was preach. But neither the Presbyterian Church of America (my denomination) nor the Christian Reformed Church ordained women. Still, I pursued a theology degree, thinking to myself, "One day I'll preach."

One morning, listening to my car radio, I heard of the Miss Greater Grand Rapids Scholarship Pageant. That announcement changed my life. Out of curiosity, I went to the informal introductory meeting and, much to my surprise, I signed up to be a contestant.

While in college, I was always looking for ways to make money. In addition to being a nanny and modeling in TV commercials as the Subaru girl-next-door, I was a restaurant hostess and a babysitter. Suddenly a beauty pageant offered me a chance to make a lot of money quickly, pay-ing for one or even two semesters of seminary. The idea excited me as I realized I had a shot at winning.

Since I jogged every night, I was physically fit. Checking through my closet, I decided my shiny purple bathing suit with thin spaghetti straps, worn with the four-inch beige heels left over from my modeling days, would be good enough. For the evening gown competition, I had my mom's sexy purple gown, which a girlfriend had glamorized by adding silver rhinestones and sequined appliqués. I even had silver heels to match. Mom was a piano teacher. I had studied piano since childhood and knew I could quickly work up a version of Chopin's "Valse in C# Minor" as my talent performance. For the "little blurb" about myself, I would speak about my love for God, music, travel, and people. I could sound like the syrupy, well-rounded, all-American, Christian good girl and, maybe, the next Miss Greater Grand Rapids. At this point I never dreamed of anything more.

On the big night, I was just myself. My shoes weren't dyed to match my evening gown; my answers weren't prepared "pageant style." Yet I won.

Winning the city contest made me eligible for the state pageant. And whoever won the state pageant would be a contender for the Miss America crown. I was about to experience the real world of pageantry. The board of directors from the Miss Greater Grand Rapids Pageant made it their business to coach me in how to be … perfect. I was instructed to fly to New York City, the home of the one designer who really knew how to do the Miss America gown. Then I flew to Chicago, where I could get the "right swimsuit, Miss America style."

My dad, who said he would not fund my graduate education, eagerly financed all of this. In his eyes, schooling beyond a college education was not essential for the domestic life he believed would make me happy. He assured me now that he would take care of all the expenses related to the pageant; it was up to me to do the rest. I practiced the piano three hours a day. When I wasn't playing Rachmaninoff or flying off for a fitting, I was swimming, jogging, or lifting weights. I spent two hours every day reading magazines and newspapers to prepare for the interviews. As Miss Greater Grand Rapids, I also had public appearances to make. I performed in local concerts and fairs. I rode in the Strawberry Festival Parade and helped to open the Gerald R. Ford Museum. I was interviewed on radio and television. Becoming Miss Michigan became my all-consuming goal.

Meanwhile, I was maintaining a 3.8 at Calvin Seminary, where few cast a skeptical eye on my efforts to become a beauty queen. My professors and fellow students smiled with pride when I practiced my talent routine on the school's old, brown upright piano. They saw my attempt to become Miss America as a "worthwhile evangelistic venture." I would be a missionary right here in this country.

I believed I would be unique among pageant contestants, as I had not been a little girl who watched the Miss America Pageant every year, dreaming of wearing that crown. Since this had never been a vision of mine, I became convinced that my quest must be a vision from God. I even had the backing of scripture. To me and to those in my church, it seemed God was preparing me to "come to the throne for just such a time as this" (Esther 4:14). God was calling, and my only job was to respond obediently. Looking back with newfound awareness, it is fascinating that, of all the women in the Bible, I clung to Esther as my mentor. She was that savvy beauty, who knowingly submitted herself to a power game — an exchange men and women have been playing through the centuries. Esther used her looks to navigate a hostile environment, willingly giving King Ahasuerus what he wanted in order to gain power both for herself and for her people.

No one close to me questioned my pageantry decision or encouraged me to question it. No one within my Christian circles challenged me to look deeper, to explore my ambitions and desires, to think about my past and what might have driven me to so strange and radical a turn in my life. Instead, I had the Protestant work ethic preached to me: work hard for God and let God take care of the rest. Some Christians even drew analogies between my evangelistic efforts and those of the Rev. Billy Graham, only I was a woman, and he was a man. Therefore, I would evangelize through a beauty pageant and he, an ordained minister, through a legitimate pulpit. Given our distinct "pulpits," maybe God would use me to reach the population of lost souls that Billy, a middle-aged man, never could. As a result, more lost souls would be won for the Kingdom through my beauty. And this was not a bad thing, for all things were to be used to advance the Kingdom, whether it was my beauty or my body or my womanhood or my soul.

While I was busy preparing to be Miss America, at a ceremonial banquet I met the reigning Miss America, Cheryl Prewitt, a Pentecostal Christian. She was a perfect Southern belle, with lush, shoulder-length, dark hair and beautiful bright blue eyes. She encouraged me in my dream. After meeting Miss America, the possibility of winning the crown began to feel like a certainty. My Christian friends were convinced that using this platform to reach the "lost world" was God's will.

The church was a place where narcissism and a desire for fame could be cloaked under a banner of service to the Lord. I urged myself to be a servant and to use my "God-given beauty and talent" for Christ. In retrospect, I see this as the only way I could justify my shameful desire for fame and fortune. In this fundamentalist system, I had learned to encase my "sinful longings" in pure and Godly motives. Then, I was told, reward from God was guaranteed. In fact, my reward would be a crown, a symbol of Christ and of the eternal blessing of God in the afterlife.

Most importantly, if I won the Miss America crown, I would break through the stone wall my church had placed in the path of my ordination. I would have an actual crown on my head to prove that Almighty God had found me worthy and called me to pastor not just a church but a nation. And I would do it all with a big Miss America smile on my face. The same church that had frustrated my efforts to preach to a congregation would now support my position as pastor to the entire country. The same church that had shamed me as a teenager for exposing my body in an ordinary bathing suit would point to me as a role model for Christian women as I strutted down the Atlantic City runway in a suit especially designed to highlight the roundness of my breasts and to accent my derriere. To serve God, all I had to do was stand tall, look pretty, and smile in a bathing suit and high heels.

The Miss America system reinforced the values I had learned in my home and in my church, the blaringly obvious, yet unnamed truth — that woman exists for man's lustful pleasure. She is taught to obediently act out this belief with no voice of her own. Fundamentalist men know this, and fundamentalist women comply. This covert, contorted contradiction defines women in this maddening system.

Now, in addition to being a missionary for the church, I became an evangelist for the pageant system. The two had much in common: both purported to have women's best interests at heart; both waved the banner of what was to come if only women obeyed the rules; both had rigid expectations of the role women should play; both, at their core, silenced women's souls while pretending that they did not.

What I did appreciate about the pageant system was that Miss America's beauty was not labeled "an occasion of sin." In fact, beauty only increased her score. Given my experience in fundamentalism, this was a relief. And so I became a convert for the system, mimicking its insistence that this was not a beauty pageant at all but was, rather, a scholarship pageant, one that valued a woman's talent, intelligence, and maturity. I wanted to believe that my face and my body weren't all that mattered, and I heard that "fact" repeated to me over and over again: this was a scholarship pageant, and talent counted for 50 percent of the total score. Whenever anyone referred to it as a "beauty pageant," I politely corrected the error: "No, this is a scholarship pageant. This is not a beauty pageant." This odd contradiction made sense to me at the time. I had learned to believe (and wanted to believe) that things were what others told me they were. That's just how it is in fundamentalist systems: young women are to believe what they are told.

I convincingly "witnessed" to other women about the pageant, telling them what a wonderful thing it was. Women were given a chance to excel and win thousands of dollars in scholarship money. Like playing with baby dolls and baking apple pies, the Miss America Scholarship Pageant provided a chance for young women to learn the necessary skills in the art of being successful women. Here, being female was the paramount virtue — provided you were female "their way."

I arrived in Muskegon for the Miss Michigan Pageant excited and eager. God was with me, I knew. Then, the bottom dropped out. I met a handful of other contestants whose stories were similar to mine. They, too, believed God was with them. Some of them boldly shared their belief that God meant them to be Miss Michigan, too. How could this be? Suddenly, I felt all alone. I was in a town I didn't know, in a competition with forty-one other young women who looked good, who were talented, and who spoke with conviction and confidence. While they seemed to smile unceasingly and effortlessly, I didn't. My face hurt from smiling so much. Although we were instructed to rub Vaseline inside our lips to help us hold a smile, it didn't work for me. The other contestants' makeup looked perfect and their hairspray held tight. I felt awkward while they looked poised. And I knew I was in this alone.

I'll never forget meeting the woman I thought was my main competitor. She was also born again. I was bewildered. Would God betray me? What about everything my church friends had told me? Surely she was not going to win ... was she? I became unnerved when I heard how she, too, believed that God had brought her to Muskegon; she even referred to the same Bible verse about Esther. She was older than I and was, I felt, much more mature. She had a look of self-assuredness and she sang beautifully, a song with God in it. I knew the judges would love that. Where was God for me now? For that matter, where were all those people who had told me they knew how this was going to turn out? They weren't living this awful week with me, and it *was* awful.

We were judged from the minute we woke up to the minute we laid our heads on our pillows each night, every day for a week. We were taken out and put on display by the pageant's directors. How did we interact with the public? Did we say the right things? Smile enough? Did our talent have the right effect on the audience? And the audiences went on and on. Rooms full of men — the Jaycees, the Lions Club, the Men's Business Club, the Rotary. The calendar was booked. When we weren't being taken out to perform, we were taken out to play ... and to be watched while we played. They took us to amusement parks and filmed every minute of the "fun." We ate cotton candy and smiled. We rode the merry-go-round and smiled. The film would be taken back to Muskegon and used to show how much fun we all had during our week in hell. We were to be the perfect blend of beauty and playfulness — like Playboy Bunnies. Through it all, I continued to believe that God wanted this for me and was proud of me.

I ended my week of pageantry physically exhausted and ten pounds lighter, a change in physique that I later learned caused one judge to deduct points because he could see the bones in my shoulders. As we dressed for the big night, I saw other women using masking tape to create the illusion of fuller breasts, more cleavage. I saw women taping their butts up for a fuller, rounder look in their custom-tailored swimsuits. Every outfit worn throughout the week had been as carefully designed as the bathing suits. Shoes were dyed and earrings selected to match flawlessly. Points were lost for each infringement of what the judges deemed perfection. Their critique of me felt frightful and, yet, in a strange way, comfortably familiar. Their judgments and expectations for perfection were designed to keep me on my toes, to help me be my best. I knew that in order to excel in this system, I had to characterize with great ease these paradoxical, contradictory messages. I had to please the judges and give them what they expected, while at the same time, somehow just "be myself."

Thursday of that week the pre-competition began. Thursday and Friday were focused on talent, evening gown, and swimsuit competitions. Saturday morning was spent focusing on interviews. I remember that horrible morning. My memory of the interview is pretty vague, except for the first question: "Who are three people in your life whom you most admire?" Of course, my first response was Jesus Christ, "because he was such a great revolutionary." Then I mentioned someone I can no longer remember, and, finally, who was that lady who took so much flap for the war? Oh yeah, Jane Fonda. Yes. I actually said this in a Miss America state pageant. I said that I admired Jane Fonda's determination, her willingness to take a stand, and her courage to speak out for what she believed was true. Analyzing this response now brings to light a central theme of my life experience: struggling to be true to my authentic self while remaining attached to systems that do not value or reward this behavior.

I remember a long silence after that statement. What more did they need to know about me? My response pretty well summed it up. This year I would not be walking away with the crown. I obviously needed more seasoning. Somehow, I was testing to see if I could win on my own terms. Yet a timid, angry part of me buried deep inside was thrilled at the prospect of not winning. But I had to carry on. I still had to live through Saturday night.

Dear God, do I remember that night? We all hit the stage in red high heels and red leotards with bouncing fringe, dancing and singing a medley of Broadway hits. Then all forty-two of us stood frozen in position while the master of ceremonies welcomed everyone and laboriously explained that this was not a beauty pageant. He concluded by addressing the central question: "Many of you might be wondering, if this is not a beauty contest, then why is there a swimsuit competition? Being a Miss America, you see, means being the living symbol of the best of today's youth, and that means not only being outstanding in personality, talent, and intelligence, but being well-rounded in physical fitness as well."

There we were, a bunch of beauties being told we weren't just beauties, all standing on stage, red lips smiling prettily, Vaseline smeared all over, waiting to hear the verdict. My name was called. I was one of the final ten. This was really happening. I quickly ran backstage to dress for my talent performance.

The convention hall was packed. Thousands of people listened to me play Rachmaninoff's "Prelude in G Minor." I sat in front of that beautiful black Steinway in a costume that I'd proudly chosen for myself against the advice of the board back home. Instead of the traditional Miss America gown, I wore a gold metallic shirt with thin straps and black silk harem pants with gold, purple, green, and red stripes running through. I finished the European gypsy look (a nod to my Hungarian heritage) with a gold flower that held back my hair.

I really don't know if the harem pants killed my chances of being Miss Michigan, or if they had died in the interview room, but I'm certain that what happened next definitely arrested my march toward Atlantic City. Halfway through my performance, I remember having a remarkably lucid conversation with myself. "What are you doing here?" I needed to know. "Why are you here?" I asked myself. This conversation cost me my place in the song. I had the soothing thought of just quitting, walking off the stage, and putting this all behind me. To my surprise, I had admitted to myself that there was some part of me that did not want this crown, after all; the price was too great. I remember that moment like a freeze frame, those brief seconds in which my conflicted interests and choices became conscious. Eventually, I found my place and decided to keep playing.

I went backstage for makeup, hairspray, and a fast change. I continued with the swimsuit portion and then the evening gown. I walked smoothly, turned gracefully, stood tall, and smiled pretty. Yet even while planting each foot firmly in front of the other in those four-inch heels, I still remember the vibration from the tremor in my calves and thighs. I was reminded that I was vulnerable up there, in front of judges, in front of thousands … in front of thousands of judges.

By midnight, the top ten had all competed. It was now time to stand, hold hands, and form a line across the stage, waiting for our names once again to be called, or not. I remember that moment right before Miss Michigan's name was called. The fourth runner up is … the third runner-up is … the second runner-up is … the first runner-up is. … I looked at the six of us who remained and realized that the other woman, who also looked to Esther as mentor, was still standing. I remember seeing her fingers tightly squeezing the women's hands on her right and left and thinking, "Okay, God, which one of us is it going to be? Which one of us will you choose to wear your crown?" And then her name was called. I was not in the top five. It was all over. She was the chosen woman and I was not. I was devastated. I went from believing I was destined to win to feeling like a total failure, and I blamed God. What had gone wrong? I didn't understand. I was supposed to win. God was the one responsible for this loss, not me!

After the main show was over, the contestants were still choreographed. We walked out a set of double doors and faced the huge crowd of family and friends who had come expecting each of us to win. I walked out in tears and ran into my daddy's arms. He had shared my dream. My victory was supposed to give his middle-aged years meaning. He was as upset as I was. I had let him down. God had let both of us down. I would not be Miss Michigan or Miss America, at least not in 1982.

When I didn't win, I decided to leave Grand Rapids and move back home to Florida. This move was pivotal, interrupting my seminary study. I was so humiliated about the loss that I couldn't return to seminary and face the people who had assured me I would win. I didn't know what I wanted anymore. I thought the geographical distance would help me survive the experience. My passion for theology was, at best, a smoldering ember, a memory of what had once burned so brightly.

I needed to "re-strategize." I had learned a lot, including the fact that contestants frequently moved from state to state to compete, creating residency in states where competition was deemed easier and hoping to win at any state level in order to make it to Atlantic City. Now I knew the rules. In spite of my ambivalence, I also knew I needed to prove something to myself … and to God. I was hooked. Even though my heart wasn't in it, I persisted. I went through the motions. I knew how to play the piano, and now I knew how to play the pageant game. The cost didn't matter, because I was now dead inside. I eventually became Miss Boca Raton — a ride in the back of a Mustang convertible in a local parade, my picture on the front page of the newspaper. By then, I was too unplugged to care. I became one more woman among the crowd of women going through the motions.

After the loss of Miss Florida a year later, I said goodbye to the pageant world of glitter and four-inch heels. I sold some of my gowns at a consignment shop in Fort Lauderdale. I remember a beautiful, red-sequined gown that fit my body like the skin of some exotic snake. This was the gown, although no one expressly admitted it, designed to titillate the men. This was the one specifically sewn to send men into that erotically, paradoxical state: "There she is, our sweet and innocent Miss America; there she is, our sexy whore." On some level, I knew this was the acceptable exchange in this system: the unspoken agreement was that I would give them what they wanted (chastity masking carnality) in the hopes that, in return, I would get what I wanted — the crown of approval, the chance to speak.

Today, I am intrigued by that snake-like gown I chose, and its connection with Eve. Apart from my awareness at the time, I joined the lineage of Christian women who paraded themselves or were paraded as the "typical" female, the seductress. Without conscious awareness, I obediently acted out fundamentalism's unnamed and unspoken rules for Christian women and female behavior. I tried to seduce the judges and the audience in order to win the prize; yet, at the same time, I had to appear as though I was not seducing them — for seduction, I had been taught, was not Christian. My outward compliance with their rules was mixed with an inward defiance of their demands. I knew I needed to comply in order to survive, yet I also needed to defy in order to survive … a lot like Eve. I was complying by portraying myself as a seductress and yet defying by secretly doing what I could in my own way, unable to submit myself fully to their rigid rules for my female expression.

It was easy for me to get rid of that red-hot gown; I think I sold it for a hundred bucks. I don't miss it. I'm glad it's gone. But there was another beautiful long, flowing white silk and chiffon gown. It had a scarf that I draped dramatically around my neck. That one, I kept. I still have it in my closet. I just couldn't sell it. I had to hold on to something of my own from this experience. This gown represented my femaleness defined my way, and my soul's purity, which I would one day recover.

For at least a decade, my participation in the Miss America Pageant system became my secret shame. For a long time, I mentioned it to no one ... except those I knew intimately and trusted deeply. I was ashamed that I had spent three and a half years in such a demoralizing endeavor. I was angry that I had "wasted" so many years living out the conflicts I had internalized from Christian fundamentalism.

I was also ashamed that I had lost. It didn't matter that other people viewed this as an accomplishment and a valuable life experience. I felt duped by the pageant system, my church, God, fundamentalism — and, most importantly, myself. Why had I so blindly believed what they told me? Why did I allow the disruption of my education? In spite of my own apparent choices, what family and church dictums was I unconsciously acting out? And why had I remained so unaware of and unresponsive to my soul's needs?

Embodying Conflictual Splits

The promotion of Eve as the Bad Woman and Mary as the Good Woman by the early church fathers is the polarized split imprinted on us. Tragically, Eve's curiosity and inquisitiveness were rewritten and reframed as something evil. It is as tragic to create Mary as an icon, a sinless woman separated from her humanity, as it is to create Eve as a symbol of sin, a woman separated from her divinity. In each case, the woman is denied her integrated self and therefore her wholeness, her holiness. As a result, both are diminished in the expression of their full female power. We reclaim Eve as a mentor. Mary cannot replace Eve. We choose to remember Mary as Mary, a woman and a mother, embodying both humanity and divinity. Fortunately, Jesus came to remove crusty and rigid categories for people with judgmental labels and polarized distinctions. We want to mirror Jesus' behavior in our rejection of Mary as the new Eve.

In our years of work with Christian women, we have observed these polarized splits both within the woman (intrapsychically) and among women (interpersonally). This observation is directly related to Christian fundamentalism's demand that women be the role. The submissive, tame, polite, passive, dependent role is heralded as the Good Woman. The unconfined expression of a woman as bold, outspoken, and unbridled is the independent, on-the-edge Bad Woman. In the fundamentalist system, the aggressive independent is the woman who secretly wants power (the same voice as men); but in this system, this thought must remain a secret shame. She should *not* want power. She should *not* want money. She should *not* want prestige or recognition. She should be humble and meek — female, by their definition. In this system, only men hold the power. A woman is forced to find ways to exercise her power covertly, remaining confined to her limited box.

This external division and polarization mirrors the internal split women experience as they try to define themselves (and peg other women) as either Mary or Eve. They are forced into the role of the meek, passive, and dependent in order to fit in. The woman who chooses to be daring, aggressive, and independent usually experiences such isolation and shunning that she eventually leaves the system.

We asked a friend, a Catholic priest, to freely associate Mary with Eve. Here is his raw commentary, spoken spontaneously. We believe it reflects much religious pigeonholing of women.

The Good Woman/Bad Woman Split

Mary	Eve
The good woman	The bad woman
The mother	The harlot
Superhuman	Subhuman
Faithful to God	Faithful to self
Strong	Weak
Holy	Evil
Disciplined	Undisciplined
Sacrificial	Self-indulgent
Kind	Cunning
Obedient	Disobedient
Chaste	Wild
Virginal	Temptress
Compliant	Defiant
Transcendent	Animalistic
Pious	Hedonistic
Honored to serve God	Selfish pleasure seeker

These candid comments define the split that the Christian church has held up for women. In fact, this friend recalled hearing his mother say over and over, "Remember, there are two types of women in the world: There are the Marys and there are the Eves. Stick with the Marys." This dichotomy is clearly what is communicated within fundamentalism and it pervades the entire culture.

When the church makes Eve all bad and Mary all good, it denies women the possibility of having both aspects of femaleness powerfully experienced and fully integrated within the self. Many women are forced to live their lives bound, unable to freely express the fullness of both Mary and Eve within. Fundamentalist women live lives of internal conflict as they play out this split. When the church infers that sexuality is bad and chastity is good, all people are subject to fragmentation.

By reframing and renaming some of these polarities, perhaps we can more easily imagine the integration of our wholeness as women. These qualities exist in all women more on a continuum than in exclusion. The fragmentation occurs when, in compliance with the expectations of role, women disconnect from important and useful parts of themselves. Qualities of Eve, when not framed in the language of shame, are as truly a part of our fullness and our goodness as those of Mary.

The Eve/Mary Continuum

Mary / Eve

quiet / vocal

stop / go

chaste / sensual

disciplined / carefree

feminine / masculine

stillness / movement

motherly / girlish

obedient / defiant

passive / aggressive

nurturing / withholding

sacrificial / self-indulgent

the good woman / the bad woman

willing to suffer / seeker of pleasure

faithful to God / faithful to self

slow to act / spontaneous

yielding / insistent

compliant / bold

Much of Christian doctrine about Jesus focuses on his divinity at the expense of his humanity. Ostensibly, the Christian church teaches that Jesus was "fully God and fully human," yet his divinity and his humanity are not allowed to mutually coexist; instead, they are treated as separate, distinct compartments. When Christian fundamentalists ignore Jesus' humanity, the possibility of his sexuality is quickly bypassed. The split mentality that is directed toward women also is projected onto Jesus, in that his divinity is emphasized and preached about as something entirely separate from his humanity.

Consequently, fundamentalist men and women are left devoid of a healthy model of integrated sexuality, spirituality, and humanity. Both women and men, learn early on to split off from their bodies, denying the fullness of their passions and sensualities. Unfortunately, this compartmentalization minimizes the depth of their spirituality. It is in the experience of one's sexuality and in one's body that one truly encounters the spirit world, the place of "oneness" where sexuality, physicality, and spirituality truly meet — this is the place where authentic surrender, vulnerability, and unity come together.

The Curse

Unfortunately, many women, whether fundamentalist or not, have been raised in homes that instilled the belief and expectation that all spontaneous emotion must be stifled and controlled. As Good Women, we are especially expected to repress our anger and suppress our power. Consider an article by Stephanie Bender, director of Full Circle Women's Health (a clinic offering counseling for women), in the May 1996 magazine issue of *Focus on the Family*. In "The Once-a-Month Blues," Bender discusses the PMS "affliction." She evaluates women's normal and expected human emotions: "anger, sudden mood swings, emotional over-responsiveness, unexplained crying, irritability, anxiety, forgetfulness, confusion, and sensitivity to rejection." She then equates these emotions with an "overly emotional female state," which she calls "PMSing."[30] The absence of feelings (emotional numbness) is normalized through teachings such as this: "God often removes our feelings so we won't depend on them."[31]

Negative attitudes about the emotional variability of premenstrual syndrome have only helped to promote the belief that a woman's menses are not to be honored or valued. Menstruation, similar to labor pain, is seen as the result of Eve's sin — hence, the reference, "Eve's Curse" — a consequence of being female that simply must be endured, as if the shedding of blood is atonement for female folly. Could it be that during her PMS emotionality a woman is merely verbalizing the craziness of a system that seeks to dominate and stifle her emotions rather than welcoming their expression? Perhaps the emotional display of PMS represents the only time she can come to life, the only time her emotional fullness is tolerated.

Compare Dr. Christiane Northrup's straightforward, empowering assessment where, in her book, *Women's Bodies; Women's Wisdom*, she states:

> "Once we begin to appreciate our menstrual cycle as part of our inner guidance system we begin to heal both hormonally and emotionally. There is no doubt that premenstrually, many women feel more inward and more connected to their personal pain and the pain of the world. Many such women are also more in touch with their own creativity and get their best ideas premenstrually, though they may not act on them until later… . Premenstrual syndrome results when we don't honor our need to ebb and flow like the tides."[32]

In ancient communities, both women and menstruation were valued as honorable. They believed that during this time women were "in their moon," or more deeply in touch with their female fullness and their instinctive, earthy powers. In native cultures, women, with their heightened wisdom during this time, were perceived as catalysts for the community, able to shed light on darkness. Women's inner reflectiveness and introspection were validated, and the resulting insights and wisdom gained by the community were revered. Often, women's dreams and visions were used to guide the tribe. In the Native American moon lodges, bleeding women came together for renewal and revisioning and emerged afterward inspired and able to inspire others.

Women must be free to emote with the wind, to cycle with the moon, to ebb and flow with the tides, to rhythmically dance with nature. What would it take for women, and our culture, to view menstruation as it once existed, ceremonially celebrated as a time when women pass into their greatest peak of power and femininity.

Compare such emotional expression with how Jesus, the human one, bore witness to real humanity. As depicted in the New Testament, Jesus set an example of a human being who demonstrated the full gamut of raw emotion. He was loving and kind to little children; he was enraged with the money changers in the temple; he wept; he was impatient at times with his followers, calling them "little-faiths"; he openly expressed his anguish in the garden of Gethsemane when he prayed, "Let this cup pass me by" (Matthew 26:39). Yet, Christian fundamentalism views emotional containment and repression as synonymous with spirituality.

In fundamentalism, the "will of God" supplants the human emotional state, as if one can compartmentalize one's being and discern God's will exclusive of one's emotions. Fundamentalists' concerns about women and their emotions are rooted in their fear of Eve. If they were to chew the fruit of greater emotional consciousness, few fundamentalist women, using their feelings as a primary guide, would choose to stay in a system that requires them to disown and repress so much of their emotional selves. Instead, they might follow in Eve's footsteps, refusing to remain emotionally numb. Eve's response to her own emotions and intuition — propelling her to act in a curious, defiant, and daring manner — is a model for women today.

Creation: "I will bless the body; bless the cup;
bless the feminine; bless my sexuality and emotionality."

New Covenant/Naked Truth

"Then, taking a cup, he gave thanks and said, 'Take this and share it among you, because from now on, I tell you, I shall never again drink wine until God's domination-free order comes. ... This is my body given for you. ... This cup is the new covenant in my blood poured out for you.'" (Luke 22:17–20)

The sacral chakra involves the reproductive and sexual organs and the lower back. We focus on this chakra to celebrate sexuality, the ability to feel, the creative core. The color is orange and it is associated with water. Take a drink of water. With each drink, remember Jesus' blessing of the body and the cup in what we have come to celebrate as Communion. Blessed be our bodies. Blessed be our feelings. Blessed be our sacral chakra. Blessed be the womb. Blessed be our sexuality.

Think about what it means to commune with God, with another, with your community. Imagine the breadth and wealth of your emotional life. Do you give permission for all of your feelings to be acknowledged and honored? In thinking about the characteristics and commandments, have you become aware of the integrity of your sexual self being violated in any way? How has that affected your life and relationships? How might the water in the vessel of your being be transformed into wine? Imagine a flow of release and renewal. As you saunter through the day, feel the freedom and the pleasure of moving your hips. Welcome the beautiful moistness and fertility of your creative womanliness.

Vagina Theology

In support of an integrated, embodied spirituality, in which human flesh is reclaimed as divine, and theology lives incarnate, we offer this intimate reflection of renewal.

Serena

She had been married a little over a year, living in a tiny, one-bedroom apartment in Massachusetts. The living room, which they called "the big room," overlooked a fake water sculpture in the middle of a perfectly circular, humanly constructed pond. There she sat, alone (or so she thought) with her theology textbooks and the very old, garage-sold, green tweed loveseat, pleasuring herself for the very first time. Why was this happening now, she thought? Why hadn't she discovered this beauty years before? Here she sat, newly married, her stamp of approval on her certificate for sex. She now retained legitimate permission from the church and the state, at all of twenty-seven years of age, to discover her *cunta*, her holy well.

New Testament. Old Testament. The Nature of God. You name it, she was excited. She felt awakened. Curious. Full of wonder, even girlish, in her open vulnerability to learn more about her world. Theology lit a fire in her that was undeniable. She remembered thinking to herself, "This is nuts. No one will ever understand how much theology turns me on!" Memories of her previous seminary professors flashed briefly across her mind. What would they think? Would her conservative Christian family and friends all have a disapproving, judgmental scowl to offer in light of her newfound pure delight?

But today, this new day, in broad daylight, none of that mattered, because she was free. Free to discover herself in a way that was completely surprising to her. And God was with her. She was sure of it. She felt God's presence — just like she did when she took Communion. She was stirred from the inside, just as she was every time she took "the body and the cup." This day, she was alive for her. Christ's body and blood were alive for her as well. She knew it. Here, amid the pond's fake fountain and the big room's "flip-the-switch" fireplace, she was finding the fire that had never been free to dance because her body was bad. Her body had caused men to lust. Her body had housed temptation. Her body held truths that she was supposed to forget. Only this day, for the first time ever, she was free to remember her own body, to know and be known, while she studied theology, with God, with herself, with her body as both participant and observer. And God declared it good. She just knew it. She felt deep approval and pure joy, confirming, "Finally! I created this body for your pleasure, for your sanctification."

Her cunta. Her pleasure. Her sanctification? Her holy well with sanctified waters flowing? Of course, her cunta was awakened while she pursued her passion of knowing more deeply the nature of God. Aren't they one and the same? Aren't our bodies the temples that God inhabits? Vagina and womb, from whence life itself is birthed? That day she knew the truth. She knew she had been misled. She had believed her body was bad. This belief kept her from remembering to explore and discover and inhabit herself. This bodily pursuit, once ordained off-limits, would open her to God in ways beyond anything she could imagine. She felt her warmth. Her womb. God's womb. The "I AM" where all things create and are created, again and again. This was the one true moment when she knew more about being born again than she had ever known. Thoughts became clearer, insights deeper. She was now certain God was not male. God was beyond male, beyond mystery. Her cunta knew more about that mystery than anything her upbringing had ever taught her. For a young woman raised to believe such pleasure was a sin, this was ascension beyond heaven. No wonder people cry out in orgasm, "OH, MY GOD!"

Hildegard of Bingen, in the twelfth century, wrote of her own mystical experience, complete with flowing waters and even a sort of redemption of the contempt of Eve:

> And behold! In the forty-third year of my earthly course, as I was gazing with great fear and trembling attention at a heavenly vision, I saw a great splendor in which resounded a voice from Heaven, saying to me... "Cry out and speak of the origin of pure salvation until those people are instructed, who, though they see the inmost contents of the Scriptures, do not wish to tell them or preach them, because they are lukewarm and sluggish in serving God's justice. Unlock for them the enclosure of mysteries that they, timid as they are, conceal in a hidden and fruitless field. Burst forth into a fountain of abundance and overflow with

mystical knowledge, until they who now think you contemptible because of Eve's transgression are stirred up by the flood of your irrigation."[33]

Throughout religious tradition, from the Song of Songs to the poetry of Hafiz, we discover the use of the "erotic aesthetic" in "myth and symbol, dance and music, story and theology, and painting and sculpture to refer to the divine."[34] A provocative Bernini sculpture of the ecstasy of sixteenth century Theresa of Avila can be found in Cornaro Chapel in Rome, Italy. Here is Theresa's description of her experience:

> Beside me on the left appeared an angel in bodily form.... He was not tall but short, and very beautiful; and his face was so aflame that he appeared to be one of the highest ranks of angels, who seem to be all on fire.... In his hands I saw a great golden spear and at the iron tip there appeared to be a point of fire. This he plunged into my heart several times so that it penetrated my entrails. When he pulled it out I felt that he took them with it, and left me utterly consumed by the great love of God. The pain was so severe that it made me utter several moans. The sweetness caused by this intense pain is so extreme that one can not possibly wish it to cease, nor is one's soul content with anything but God. This is not a physical but a spiritual pain, though the body has some share in it — even a considerable share.[35]

This considerable share is worthy of affirming anew. As often as we eat the bread and drink the cup, we can remember that Jesus blessed and honored the body in this meal. Jesus, who had turned water, an ancient symbol of the feminine, the source of all life, into wine, took the cup, another ancient symbol of the feminine, the chalice, the womb, and blessed it.

Theologians have argued for centuries over the meaning of the bread and cup, using concepts like consubstantiation and transubstantiation. We would merely suggest that the mystery and meaning of the bread and the cup have something to do with Jesus' overriding message of bringing about God's domination-free order within us — in our bodies, and among us, the body of the church — supporting our own incarnation, our human vulnerability, the goodness of our flesh, and the God-likeness of our sexuality. We are invited to share in this meal, and in this intention, acknowledge Jesus' death and his resurrection even as we participate in our own.

When we open to embracing the potential aliveness of our own sexuality without judgment, we access the fullness of integrating our sexuality with our spirituality. We can no longer endorse domination-based systems that proclaim to know the the right way for others' sexual and spiritual expression. Through the daily incarnation of our sexual selves, we create lives and systems rooted in balance and wholeness — systems that support our spirits soaring and keep our bodies grounded.

Dance: Choose a piece of music that speaks to you of sensuality, passion, fertility, and life. Wear an orange dress or tie an orange scarf around your hips. Give yourself permission to embody your sacral chakra through the beauty and creativity of your dance.

Community Creation Circle: This activity is planned for a group with the intention of developing trust, mutuality of purpose, and vision. A specific creative intention may be named by or for the group at the beginning. Members sit on the floor (or on a pad or pillow if needed) in a circle with feet on the floor and knees up, touching those of the adjacent persons. Choose a piece of instrumental music that supports the intention. To begin, have the group members touch hands, palm to palm, giving light pressure to the person on each side. Lead the group in breathing in unison for three or four breaths. Invite the group members to invoke the common intention through creative movement of the dominant hand, (allowing the other hand to rest) as if the hand were a dancer or a musical conductor or a sculptor bringing vision to life. After a minute or so, instruct the members to bring their creation to rest and allow the expression to continue with the non-dominant hand. Continue for another minute. Allow both hands to come to rest. Have the group complete the artistry using both hands. As the music finishes, bring palms together again, breathe in unison three or four breaths, and allow the hands to come to rest on the knees where they meet. Allow time for conversation among the group members.

Sculpting and Yielding: In this exercise, partners will share an intimate experience of mutuality and artistry. During the first piece of music one of the partners will be the sculptor and the other will be like clay. The sculptor will gently touch a part of the partner's body to indicate in which direction she should move that part. It might be her hand, her shoulder, her hip. She should move toward the touch. She will continue to move in the same direction until she can take the movement no further or until the sculptor indicates a new directive. The person moving as clay will work to yield to the suggestions of the sculptor. Switch roles for the second piece of music. Talk about the experience. Was it difficult to be molded? Did the sculptors find the clay malleable? Were the sculptures breathtaking?

Giving Birth to the Feminine: This movement ritual can be adapted for giving birth to anything you wish to bring to life, but it will be described in terms of imagining the feminine as an entity to welcome, deliver, and integrate into your life. When the gifts of the feminine are devalued by our families or other institutions, we may suffer from our own un- conscious judgment and lack of welcome for these qualities. This op- portunity is especially helpful for life partners as they share and support each other through this experience. A lot can be embodied through this exchange, both in a physical and an imaginal dimension.

This ritual can be done in pairs in a group setting. One person will be giving birth and the other acting as a coach, midwife, or partner. When complete, the exercise can be repeated with the roles reversed, if desired.

Choose three pieces of music: one to accompany the concept of the annunciation and the pregnancy, one to evoke the travail of the deliv- ery, and a third that captures the wonder and delight of welcoming the newly born into one's arms and life. Tell the participant giving birth to imagine receiving news that she or he is to bear and deliver the incarna- tion of the feminine, as if it were a baby. The participant is to move according to these three expressions while the partner gives support and nurture through creative movement. Afterward, they may discuss what the birth-giver experienced in the process of receiving both the fruit of the birth and the support of the partner. They may discuss what the supporter came to understand better through the dance.

Mary and Eve: This dance experience is planned for partners, perhaps working in a group setting. You will need two pieces of music for danc- ing Mary, two pieces for dancing Eve, and one for integrating the two characters. Before beginning, invite each dancer to name one quality of Mary she would like to express through her dance. When the first Mary music begins, one partner will begin to dance her characterization of Mary for about a minute, then the partner will reflect her movement back to her, showing what she "heard" in the first person's dance, again for about one minute. The first dancer then dances again, taking her movement to another level, with the partner reflecting again. When the music has finished, the partners do the same thing again with the second piece of Mary music. This time, the second partner begins. Allow a few moments for conversation.

Repeat this entire process using the music selected for Eve. Again allow time for some discussion both before and after. Bring the group together (if there is a group) and brainstorm a list of qualities that seem to describe Mary. Create another list for Eve.

For the last dance, let the music play longer, especially if you have a group of dancers. Have the group stand in a circle around a common dance space. One dancer may begin to dance an interpretation of either Mary or Eve. A second may join her to offer a complementary movement. They may both be dancing Eve, or one Mary and one Eve; it doesn't matter and will not be named. The dancers may move in and out of the circle, supporting two dancers at a time. The experience should invite a celebration of the qualities of both of these women in a dance of integration.

Blood Ritual: The effects on women from pervasive negative messages are not easily or quickly resolved. The process of self-understanding and the practice of new behaviors are ongoing tools for the resurrection journey. This ritual is for menstruating women. It is an opportunity to spend a few days each month experiencing a kind of death and rebirth metamorphosis.

On the first day of your period, or at the new moon if your bleeding days are done, take a ritual bath. Use salts, candles, incense, soft light, music, whatever will help you create a space and time set apart for reflection and honor. Touch and treat your beautiful flesh lovingly and tenderly. Notice what kind of touch you like. Welcome the sensitivity that comes with the hormonal shifts of this time and acknowledge the insights and grievances you may otherwise push aside. Be compassionate with yourself. Grieve with your bleeding uterus for the pregnancy not meant to be this month, whether by or in spite of your hopes or intentions. Grieve for a moment with all women's bleeding, with all women's grief. When you are finished, purpose to welcome these days of bleeding as a time for letting go of what no longer serves and a time for preparing to create what is new and life supporting. Make a note in a journal of any ideas or new awareness you encountered.

On the final day of your period, take another bath, this one celebratory. Add any beauty treatments that support you in feeling renewed — a manicure, pedicure, facial, hair-do, body lotion, whatever works best for you. Reenter your life with a new appreciation for your feminine beauty, your body's cycle, your emotional resources, and the life-affirming power of resurrection. In this new month, behave in one new way that reflects your rebirth. Journal your journey if you like.

My Bawdy Zone

Erotica
Exotica
Infusing all of me
With energy
And synergy
Delicious ecstasy

A sacred gift
I ache with it
This deep abiding passion
For birthing, loving,
Playing, dancing,
Self-expressive fashion

This zestiness
And testiness
That permeates my being
I can't give up
I won't give up
This wonder I am seeing

This part of me
This mystery
Defying all refinement
I celebrate
My bawdy zone
My body's own excitement

Notes

1 Meredith B. McGuire, *Religion: The Social Context, 5th Edition* (Belmont, CA: Wadsworth Thompson Learning, 2002), 29.

2 Teresa Whitehead, "Conservative Christian Women are Watching Cindy Sheehan...and Seeing Themselves" BuzzFlash, www.buzzflash.com/whitehurst/05/08/whi05007.html (accessed August 14, 2005).

3 Walter Wink, *The Powers That Be: Theology for a New Millennium* (Minneapolis: Augsburg Fortress, 1998), 76.

4 Suzanne Woods Fisher, "The Stay at Home Dad," Christianitytoday.com, www.christianitytoday.com/mp/2000/003/11.24.html.

5 Dan Kindlon and Michael Thompson, *Raising Cain: Protecting the Emotional Life of Boys* (New York: Ballantine Books, 1999), 257.

6 Frederick Clarkson, "Righteous Brothers," *In These Times* (August 5, 1996): 14.

7 Ibid., 15.

8 Mary Stewart Van Leeuwen, "The Promise of Promise Keepers," *Capital Commentary* (October 13, 1997): www.cpjustice.org/stories/storyReader$205.

9 Carolyn Holderread Heggen, *Sexual Abuse in Christian Homes and Churches* (Scottdale, PA: Herald Press, 1993), 73, 90.

10 James Alsdurf and Phyllis Alsdurf, *Battered into Submission: The Tragedy of Wife Abuse* (Downers Grove, IL: Intervarsity Press, 1989), 67.

11 Ibid., 75, 76.

12 James Dobson, *Love Must Be Tough: New Hope for Families in Crisis* (Dallas, TX: Word, 1983), 149-150.

13 Kersti Yllo, "The Status of Women, Marital Equality, and Violence Against Wives: A Contextual Analysis," *Journal of Family Issues*, 5 (September 1984): 316-317.

14 Malcolm Gladwell, *Blink* (New York: Little, Brown, and Company, 2005), 33.

15 ThinkProgress, "Ted Haggard on Homosexuality: Jesus Camp," ThinkProgress.com, http://thinkprogress.org/2006/11/03/ted-haggart-on-homosexuality/.

16 Jane Doe, "Letter." *Time*, March 5, 2004, www.lgbtcenters.org/news/news_item.asp?NewsID=1097.

17 Intersex Society of North America, "What is INSA's Mission?" http://www.isna.org/node/728.

18 Karen McCarthy Brown, "Fundamentalism and the Control of Women," in *Fundamentalism & Gender*, ed. John Stratton Hawley, 197 (New York: Oxford University Press, 1994).

19 Randall Balmer, "American Fundamentalism: The Ideal of Femininity," in *Fundamentalism & Gender*, ed. John Stratton Hawley, 49 (New York: Oxford University Press, 1994).

20 Anna Quinlan, "Now Available: Middle Ground," *Newsweek*, July 11, 2005.

21 Judith Graham, "Contraception Becomes New Rallying Point for Abortion Foes," *Chicago Tribune*, September 28, 2006.

22 Dr. Glen Harold Stassen "Pro-Life? Look at the Fruits," *Sojourners*, www.sojo.net/index.cfm?action=sojomail.display&issue=041013, (accessed October 13, 2004).

23 James Dobson, *Dare to Discipline* (Wheaton, IL: Tyndale, 1970), 176.

24 SilverRingThing, Home Page, www.silverringthing.com. www.silverringthing.com.

25 Guttmacher Institute, "Recent Findings from the 'Add Health' Survey: Teens and Sexual Activity," *The Guttmacher Report on Public Policy* 4:4 (August 2001), www.guttmacher.org/pubs/tgr/04/4/gr040401.html.

26 Gene V. Robinson, "From the Closet to the Episcopate," The Earl Lecture, Berkeley, CA, January 25, 2005.

27 James Dobson, *Dare to Discipline* (Wheaton, IL: Tyndale, 1970), 178, 179.

28 Advocates for Youth "Abstinence-Only-Until-Marriage Programs," www.advocatesforyouth.org/abstinenceonly.htm www.advocatesforyouth.org/.

29 Simone DeBeauvoir, *The Second Sex* (New York: Vintage Books, 1952), 167.

30 Stephanie Bender, "The Once-a-Month Blues." *Focus on the Family* (May 1996), 12.

31 Rick Warren, *The Purpose Driven Life* (Grand Rapids, MI: Zondervan, 2002), 109.

32 Christiane Northrup, *Women's Bodies, Women's Wisdom* (New York: Bantam Books, 1994), 103.

33 Ronda E Sola Chervin, *Prayers of the Women Mystics* (Ann Arbor, MI: Servant Publications, 1992), 17-18.

34 Joseph Runzo and Nancy M. Martin, eds., *Love, Sex and Gender in the World Religions* (Oxford: One World, 2000), 16.

35 Art and Architecture of Venice, "Cornaro Chapel." www.boglewood.com/cornaro/xteresa.html.

10

The Cost of Belonging

Root Chakra: Belonging

Family Textile

Wrapped in the warmth of a family and
Snuggled with family lore
Bundled with noise and ideas
Comforted to the core

Such exquisite patterns of color
Displayed in this tapestry
Filled with wit and passion and laughter
Fine as home entertainment can be

Each person with something to offer
From the smallest to the old
Questions, opinions, and stories
The fabric of lives unfolds

When everyone has a moment
To uncover a deep concern
The joy of love and belonging
Through experience is learned

But when ideas are mocked or minimized or
Muffled and never heard
The voice that spoke becomes smaller,
More quiet, more unsure

If anyone cared to notice
One could glimpse the tiny death
On the face of the one who was trying
To find a place in the weft

That's when it starts to unravel
This comforter called a home
The quieted ones aren't really silenced
As they're watching and feeling alone

It may seem that they wish to be distant
They may turn their interest away
Or bury themselves in activity
The doing that weaves through the day

But bound by a family's binding
They will still make the impact they can
They may struggle or wiggle covertly
Perhaps use an indirect plan

Or they may find a way to be noticed
By cutting or tearing away
Leaving the rest feeling furious
Too late to hear what they'd say

They may turn their frustration all inward
Giving themselves all the blame
Believing somehow they deserved all
The judgment, the laughter, the shame

And so the whole piece ends up damaged:
The bleeding, the tearing, the stains
Broken trust and loss of belonging
Small remnant of comfort remains

So much is destroyed in the process
Such pain and confusion the cost
If only from the beginning
No voice was threatened or lost

These heirlooms can be rewoven or
Mended, or patched, or glued
But too often they just end up smaller:
Tattered, Faded, Subdued

Characteristics: Us against them mentality; insistence on rigid adherence to the law; rooted in judgment.

Within the fundamentalist Christian culture, life is to be lived in a narrowly defined way. Much, if not all, of the outside world is considered suspect. For the fundamentalist Christian,

> [T]here are only two kinds of people in the world: the righteous and the rest. To lead the best, most meaningful life, one must belong to the one, true religion. It is even more important "to believe in God and the right religion" than to be a good person. These "good people" have "a special relationship with God" because they believe in him the most and do the best job following his laws. "God will punish most severely those who abandon his true religion" in this world filled with nonbelievers and Satanic temptation. [1]

This orientation feeds divisiveness in the world community (you are with us or against us), within American society (for or against "family values"), and within the individual (who is separated from her true self). The doctrine itself promotes polarities. An us-against-them mindset causes members to respond from a stance of defensiveness, anticipating a debate or an argument that they must win for the cause of Christ. This internal posture breeds rigidity. Individuals expect to be tempted. They are fearful of succumbing to worldly seductions, which could result in the loss of eternal salvation (or, at the least, start the backslide down the slippery slope). As a consequence, human relationships are impaired as members live with the silent threat of condemnation and the fear of being cast aside or judged. Members suspiciously keep others, who are different, at a distance.

This mentality is foundationally rooted in a philosophy of exclusivity, preventing anyone and anything that is perceived and experienced as foreign from full participation. This isolative behavior, in turn, increases members' dependency on the system. In exchange, they receive a sense of belonging, set apart from a world where they are taught they do not and should not fit in.

In contrast, Jesus treated those judged by others as outcasts as his friends and equals. He welcomed diversity and responded to the disenfranchised with an expanded, open mind. We see many times throughout the gospels that Jesus dealt with a very diverse population: from tax-gatherers to sinners to those possessed by demons, from children to the sick and dying.

And as Jesus passed on from there, He saw a man, called Matthew, sitting in the tax office; and He said to him, "Follow Me!" And he rose, and followed Him. And it happened that as He was reclining at table in the house, behold many tax-gatherers and sinners came and joined Jesus and His disciples at the table. And when the Pharisees saw this, they said to His disciples, "Why does your Teacher eat with the tax-gatherers and sinners?" (Matthew 9:9–11)

This gospel account in Matthew describes Jesus' treatment of people as humane and welcoming. He socialized with the marginalized, those whom the fundamentalists of his day deemed sinners. Jesus refused to live as an arrogant religious separatist and consequently threatened the social order of his day. He served within God's domination-free realm and no one was excluded ... not the children, not the prostitutes, not the tax-gatherers.

This baffled the Pharisees, who maintained an isolated position in the world. The Pharisees believed themselves and their rules to be righteous; everyone else was not. Jesus sought to refocus these Pharisees, moving them from this mentality to one of unity, acceptance, and love. Jesus and his followers were catalysts of change and transformation, incorporating new and inclusive practices in the community, which included breaking down gender and cultural barriers — contrary to the pharisaical traditions and actions of the day.

A woman drawn to understand Jesus today, knowing he offered such grace and acceptance in his day, may hope to find the same in the family of a church. Looking for belonging, she seeks support for making sense of the complexities of her life and the trouble in the world. In some church communities, she may learn that she must accept Jesus Christ as her personal lord and savior to relieve the fear of hell, the burden of guilt, and the anxiety of uncertainty. In a fundamentalist system she is offered a simplistic package solution, sometimes framed as the Four Spiritual Laws:

1. God LOVES you and offers a wonderful PLAN for your life.

2. Man is SINFUL and SEPARATED from God. Therefore, he cannot know and experience God's love and plan for his life.

3. Jesus Christ is God's ONLY provision for man's sin. Through Him you can know and experience God's love and plan for your life.

4. We must individually RECEIVE Jesus Christ as Savior and Lord; then we can know and experience God's love and plan for our lives.[2]

Her belonging will be predicated upon her acceptance of these teachings and the assumption of her proper role. A Good Woman obeys the authority of God and men. In this system she will be programmed not to have an autonomous voice. The rules of the game are not to question the rules of the game, at any cost. Blind obedience is what is valued and required of female members within such a system.

This rigidity is most obvious in traditional religious wedding vows, by which a woman promises to love, honor, and obey her husband "'til death us do part." She then is hostage without a safety net. What if he tells her to do something crazy while intoxicated? What if he repeatedly and unilaterally invests the family savings (against her better judgment) in a way that puts the entire family at risk? What if he disciplines their children in ways she finds harsh and destructive? What if she finds her dominated self slipping away? What if she begins to outgrow the fundamentalism while her partner rigidly clings to controlling practices? She has few options if she hopes to remain a part of the family.

Commandments: You must keep up appearances and not be an embarrassment; you will belong if you are judged obedient.

As a religious group in Jesus' day, the Pharisees demonstrated a fundamentalist religion that degenerated into an assembly of unrighteousness and sectarianism. Religious hypocrisy became their glaring sin, which called forth from Jesus some of his most scathing denunciations. If it seemed that Jesus displayed an extraordinary tolerance for the sins of the publicans and harlots, he made up for it in his blunt exposure of the Pharisees' lack of genuine righteousness and sins of a religious nature. Jesus scorned their ostentatious, holy-looking dress; long, insincere prayers; and inauthentic sermons.

The Pharisees were preoccupied with deception, presenting themselves as upstanding, religious people yet acting in unjust and unloving ways. Although they would deny it, many Christian fundamentalist churches today are also rooted in the same deceptive religious practices. Their primary concern, like that of the Pharisees, is a publicly righteous image; their interest is to portray to the external world a good and pious front. Often this front is a tightly constructed and well-contained cover-up for their underlying intent to preserve the structures of domination and hide less-than-perfect human realities. Theirs is a strict standard of religiously defined perfection, designed to deceive. Jesus spoke to this directly: "And when you pray, do not imitate the hypocrites: they love to say their prayers standing up in the synagogues and at the street corners for people to see them. In truth I tell you, they have had their reward. But when you pray, go to your private room, shut yourself in, and so pray to your Father who is in that secret place" (Matthew 6:5–6).

Christian fundamentalists are quick to advertise a life in Jesus that is happy and problem-free, dangerously close to perfection; yet, at the same time, pleasure is perceived as sinful and suffering is valued as spiritual. The happy façade must be maintained at a high cost to the woman's authentic inner truth. Reality is not experienced as the truth about the here-and-now moment; reality to the fundamentalist is what might be achieved, or should be achieved, for piety's sake. This mode of experiencing life takes a lot of emotional energy, as it requires members to live a lie. When we deceive ourselves into thinking that we are just fine when we're not, we do not give ourselves permission to be fully human or fully authentic. Secrets, lies, and self-denials prevent us from living squarely in the truth. This deceptive presentation of perfect piety inhibits members from knowing and embracing their authentic selves. Women, in particular, are required to censor their truth in order to align themselves with what the system expects and judges as pious.

Christian fundamentalist churches insist that their members look good and appear to be decent. Whereas actually being good is minimized in value as an attempt to gain "salvation by works" or "works righteousness," learning *what to say* and *how to act in public* is crucial for being accepted as a respected member. Members are taught early on that they are not to embarrass the system by being disobedient to its agenda. When an emphasis on goodness is carried to this rigid extreme, true goodness is cast aside and replaced by a false presentation of decency.

Scott Peck writes in *People of the Lie: The Hope for Healing Human Evil*: "[T]he words 'image,' 'appearance,' and 'outwardly' are crucial to understanding the morality of evil. While they [evil people] seem to lack any motivation to BE good, they intensely desire to appear good. Their 'goodness' is all on a level of pretense. It is, in effect, a lie."[3]

With the public concern of appearing good to others, it makes sense that evil people would be found within religious organizations that promote a holy public image. Altemeyer and Hunsberger explore this issue based on their research: "Are religious persons usually good persons? The answer in this study at least, appears to be 'no,' if one means by 'religious' a fundamentalist, nonquesting religious orientation, and by 'good' the kind of nonprejudiced, compassionate, accepting attitudes espoused in the Gospels and other writings."[4]

They elaborate on their findings, and when referring to "evil people," they report:

> They are likely to exert themselves more than most in their continuing effort to obtain and maintain an image of high respectability. They may willingly, even eagerly, undergo great hardships in their search for status. It is only one particular kind of pain they cannot tolerate: the pain of their own conscience, the pain of the realization of their own sinfulness and imperfection.[5]

This drive to appear perfect prevents members from honestly facing any aspect of themselves that is less than perfect. This unwillingness to face one's flaws in the light of truth creates the need for a psuedo-perfection, a good Christian image. Peck continues, "The evil in this world is committed by the spiritual fat cats, by the Pharisees of our own day, the self-righteous who think they are without sin because they are unwilling to suffer the discomfort of significant self-examination."[6] The result of this lack of self-examination is a system rooted in silence and shame. Individuals cannot act in integrity and authenticity when they feel their choices are dictated by the image they must promote. One teen-ager reported:

> I could not believe it when I got pregnant. ... My church is very pro-life and very, very down on abortion. I've helped people pass out pro-life brochures in front of a Planned Parenthood. But when I got pregnant, after I got over the shock, I didn't see many options. I shouldn't have had sex with the guy, and I sure didn't want to mess up my life by marrying him. If I'd gone ahead and had the baby, people in my parish would have been so disappointed in me. The shame would just have killed me. ... I finally broke down and talked to my mother. She didn't believe in abortion either, but she agreed with me that it was the only option that made sense. And we never did tell my father that I had been pregnant or had an abortion. He couldn't have handled it. He probably would have kicked me out of the house.[7]

True integrity dissolves in a system where the *appearance* of what is right is valued more highly than actually doing right. The question of whether or not an individual would seek an abortion in a crisis situation is irrelevant to the system's requirement of opposing a woman's right to choose. In reality, the emphasis on appearance and the inherent intolerance of the system is what actually creates such situations of crisis. The inability to acknowledge what is really going on forces members into behaviors and decisions that must remain hidden. One's place in the system is dependent on the veneer of compliance.

Paula

Belonging to the group is the promise of fundamentalist systems. I remember many evangelistic events where, influenced by the music and powerfully persuasive speakers and wanting to be a part of it all, I confessed my sins and committed myself over and over again to deeper faith and obedience to the edicts of the system. I was caught up in the great feeling of camaraderie and being right. Even now, exposure to these situations can be almost hypnotic and strangely enticing, while at the same time, truly frightening. I hear once again of our human unworthiness, the familiar ABCs of "salvation," and the rigid requirements of submission to men, to authority, and to a rigid set of beliefs. Now I can consciously recognize the exclusivity in the message and its dissonance with my present understanding and experience of God. For years, though, I was a willing participant with the crowd rather than dare to question, to risk ostracism, or even to hold onto myself.

Chris Hedges explores a similar phenomenon as it relates to patriotism in his book *War Is a Force That Gives Us Meaning*, and in the following excerpt from his interview with Amy Goodman in the *Democracy Now!* studio on May 21, 2003.

> It is about the suspension of individual conscience, and probably consciousness, for the contagion of the crowd for that euphoria that comes with patriotism. The tragedy is that — and I've seen it in conflict after conflict or society after society that plunges into war — with that kind of rabid nationalism comes racism and intolerance and a dehumanization of the other. And it's an emotional response. People find a kind of ecstasy, a kind of belonging, a kind of obliteration of their alienation in that patriotic fervor that always does come in war time. ... I talked upon this notion of comradeship as a suppression of self awareness and self-possession to sort of follow along, locked in the embrace of a nation, or of a group, or of a national group unthinkingly, blindly. And there is a kind of undeniable euphoria in that.[8]

There is a cost for this euphoric experience of belonging. It can mean denying one's deepest personal convictions or even one's own children. A graphic example is found in families that are unable to accept or even acknowledge a homosexual daughter or son because of religious intolerance. A woman who dares to discover her own path is commonly cut off, with little hope of true reconciliation. To choose a different life-style, break some family or church taboo, disagree with the party line, vote independently, discover an alternative sexual expression, or even stop attending church regularly is apostasy. The fear of the resultant judgment and alienation is a powerful deterrent to authenticity. The lure of the comfort of comradeship and the experience of the ecstatic are equally powerful disincentives to change.

Many political groups have aligned themselves with Christian fun-damentalists' militaristic principles and behavioral compliance. While few fundamentalists perceive themselves as white supremacists, many white supremacist groups hold fundamentalist beliefs, quoting the Bible as their rulebook and God as their authority. In both groups, obedience without question is a requirement for membership. In *The Purpose Driven Life*, Rick Warren, spells out clearly this requirement to obey: "You will give an account to God of how well you followed your leaders."[9]

In *The Subtle Power of Spiritual Abuse*, David Johnson and Jeff Van Vonderan compared this dominating and overpowering system, perpetu-ated through the fundamentalist family, to the astronomical phenom-enon of black holes: "A black hole is a star whose mass got so incredibly dense that it actually 'imploded' — that is, instead of exploding outward it exploded inward. Now its gravity has grown so strong that it prevents even light from leaving. Hence the term 'black hole.'"[10]

The gravity of this system makes it hard for people to get out; even truthful information about the system has difficulty escaping. A wom-an's identity is defined by whom she remains attached to: her church, her man, her children. If she tries to leave, she might find taking initia-tive or responsibility for her own life frightening and unfamiliar, even sinful.

The emphasis on appearance and the requirement of obedience to ensure belonging stand in stark contrast to the teachings of Jesus. He did not demand unquestioned obedience from any who followed him. He did not threaten or shame to motivate compliance. Jesus spoke in parables, which opened people to their own stories, inviting them to question and find their own truths. Jesus himself questioned and ignored the traditions and rules of the patriarchal political system. Acting in an inclusive and egalitarian manner, he did not participate in the sexism, racism, and separatism of his own day. Rather, he embodied light and welcome, as his stories tell.

Creation: "I will create circles of welcome and grace; born of spirit; embodying truth; secure in the family of God; willing even to die."

Ancestral Inheritance

"Arise, shine out, for your light has come." (Isaiah 60:1)

"God forbid that I should give you my ancestral inheritance." (1 Kings 21:3)

The promise of our inheritance is to be children of light; we can be born of spirit, into the family of God. Our call to stand up, to walk and shine our light, is preeminent to our behavioral performance or our agreement with any particular religious requirement. Our physical experience of this belonging resides in the root chakra, the legs, hips, and base of the spine. The color of this chakra is red.

Bring your attention to this part of your body. Notice any sensations or messages that arise. Reflect on those who have come before you. Think of the great cloud of witnesses spoken of in Hebrews 12. Imagine mother after mother nurturing her child until the child is you. How amazing that your lineage has survived to the present. Claim the value of the inheritance of your life, your ancestry, and all the qualities that make you human. Think about nature and the support the earth offers to you. Appreciate your connection to the whole creation and your unique place in it. Wonder about how you have experienced belonging in your life. Think about the space for belonging you have created in your home. What do you claim as your ancestral inheritance? Envision yourself walking in confidence, feeling your feet firmly planted and supported by the earth — God's earth, your earth, the same earth where Jesus walked.

Our very existence is proof that each of us is the legacy of an unbroken line of sexually expressed women. These mothers and grandmothers of ours were powerful, creative, and supportive of the life taking shape within their wombs. In that succession of wombs, we each have swum in the mystery of our becoming. We may hope that each ancestral conception resulted from a passionate and loving moment of mutuality and delight, but at the least we know that each woman before us was a survivor and a creator of life out of life. This strong heritage is rooted in feminine physicality. Our foremothers, often with the support of male partners, have given us this inheritance: our sexual selves, our creative potential, our unique and safe place in God's family.

Our life in this moment is our own to create, with all the beauty and fullness we can imagine. As we affirm our own belonging, we can invite others to belong without judgment. We can create new families of belonging. As we make our homes places of acceptance and honor, where each person receives the permission and the support they need to become all God has imagined them to be, we extend this offer of belonging to others in our circles of love. In telling the stories of the women who have come before us and in creating the stories of our own lives with courage, we pass on the truths we have discovered and the blessings we have shared. By affirming who we are and fully inhabiting the vessels of our bodies, we exercise our belonging as a daily practice.

We might think of our invitation into the full expression of who we are meant to be as a baptism. We were born from the waters of birth, perhaps sealed in sacramental waters of a ritual baptism. We may continue to be reminded each time we take a shower or enjoy a drink of water or swim in the ocean that we belong to God, and we are surrounded by God, not because we agree with the right creed, but because that is our ancestral inheritance as creations of God. As women, we have been given our selves and our bodies by design. We can celebrate this gift as well as our related-ness to Eve and to all women who have come before us. We must not give up the rights and responsibilities of our belonging. *We do belong.* Female and male together reflect the image of God. We belong in creation, and our place in creation belongs to us. We cannot suspend our consciousness or let the wisdom we bring be overshadowed by the judgment of domi-nating structures or individuals, or by the "contagion of the crowd."

Our flesh connects us to our ancestors. Those who came before en-sured that we would live. We bear their genetic code and manifest a pat-tern of their likeness. From the past, and perhaps through transcendent presence, we can claim their blessing as we honor and thank them for the gift of our lives. Perhaps our experience of belonging in our family of origin prevents us from fully believing in the possibility of belonging in God's family. To enter into our resurrection, we must first be willing to acknowledge what has died within us as well as what domination still seeks to control us. Wink offers this wisdom:

> We are dead insofar as we have been socialized into patterns of injustice. We died, bit by bit, as expectations foreign to our essence were forced upon us. We died as we began to become complicit in our own alienation and that of others. We died as we grew to love our bondage, to rationalize, justify, and even champion it. ... At some point we must begin to become our-

selves. And to do that, we who are dead must die to our learned preferences for domination. ... One does not become free from the powers by defeating them in a frontal attack. Rather, one dies to their control: "Those who try to make their life secure will lose it, but those who lose their life will keep it" (Luke 17:33). Here also the cross is the model: we are liberated, not by striking back at what enslaves us — for even striking back reveals that we are still controlled by violence — but by a willingness to die rather than submit to its command.[11]

We can make this choice inspired by our mentors, Eve and Jesus. We can appropriate our resurrection through our willingness to die to what would control us.

Like Eve and Jesus before us, we will face judgment and opposition. It may not be an easy path, but together we are many. We have come from the bodies of women. Let us honor the bodies of women. As we embody the gifts of our ancestors, we shape the stories of God.

Dance: Choose a piece of music that speaks to you of belonging, earthiness, your ancestors, and groundedness. Wear a red dress or tie a red scarf around your hips. Give yourself permission to embody your root chakra through the beauty and rhythm of your dance.

Circle of Sharing: This is described for use in a group setting. It allows each person to be recognized and validated in the group as their movement is shared collectively. Gather the members into a circle, and while an instrumental piece of music is playing, invite one member at a time to express a movement. It could be as simple as moving the hands or arms or legs in a certain way. The group will then take on the movement of that person repeating it a few times. Proceed around the circle until each one has shared at least once.

Connecting to the Earth: This activity requires music with a strong drumbeat. Have participants cross the room, one or two or three at a time, using only the lower body to interpret the music. Movement can be forward, backwards, sideways, quick or slow, feet, hips, knees, working with the earthy beat of the music. Repeat until the song finishes. Reflect on what it is like to move in this uncharacteristic way.

Soothed

Aching need
When sooner soothed
The lesson learned
Is less confused

There is a God
Someone who cares
Whose milk is warm
Who softly shares

They are so few
These absolutes
This one she knew
Must be the truth

Notes

1 Bob Altemeyer and Bruce Hunsberger, "Authoritarianism, Religious Fundamentalism, Quest, and Prejudice." *International Journal for the Psychology of Religion* 2 (1992): 127.

2 Campus Crusades for Christ, "The Four Spiritual Laws," Global Media Outreach, www.greatcom.org/laws/english/.

3 M. Scott Peck, *People of the Lie: The Hope for Healing Human Evil* (New York: Simon & Schuster, 1983), 75.

4 Bob Altemeyer and Bruce Hunsberger, "Authoritarianism, Religious Fundamentalism, Quest, and Prejudice." *International Journal for the Psychology of Religion* 2 (1992): 124.

5 Ibid., 113-133.

6 M. Scott Peck, *People of the Lie: The Hope for Healing Human Evil* (New York: Simon & Schuster, 1983), 72.

7 Steve Clapp, Kristen Leverton Helbert, and Angela Zizak, *Faith Matters* (Fort Wayne, IN: LifeQuest, 2003), 69.

8 Chris Hedges, Democracy NOW, www.alternes.org/story/15982

9 Rick Warren, *The Purpose Driven Life* (Grand Rapids, MI: Zondervan, 2002), 166.

10 David Johnson and Jeff Van Vonderan, *The Subtle Power of Spiritual Abuse* (Minneapolis: Bethany House, 1991), 73.

11 Walter Wink, *The Powers That Be: Theology for a New Millennium* (Minneapolis: Ausburg Fortress, 1998). 93-94.

11

Jesus

The Light Is Come

On Christmas
Eve
The light is born
To live in us again
Soft and naked flesh has come
Our hearts to enter in

Inspiring us to ponder
The wonder of a choice
Awakening our consciousness
Empowering our voice

This body of divinity
Enables us to see
The beauty of the image
Manifest in "he" and "she"

The grace of life is dancing
In the warmth of every breath
Though destiny for humanness
Will surely come to death

The cup that would not pass away
A blessing has become
In birth and resurrection
Renewal has begun

The birth of Jesus as a vulnerable infant, welcomed into life on the road and honored by magicians and shepherds alike, creates a challenging vision of a child-centered family. His complete dependence on his significant adults reveals his fragile and lovable humanity. Their willingness to adjust their lives for the sake of his security provides a model for every family. His precocious inquisitiveness presaging his poignant message aligns decidedly with the boldness of Eve. He lived and resurrected her story of evolving consciousness in the context of his own family and community life.

The gospel of Luke reports that as Jesus "grew to maturity, he was filled with wisdom; and God's favor was with him." One can imagine him going to Hebrew school, learning to read the Torah, and thinking for himself about the rich meaning of the myth and history he encountered. By the time he was twelve, he was accidentally left "home alone" in Jerusalem following the feast of the Passover. His parents found him after three days "in the Temple, sitting among the teachers, listening to them, and asking them questions; and all those who heard him were astounded at his intelligence and his replies" (Luke 2:40-47). Perhaps he was already grappling with the nuance and mystery he found in the Book of Moses. Later we hear Jesus saying: "From the beginning of creation [God] made them male and female. This is why a man leaves his father and mother and the two become one flesh." While some have cited this Genesis text as the inauguration of the "traditional family," Jesus' further teaching instead promoted a radical feminist ideal. He proposed that a man who divorces his wife is guilty of adultery against her and a woman who divorces and remarries is as guilty of adultery as a man would be. At the time, a man could only commit adultery against a woman's husband, not against her, and no woman could divorce her own husband. Assuming a woman to have equal consideration in the matter was unheard of.[1] Apparently, Jesus recognized much more in the creation story regarding the essential equality of men and women than the patriarchal arrangements so many cultures have supported.

Although Christian fundamentalism professes to structure family in accordance with Christian values, its view is quite contrary to the kind of family Jesus and his early community envisioned. Jesus himself left his family and invited his followers to do likewise. He created a new family among those who shared similar philosophies and sensibilities. As he marched to the beat of his own drum, Jesus modeled for us the psychological and theoretical concept of separation and individuation. As we see in this passage from Mark, Jesus put the traditions of his time to the test:

Now his mother and his brothers arrived, and, standing outside, sent in a message asking for him. A crowd was sitting around him at the time the message was passed to him, "Look, your mother and brothers and sisters are outside asking for you." He replied, "Who are my mother and my brothers?" And looking at those sitting in a circle round him, he said, "Here are my mother and my brothers. Anyone who does the will of God, that person is my brother and sister and mother (Mark 3:31–35).

Of course, Jesus didn't forget about his mother — indeed, he was concerned about her care from the cross — but he was radically redefining family. Biology was transcended and *family* now referred to those people with whom he was intimate, with whom he shared God's work. Walter Wink explores Jesus' family values in this way:

> Jesus renounces the family as constituted by genetic family bloodlines, and offers an alternative: a new family, made up of those whose delusions have been shattered, who are linked, not by that deepest of all bonds, the blood tie, but by solidarity in the work of God. ... In the new family of Jesus there are only children, no patriarchs. As feminist scholar Elizabeth Schüssler Fiorenza remarks, by reserving the name *father* for God, Jesus subverts all patriarchal structures. No one can now claim the authority of father, because that power belongs to God alone.[2]

Jesus' example inspires us to welcome and support alternative families. For countless reasons, many people simply don't have a traditional family. But family units, whatever their constellation, are the small communities where we live in the flesh together, touching, sensing, nurturing, and blessing one another. In this work, we do the will of God together, as brothers and sisters and mothers of Jesus. In these most intimate of relationships we develop and change. When these families nurture our well-being and wholeness, we can move from them to bless and transform the world.

Jesus' experience is parallel to the experiences of many people today. The well-adjusted among us create a psychological separation from our parents in young adulthood. We move on to create new family commitments and groupings. In this way, we define ourselves as unique individuals. If, as adults, we have not done the work of separation and individuation, we run the risk of being just like our parents — or we live in rigidified reaction against them, their polar opposites. We need a healthy emotional distance to discover who we are apart from our parents; we must separate from the dictates of our families.

In fundamentalist families, this separateness from the system is simply not allowed.

Jesus acted against the religious norms of his day, but the Christian fundamentalist church refuses to accentuate this reality. Neither does it follow in his footsteps in its treatment of women. Born a Jew into a world under Roman rule to a woman whose character was considered questionable because she had conceived a child out of wedlock, Jesus became familiar with the treatment accorded women by religious and secular rulers alike. Perhaps he was sensitized and had developed empathy for women through his personal observations as a boy, experiencing his mother's plight as an atypical woman of her time. Under Roman law, operating at the time when Jesus was born, women were under the perpetual tutelage of their male relatives.

Jewish women led restricted lives — they could participate only to a limited extent in their religion. Susan Haskins candidly portrays the Jewish woman's situation:

> Whilst women are known to have supported rabbis with money, possessions and food, their participation in the practice of Judaism was negligible. Although they were allowed to read the Torah at congregational services, they were forbidden to recite lessons in public in order to "safeguard the honor of the congregation." In the first century AD, one Rabbi Eliezer was quoted as saying, "Rather should the words of the Torah be burned than entrusted to a woman!" It was for much the same reason that in the synagogue itself, women were seated apart from the men.[3]

Jesus was a catalyst for changing both Roman law and Jewish practice. Through Jesus' actions, the elevated position of women and the character of the relations between husband and wife, with an emphasis on the absolute sacredness of such a union, became clearer. The character and teachings of Jesus and the early church brought about a vast change in women's place in the home and society at that time. Yet, paradoxically, down through the ages, Jesus' "followers," who call themselves the "Christ-ones," continue to oppress women in the name of Christianity. This is very different from what Jesus lived and taught. As Herbert Lockyer wrote in *Everything Jesus Taught*: "Through the influence of the great Friend of women, their (women's) changed position resulted in continual reproach by the early enemies of the Christians because they (the early followers of Christ) gave their women high position in the church."[4]

This practice of honoring women was certainly a result of the example Jesus had set. Consider the story of the woman with an alabastar jar, of whom Jesus said:

> You see this woman? I came into your house and you poured no water over my feet, but she has poured out her tears over my feet and wiped them away with her hair. You gave me no kiss, but she has been covering my feet with kisses ever since I came in. You did not anoint my head with oil, but she has anointed my feet with ointment. For this reason I tell you that her sins, many as they are, have been forgiven her, because she has shown such great love. It is someone who is forgiven little who shows little love. (Luke 7:44–47)

The following verses in Luke describes the women who followed Jesus — independent, bold, committed women:

> Now it happened that after this he made his way through towns and villages preaching and proclaiming the good news of God's domination-free order. With him went the Twelve, as well as certain women who had been cured of evil spirits and ailments: Mary surnamed the Magdalene, from whom seven demons had gone out, Joanna the wife of Herod's steward Chuza, Susanna, and many others who provided for them out of their own resources. (Luke 8:1–3)

And we know from the books of Acts and the Epistles in the New Testament, women came to exercise a strong influence in the early church. The teaching of Jesus concerning women and his treatment of them caused the Pharisees, whose approach to women was so unlike his own, to rise up in protest against his respectful and sympathetic understanding of them. Each contact Jesus had with women was a revelation and a testimony to the sacred esteem in which he held them. Yet the fundamentalist church today is a system that requires women to be subservient to men. Within and without the church, women still are not free to enjoy full leadership and active participation equivalent to men.

Today, fundamentalist Christianity has settled for the safety and security of systematic theology — an outline of beliefs spelled out clearly through black and white, good versus bad — otherwise known as *orthodoxy*. In essence, this is the "Law" of our day. There is no guesswork in this kind of belief system. These rules and regulations serve as the determinants of who is inside the system and who is an outsider.

The church remains an exclusive club, promoting sameness among its members instead of embracing and welcoming all kinds of people wherever they may be on their spiritual path. With this kind of closed theology, members indulge an arrogant belief that *they* know the answers to life's mysteries, that only *their* eternity is secure in heaven, and that *their* religion is superior — is, in fact, the *only* true religion. They believe they are the good people, special people, hand-picked by God. They are "in" while others are "out." They have been found while others remain lost. This theology provides a sense of security and order to their lives, neatly packaged and divinely tied with a bow.

Men know where they belong in the system (on the top), and women know their place (on the bottom). And although women may be subordinate, for many fundamentalist women there is still a certain amount of comfort and belonging in knowing where they should be and how they should act at all times. There also is a false exaltation by means of subordination in this system. A good, obedient, submissive wife and attentive mother earns a token honor, respect, and affirmation for the role she is performing. Although she may have to bury some of her talents and remain silent about her heart's desires, there is nothing in the system valued as more important than the Good Woman role. The higher law of religious duty is valued more than personal fulfillment.

But Jesus' religious beliefs were not based on the Law. He did not follow a set of rules. His theology was not rooted in creeds. In fact, he said repeatedly, "You have heard how it was said ... but I say this to you ... " (Matthew 5:38–39, 43–44). Jesus did not allow for just one possible interpretation of his message. His theology unfolded through the parables he told and the life he lived. Jesus chose to share himself and his teaching with those around him through the paradigm of story, sharing through the media of parable and metaphor, not edicts and rules. Story is theology and mystery intertwined. It is multidimensional and multifaceted.

When a story is told, its meaning is not static and rigid. Its truth is not absolute. Beliefs become soiled with real circumstances, real settings, and real people. We understand and have compassion for the outlaws. We may even begin to identify with them. The neat package of our spotless theology begins to fray around the edges. We see human imperfection. Through story, we get in touch with our frailty and our connection with all of humanity. We get to know ourselves better, whether we like what we see or not. Stories, parables, and myths get us in touch with the opposing sides of an issue, allowing us to suspend judgment even as we seek understanding.

There are many interpretations available in storytelling. For example, the creation story, when shared as story, carries many possible interpretations. As told within the Christian fundamentalist tradition, this story has been interpreted in a particular way by the church fathers with one particular message in mind. That same story told through the eyes of a feminist spiritualist takes on new character and meaning, as is true in this book with the character of Eve.

Spiritually adventurous members with their rigorous faith probably became too challenging for the early church fathers. After all, orthodoxy needs a faith of certainty, and the early church had a mission to establish. Christianity would become the accepted religion worldwide and an institution of power within the culture. Possibly these early church fathers could not tolerate the tension of the lawless parables. It's hard to build a doctrinal structure with too many dimensions, too many possibilities, too many differing opinions. These early church fathers purported that there should only be one way — the right way, *their* way, the Christian way. Thus, the Nicene Creed was written in 372 CE, and later the Apostles' Creed, the first outlines describing what Christians inside the system must believe to be acceptable members. The parables of Jesus became mere footnotes. The tension had been relieved. The anesthetic of answers had successfully numbed the church.

All but forgotten was Jesus' teaching: immediate, sensual, rooted in the momentary experiences of everyday life and the natural world. Jesus' *passion*, by all accounts of his earthly sojourn, was his full immersion in the experience of being human at an earthy, elemental level. He was a homeless guy with a counter-culture message, full of talk and action about love and healing and forgiveness. The following words of Jesus, from the Book of Matthew, clearly outline his priorities and values:

> "You must therefore set no bounds to your love, just as your heavenly father sets none to his. ... Be careful not to parade your uprightness in public. ... If you forgive others their failings, your heavenly father will forgive you yours. ... Do not store up treasures for yourselves on earth. ... Wherever your treasure is there will your heart be too. ... You cannot be the slave both of God and of money ... so do not worry about tomorrow. ... Do not judge, and you will not be judged; because the judgments you give are the judgments you will get. ... Everyone who asks receives. ... So always treat others as you would like them to treat you. ... It is a narrow gate and a hard road that leads to life.

... Beware of false prophets. ... You will be able to tell them by their fruit. "Jesus had now finished what he wanted to say and his teaching made a deep impression on the people because he taught them with authority, unlike their own scribes. (Matthew 5:48–7:29)

Many people throughout the world, children of God, do indeed bear and share the fruit that Jesus embodied. Not all of them recite the same rhetoric, but we recognize them when they set no bounds to their love, do not parade their uprightness, forgive, are not slaves of money, do not worry, do not judge, and treat others as they would like to be treated. Jesus warned us also to recognize and to beware of those who demonstrate their falseness by their fruit.

Karen Armstrong affirms the importance of noticing the fruit of compassion to evaluate ideas about God and spirituality:

> The one and only test of a valid religious idea, doctrinal statement, spiritual experience, or devotional practice was that it must lead directly to practical compassion. If your understanding of the divine made you kinder, more empathetic, and impelled you to express this sympathy in concrete acts of loving-kindness, this was good theology. But if your notion of God made you unkind, belligerent, cruel, or self-righteous, or if it led you to kill in God's name, it was bad theology. Compassion was the litmus test for the prophets of Israel, for the rabbis of the Talmud, for Jesus, for Paul, and for Muhammad, not to mention Confucius, Lao-tzu, the Buddha, or the sages of the Upanishads.[5]

Jesus brought countless examples of such compassion to light in his storytelling. He trusted his disciples, and the multitudes, to draw their own conclusions from the parables he told. He relied on each person to hear and understand what he or she needed to hear. Jesus' use of parables appears to be related to the Jewish tradition of *midrash* — inventing story to re-envision and re-imagine the biblical texts, inviting the listener to personally enlarge and expand in accordance with his or her own subjective learning and experience. Both parable and midrash are non-dogmatic invitations, capable of imparting religious truths. Both are non-authoritarian, suggesting that truth is flexible, even elastic. Both parable and midrash stand in contrast to what fundamentalist Christianity teaches as doctrine.

As Jesus demonstrated, to be in the presence of parable and myth means to live in the presence of insecurity and the unknown, to live in the fruitful tension of *not knowing*. This kind of theology calls for truly living by faith and embracing the mysterious, trusting in things that are unseen yet known to be true. Such faith is risky business.

What risks are we ready to face in the church? What would a church in which Jesus participated look like? Surely children would be on his lap. Surely all would be welcome at the table. Those in the kitchen would sit down with Jesus and hear his stories. He would no doubt help with the dishes later. All would be learning together what it really means to love oneself and to love one another. We can imagine good food, great music, the best wine, and joyful dancing. Perhaps with more healing and feeding there would be less judging and repressing, more freeing and loving with less dogma and debate. Are we daring enough to labor in fruitful tension in our churches to bring forth the mystery of such new life and fullness?

Small community churches can be nests of nurture and bastions of blessing as individuals are supported through their joy and grief as well as their growth into wholeness. At its best, a church honors the mystery, fosters community, and radiates the light of true justice and goodness. Large or small, at their worst, churches are institutions of repression and convention, distracted by the love of *mammon* and too often complicit with powers of domination. Each woman must honestly examine her association with her own church if she has one, asking the hard questions. Does this church welcome the person I really am and allow me to express and develop my gifts? Does it reflect and stand for the values Jesus embodied? Is it committed to participatory equality rather than hierarchy? Does it welcome the power of the Spirit to bring about change and new understanding? Are my time and my treasure best invested in this assembly? Can I stay here and be a part of shining resurrection light, or am I called to move?

We can ask these same questions of any institution as we decide when to remain and when to move away from systems that are in conflict with our values. We are called into the full expression of our vitality as partners with Jesus in bringing about God's domination-free order. The brightness and beauty of our flames cannot exist under bushel baskets.

In some of Jesus' post-resurrection appearances, he was unrecognizable to those who loved and knew him well. In the same manner today, a woman owning her resurrection may seem disarming or foreign in her new embodiment. She may find herself outside the garden of fundamentalism, even experiencing a crucifixion of sorts from her family, friends, and church community. In taking a leap of faith, she will grieve the loss and feel the pain that comes with letting go and moving on. Rather than claiming a static, once-and-for-all experience of being "born again," she may find herself in a dynamic, cyclic process of dying to old ideologies and patterns of behavior, while resurrecting her soul to new possibilities. She may develop a deep respect for this life process as she discovers her own seasons of death and re-birth. She may welcome these seasonal flows as necessary, discovering that her moods, emotions, and cycles all foster growth and aliveness — the expression of her authentic soul. She will understand that new birth is a process, a daily practice, rooted in the earth, grounded in the present, touching the transcendent. Choosing resurrection is a risky, moment-by-moment choice, an evolving state of being.

We believe that Jesus came to earth for many reasons. One of them was certainly to re-envision and resurrect, for both genders, the spirit of Eve. His boldness reminds us of her autonomy, her freedom to be, and her curiosity for a higher consciousness. The life of Jesus mirrored the example set forth by Eve in the creation myth. Both Eve and Jesus functioned as revolutionary beings, imparting consciousness for themselves and for others. Both exemplified a liberated relationship with themselves, with God, and with others.

Jesus' life on this earth and Eve's experience in the Garden offer us stories and mythic truths to repeatedly learn and grow from. If we are willing to expand our consciousness and dare to bite that familiar, forbidden fruit again and again, both Jesus and Eve will act as spiritual guides — liberated beings who model for us a way of being human in the world, apart from rigid adherence to Law. Our prayer is that both Eve and Jesus will daily inspire and equip us to live our lives apart from that which wounds our souls. May our own resurrection parallel that of women throughout the earth as we rise with Eve, unveiled and un-ashamed, understanding and responding to our call to beautiful, embodied wholeness.

Paula

I am not a Hebrew scholar but I have owned a concordance since high school and have often used it to look up particular words in the Bible and see how they have been translated in different contexts. Applying this method of inquiry for the study of the second creation myth (Genesis 2:7-3:24), and trusting my own impressions about what I am discovering has made the story fresh and inspiring for me. Perhaps Jesus had a similar experience as a child approaching the Torah with his "beginner's mind."

The following retelling is my attempt to reclaim some of the nuance that perhaps has been lost in translation since the days when the monarch King James authorized the first Bibles to become available to the public in English and even before. I hope to draw back some of the layers of assumptions and misperceptions that have clouded our memory of the myth: Satan as the snake, Adam first created, Eve first to fall, blame spread all around, hell as punishment. Until we rethink the myth these assumptions live powerfully in the unconscious. Perhaps this reframe will stimulate other thinking about the mystery of our essential equality and our longing for oneness. Each of us, like Eve and like Jesus, must find:

> our own relationship to the divine,
>
> our own authoritative understanding,
>
> our own story to tell,
>
> our own loving, believing, authentic self,
>
> our own just empowerment,
>
> our true sexual nature, bliss, and responsibility, and
>
> our own place of belonging in God's good creation.

Retelling the Garden Story
(Hebrew words in italics)

Jahweh Elohim, like a potter, molded a reddish human being out of dust from the earth and puffed into its face the vital breath, divine inspiration, intellect, soul, and spirit of life. The human being became a living, breathing creature, a *nephesh*, full of appetite, vitality, and pleasure. And *Yahweh Elohiym* planted an ancient garden called Eden and there settled the human.

Yahweh Elohiym caused to sprout from the earth every tree that was precious to look at and good for eating; the tree of life was in the center of the garden, as well as the tree of the understanding of bountiful prosperity and troublesome adversity. And there was a stream flowing out of Eden, which divided into four channels. The name of the first one was the Pishon, spreading out, and it encircled Havilah, the land of the spiral dance, where there is fine sparkling gold. The other streams were the Gihon, the Tigris, and the Euphrates.

Yahweh Elohiym received the human, and suckling it gently, eased the being into the garden of Eden so it could tend, honor, and protect it;

then charged the human, declaring "Of every tree of the garden you may eat, but of the tree of the understanding of bountiful prosperity and troublesome adversity, if you eat of that one, you will die." So, at this point in the story, the human was not yet necessarily mortal.

Yahweh Elohiym declared, "It's not good that the human exists like this; I will fashion some help." Now this is the same word for help that is used in the verse "I lift up my eyes to the mountains; where is my help to come from?" (Ps. 121:1). So out of the earth *Yahweh Elohiym* molded every creature of the field and every bird of the heavens and brought them to discern what the human would call them.

The human seemed to be a natural namer, and whatever the human called each living creature, that became the creature's special name. The human announced names for the farm animals, for all the birds of the heavens, and for all the creatures of the field, including the *nachash*, or serpent. But for the human this help was still not sufficient. The being was so good at naming but not really so good at listening. Maybe the naming part of the human was somehow overshadowing the listening part. The help the human needed simply could not be accessed.

So *Yahweh Elohiym* cast the human into a deep trance, and, while the human was in this dreamy state, gently took/received the feminine portion, the *echad tsela*. Now, *tsela* is a word for a chamber or plank or even a whole side, curved perhaps as a rib. (In fact, in the first chapter of Genesis, the word used for the image of *Yahweh* is *tselem*.) *Echad* means primary or singular or united or even primordial: like the first day, or the first river. So, the *echad tsela* was received, and the *basar* of the human repaired. *Basar* is usually translated as flesh, but it also means kin or some element of sexuality, maybe even suggesting genetic pattern. In Greek it sometimes becomes *eugellion*, evangelism, the good news. Maybe *basar* means to speak to the unique message of the individual, the authentic self, the sexual soul.

Anyhow, *Yahweh Elohiym* molded this feminine portion that had been received into an *iyshshah* and presented her to the human. The human was so excited. *Pa'am!* You can imagine a bell ringing: ding, ding, ding! "She has a structure like mine and *basar* like mine! I announce that she is *iyshshah*, as she was received from *iysh!*" That namingness remained strong in the *iysh* part of the human nature. So, apparently this teasing apart of the genders speaks to why a man has strengths from both a father and a mother and a person longs to come back together with another in a mysterious loving way, to recreate that original oneness of the *basar echad*. It also touches on the mysterious paradox of sexual union and distinction in the individual and in the community of a couple.

In the meantime, the *iyshshah* and *iysh* were both naked, *arowm*, together. Perhaps they were metaphorically prepubescent, naked in the sense of being hairless, and they were not a bit self-conscious. Now, the *nachash*, the serpent, also hairless, who existed as the most prudent, *aruwm*, of the creatures that *Yahweh Elohiym* had fashioned in the land, spoke to the humans. Could this prudent creature have been a presence of *Chokmah* herself, the embodiment of the wisdom who was ever at play with *Yahweh*, the artisan, in the beginning, delighting and rejoicing among the humans? (Prov. 8: 22, 30, 31)

The *nachash* said, "Hasn't *Elohiym* declared that you cannot eat from every tree in the garden?" And the *iyshshah*, who had been listening so carefully earlier, said to the *nachash*, "We may eat of the fruit of the trees of the garden, but of the fruit of the tree that is in the middle of the garden, *Elohiym* declared, 'If you eat it or touch it you will die.'" The *iysh* apparently did not participate in this conversation.

The *nachash* declared to the *iyshshah*, "You won't really die. *Elohiym* knows in fact that the day you eat of it your eyes will become observant, and you will be like *Elohiym*, understanding both bountiful prosperity and troublesome adversity." So at this point in the story, the humans were not yet god-like in this way of seeing.

The *iyshshah* discerned that the tree was good for eating, captivating to look at, and it was a precious tree for making one wise and prudent. Fully informed, she decided to take the risk, accepting the consequences. She received the fruit, ate it, and offered some to the *iysh* and he ate it, too. This word for received, *laqach*, is also translated as doctrine or learning: "Let the wise listen and learn yet more, and a person of discernment will learn the art of guidance." (Prov. 1:5) Indeed, together their eyes became observant as they moved into a new understanding of their nakedness and vulnerability. They now possessed an awareness, both terrible and wonderful, of their full human/divine condition. To ritualize their experience they sewed fig leaves and fashioned for themselves sacred festive coverings, *chagowrs*, and danced in circles of wonder and celebration. And they heard the sound of *Yahweh Elohiym* moving about in the garden in the spirit, *ruach*, of the day. The human, who had recognized himself as *iysh* but was otherwise as yet unnamed, and the *iyshshah* huddled themselves lovingly together, bonded in each other's bosom of embrace, in the face of *Yahweh Elohiym* in the middle of the trees of the garden.

Now *Yahweh Elohiym* announced a name for the human, "Adam," and declared, "Where are you?" Perhaps Adam had come into his manhood.

Adam declared, "I listened to your voice in the garden and I was in fear and reverence because I now realize how vulnerably naked I am and I hid huddled, coupled, partnered with the *iyshshah* as we have become bound together in a most mystical way." Now, maybe a guy wouldn't say exactly that, but in the Hebrew telling it is more concise.

And *Yahweh Elohiym* declared, "Who enlightened you about your naked vulnerability? Have you eaten from the tree that I explained to you about not eating?"

And the human declared, "The *iyshshah* that you offered to me to be with me, she offered me of the tree, and yes, I ate."

Yahweh Elohiym declared unto the *iyshshah*, "What have you fashioned?"

And the *iyshshah* declared, "I am indebted to the *nachash*, who initiated me, and yes, I ate."

Yahweh Elohiym declared to the *nachash*, "For fashioning this, you will be destined, in a different way from the farm animals or the other creatures of the earth, to continue to go about on your belly and eat dust all the days of your life. And now a tension will be apparent between you and the woman; between her progeny and yours. (What was easy once will be fraught.) Humanity will attempt to veil the glory of your wisdom but still this wisdom will be manifest in the mystery of human sexuality.

The humans also would face new adult challenges. *Yahweh Elohiym* declared to the *iyshshah*, "You will have an abundance of worrisomeness with your fertility; through the vessel of travail you will bear children; you will overflow with longing for *iysh* and his approval and he will be hard-pressed not to try to dominate you. *Yahweh Elohiym* declared to Adam, "You listened to the voice of *iyshshah* and ate from the tree that I explained to you about not eating. In worrisomeness you will eat of the produce of the earth all the days of your life. Thorns and thistles will sprout and you will eat the grasses of the field. By the sweat of your face you will also be prone to feed on warring until you return to the earth from which you were received; you are dust, to dust you will return.

Now Adam called the *iyshshah* by the honorable name of Eve, *Havvah*, because she was the mother of all who live. *Yahweh Elohiym* made coverings of skins as clothing for Adam and the *iyshshah*, and declared "Behold, because the human being is united, *echad*, and understands bountiful prosperity and troublesome adversity, like *Elohiym*, he and she can no longer stretch out their hands and receive from the tree of life and eat of it and live forever." Apparently, the human being had indeed become both mortal and divine. What the *nachash* had predicted had come true.

So *Yahweh Elohiym* sent the humans forth from the garden of Eden to till the earth from which they had been received. The words for this going forth, *garash* and *shalach*, are the same two words used in Exodus 11:1 to foretell the deliverance of the Israelites from Egypt. Humanity therefore was likewise delivered out of Eden and *Yahweh Elohiym* placed cherubs and an enchanted turning sword east of the garden of Eden to protect the way to the tree of life.

Notes

1 Ched Myers, *Binding the Strong Man* (New York: Orbis Books, 2005), 265-266.

2 Ibid., 77.

3 Susan Haskins, *Mary Magdalen: Myth and Metaphor* (New York: Riverhead Books, 1993), 10.

4 Herbert Lockyer, *Everything Jesus Taught* (New York: Harper & Row, 1976), 15.

5 Karen Armstrong, *The Spiral Staircase* (New York: Anchor Books, 2004), 293.

12

Dance and Ritual for Healing

A young woman begins to weep quietly after her dance teacher tells her she has beautiful dancer's feet. She strokes her feet lovingly as she wonders about the dancer she might have been had she been allowed to study dance when she was young.

A patient comes to her appointment with her gynecologist begging for a hysterectomy. She has been miserable with chronic pelvic pain for years, and no doctor has been able to explain the cause. A clinical interview reveals both a childhood and adult history of hierarchical relationships, domination, and devaluation of her authentic feminine self.

Following a traumatic car accident resulting in physical therapy treatments for whiplash, a young woman recalls memories of which she had not been consciously aware. She begins to recall her sexual abuse at the hands of her grandfather, a Pentecostal preacher.

During her therapy session, another woman tries desperately to express herself. She knows what she thinks and feels, but she cannot muster the words or the courage to speak. Her throat becomes red and tight as she agonizes to give voice to her truth.

Clearly, our bodies do not exist separately from our souls. We are mysteriously integrated beings whose experiences affect our ideas, which affect our emotions, which affect our bodies, which affect our feelings, which affect our beliefs, which affect our behavior. The wounds to our psyches live on in our physical reality. In order to recover from damage done to our hearts, minds, and spirits, we must involve our bodies. Jesus understood this integrated way of being when he reminded the scribe to love God "with all your heart, with all your soul, with all your mind, and with all your strength" (Mark 12:29–30). Our bodies are temples of God's spirit, and as we honor them, learn from them, and attend to their healing, we become more whole.

Paula

On Sunday mornings when we sing in church, there are often a few brave tiny ones who enliven the red carpet encircled by chairs as they allow the spirit to move them. They spin and tumble with limbs outstretched, celebrating holy presence, and surrounded by their adoring community of support. It is sacred dance.

I call them brave because they follow their impulse to move in freedom and delight. As they grow older and become self-conscious, they will ignore this prompting and learn to sit still in their chairs. I have watched several who have come before them as they gradually restrained their dance. No one tells them to, but most of the time the adults around them model restraint, uncomfortable about spontaneous movement. So they will come to think that is what they should do as well.

We do dance in church at times. On most of the holy days and as often as possible, we incorporate liturgical dance into our service of worship. We usually have a group of five to eight, including children, teens, and adults. So some of our young dancers have found an outlet again. Each dance is choreographed, rehearsed, and sometimes costumed to contribute to the liturgy of the day. Rev. Bunny, who has danced in church for years, has been our wonderful support and mentor.

When I first began, I was nervous about explaining and justifying the reasons dance has value in worship. The more dance has enhanced my life, the more vital I understand and experience it to be as part of worship. My favorite moments are when the congregation moves together in some simple way that engages the congregants' bodies with their hearts and minds in praise and release. Not all, but many from the congregation comment on their delight in the blessing of dance in worship.

I also dance at a studio. Once a week I go to Robin's dance class in town. "Dancing the Heart" she calls it, but I think of it as dance therapy. Robin has had a long career as a dancer, choreographer, teacher, and mentor. She has developed and uses many of the dance activities described in this book as well as others to foster amazing dance encounters. There are all body types and ages in her classes and workshops, mostly women with a few happily embodied men. Claire says he used to think his body was just for carrying his head around. At eighty-five, he's never been happier or felt better, and he welcomes every day as a bonus. He attributes his wellness largely to the blessings of his dance.

Our faces become radiant and our bodies tell exquisitely beautiful stories of wonder as the ninety-minute class unfolds. We move in our own authentic ways as we discover our dance and take our stories to a new level of expression. There is little talking, and I don't always remember the other dancers' names, but at the end I feel a glimpse of understanding and a profound acceptance of each one. Together we have shared a deep and nurturing experience, and we go home changed — a little brighter, a little bolder, each of us renewed in body and in soul. Part of the magic is the supportive witness we offer to one another as we give each other attention. So many women are afraid to be seen, let alone to take the stage. But as we give each other audience and permission, we take permission for ourselves as well to take up space and to move in our own grace. For me, this too, is an experience of worship and a celebration of God.

In this dance experience we sometimes explore movement in terms of the ancient understanding of our bodies' chakras and the rights they represent. Like a beam of white light broken by a prism into a rainbow, we can imagine the embodiment of the spectrum in our own beings. The root chakra, located at the base of our spine and including the legs, which connects us to the earth, is red. Herein lies our right to belong. The sacral chakra, orange in color, encompasses our sexual and reproductive organs, the center of our creative potential and our right to feel. The third chakra, the solar plexus, houses our right to act, to accomplish our intentions. It is yellow. The heart chakra, green in color, resonates with our passion and our right to love and be loved. The throat chakra stands for our right to speak and to be heard. This chakra is blue. The sixth chakra, indigo, covers the area of our eyes and ears and is related to our intuition and our right to be aware. It is called the third eye or the brow chakra. Finally, the violet crown chakra, at the very top of our head, relates to mystery, our connection with the divine, and our right to know.

We may make shapes using our whole bodies, for each of the chakras, one at a time. How would you move your right to speak? How might you embody your right to see? Through this exercise we may notice one part of our body that is especially blocked, in discomfort, or in need of attention or release. Now we may spend more time with this one area, exploring how we might enhance our freedom of expression. We may experience a profound release or reconnection. Often ideas come to mind — ways an issue might be contributing to relational or professional conflict. Afterward, some are inspired to paint or to write poetry or to make music. Some experience new insights for managing a challenging relationship. I feel purged, invigorated, whole, embodied, and integrated.

Dance can be a powerful, transformative tool in a group setting. One can build awareness and support healing through individual experiences of attention to the body, movement, creative expression, and ritual. Moving the body can release buried pain and free the soul into newness. As they are released, the pain and grief must be noticed and honored as such, and then allowed to dissipate. Certain sadnesses may surface again and again, perhaps with less intensity as time goes on. As we grieve our losses, they lose their hold on us. As we give and receive empathy for our pain, we find the courage and power to change and grow. Mutual support found in a dance group, through therapy, or with a friend, a partner, a mother, or a daughter is invaluable in this process, as Eva discovered.

Eva's Dance — Continued

Years passed and Eva grew up, got married, had babies, and became very busy with mothering. She began trying to make her children fit into the same mold she'd known. She said "no" a lot, and tried to manage their strong wills; she cared more than a little about approval from her family and church. Soon enough, however, she fell deeply in love with those amazing children and started listening to them. Her husband was listening too and did not hold her back from discovering her truth. As she saw their dancing and heard their singing, honoring their questions and insights and responding from her heart, she began to recognize the voice that had been quieted and lost to her. She moved back into her body and her mind, and she remembered how she also loved to dance.

Together with her family, she began to hear and speak the truths of their Mother God once again. She started dancing, making music, speaking up, and saying "yes" to herself and to her children. She started paying attention to what was happening in the country and in the world.

She was amazed and angered at how Jesus' teachings had been twisted by people in power calling themselves Christians. Public education budgets were chronically underfunded while the military industrial complex flourished. Health care was unavailable or unaffordable to many. Government was being urged to control and interfere with women's most personal reproductive health choices. It was impossible for many workers to earn a wage adequate to feed their families or to buy a home. Protection of the environment was disappearing. Individuals of certain sexual orientations faced discrimination. The rich and powerful were given every advantage while increasing their profit from the labor of the poor. Men intent on world domination were spending lives and billions of dollars on wars and weapons. Fear reigned, and civil rights were threatened. In many churches and families, women were second-class citizens. In many homes, violence against women and children was rampant. Nuclear weapons were a hair trigger away from annihilating all the living things she cared about. Who was paying attention? How could this desperate situation be transformed? What would Jesus say? She felt so discouraged.

Still, Eva danced, and listened, and thought about Jesus' life and message, and studied to learn what was true. She questioned her church and her family. At last, her own mother told her to keep thinking for herself. She discovered that sometimes a mother knows just what you need to hear. She found a church that was welcoming to children, women, diversity, dance, and thinking.

She learned that parts of the Old Testament were written as myth or poetry to convey profound truths in timeless ways. Other parts were historical accounts, but none of it was a science book. She discovered rich metaphors there for the feminine qualities of God.

She discovered that the New Testament writings were collected almost three hundred years after Jesus' life on earth (by men, not women), and that many gospels were not included (some by women) — gospels that spoke of God's nature as both mother and father. She marveled at the diversity of the early church.

She realized how Jesus himself was radically feminist, activist, and political as he honored and included women, and challenged the conventional power structures of his time.

She came to appreciate that God alone is ruler of the conscience, and that no one else can dictate our beliefs or moral choices. Until we have a perfect world, we must listen to each other, support one another, and pass laws that are fair and safe.

She affirmed the importance of preserving the separation of church and state, so that all people can be free to understand and honor God in their own way.

She began to recognize Jesus' message reflected in the wisdom and truths of other faith traditions, and her dance expanded.

She became more courageous in speaking her views on issues of politics, social justice, and freedom of speech. She took her right to vote seriously. She voted her onvictions with her dollars, spending more locally and ethically. She began to stand with the Women in Black as a witness for peace and in solidarity with those whose lives have been devastated by war and violence.

She expected those she trusted to speak honestly, to live their beliefs, and to act for the public good — in her family, her church, her community, and her political affiliation. She began to understand how the power and influence of women, when not acknowledged, manifests subversively, but without the necessary accountability that ensures the courage and integrity of conviction. She realized that women must openly share equal partnership in power and perspective for the good of all.

Finally, Eva began to see and to believe that things would change. Jesus said, "The truth will make you free." She believed that the truth of Jesus' life and witness would be a powerful and transforming force in the world when

the compassion and courage
from mothers and others
welcomed and defended each being
in the music and dance of truth.
And every day,
Eva danced.

$\mathcal{D}$ansformation $\mathcal{I}$nspiration

From the New Jerusalem Bible

Dance

You have turned for me my mourning into dancing. (Psalm 30:11)

Ancestral Inheritance   Root Chakra

Arise, shine out, for your light has come. (Isaiah 60:1)

God forbid that I should give you my ancestral inheritance. (1 Kings 21:3)

New Covenant / Naked Truth   Sacral Chakra

Then, taking a cup, he gave thanks and said, "Take this and share it among you, because from now on, I tell you, I shall never again drink wine until God's domination-free order comes. ... This is my body given for you. ... This cup is the new covenant in my blood poured out for you." (Luke 22:17–20)

Support / Balance   Solar Plexus Chakra

It was those who were poor according to the world that God chose, to be rich in faith and to be the heirs to God's domination-free order, which God promised to those who love God. You, on the other hand, have dishonored the poor. Is it not the rich who lord it over you? Are not they the ones who drag you into court, who insult the honorable name which has been pronounced over you? ... You will love your neighbor as yourself. ... Talk and behave like people who are going to be judged by the law of freedom. Whoever acts without mercy will be judged without mercy, but mercy can afford to laugh at judgment. (James 2:5–9, 12–13)

Find Your Heart   Heart Chakra

Do whatever is in your heart, for God is with you. (1 Chronicles 17:2)

You must love your neighbor as yourself. (Mark 12:31)

In love there is no room for fear; but perfect love drives out fear.
(1 John 4:18)

Open to Creative Expression   Throat Chakra

Pray for me to be given an opportunity to open my mouth and fearlessly
make known the mystery of the gospel of which I am an ambassador in
chains; pray that in proclaiming it I may speak as fearlessly as I ought to.
(Ephesians 6:19–20)

Words flow out of what fills the heart. (Matthew 12:35)

Recognize Your Own Authority   Third Eye Chakra

Jesus said: "Why not judge for yourselves what is upright?"
(Luke 12:57)

Marvel in Mystery   Crown Chakra

In truth I tell you, unless you change and become like little children
you will never enter God's domination-free order. (Matthew 18:3)

"Let the little children come to me; do not stop them; for it is to such
as these that God's domination-free order belongs. I tell you the truth,
anyone who does not welcome God's domination-free order like a little
child will not enter it." Then he embraced them, laid his hands on them,
and gave them his blessing. (Mark 10:14–16)

You will know the truth and the truth will make you free. (John 8:32)

Chart to Facilitate DANSFORM Ritual
Root to Crown

Day/Color	Chakra/Heritage	Creation
Sunday – Black	Whole Body Awareness: Mourning into Dancing	**Dance** Psalm 30:11
Monday – Red	Root Chakra: Base of spine, legs To connect to earth and tribe Belonging Glands: Adrenals	**Ancestral Inheritance** Isaiah 60:1 I Kings 21:3
Tuesday – Orange	Sacral Chakra: Sexual, reproductive organs To give birth to, to create Sexuality, feeling Glands: Ovaries, Testes	**New Covenant** Luke 22:17-20
Wednesday – Yellow	Solar Plexus Chakra: Gut, core To mature and to act Empowerment, equality Glands: Pancreas, Adrenals	**Support / Balance** James 2:5-9, 12-13
Thursday – Green	Heart Chakra: Heart, arms, hands To love and to be loved Authenticity Gland: Thymus	**Find Your Heart** I Chronicles 17:2 Mark 12:31 1 John 4:18
Friday – Blue	Throat Chakra: Throat To speak and to be heard Expression Gland: Thyroid	**Open to Creative Expression** Ephesians 6:19,20 Matthew 12:35
Saturday – Indigo	Third Eye Chakra: Eyes, ears To value intuition Awareness Gland: Pituitary	**Recognize Your Authority** Luke 12:57
Sunday – Violet	Crown Chakra: Top of head To connect human to divine Spirituality, knowing Gland: Pineal	**Marvel in Mystery** Matthew 18:3 Mark 10:14-16 John 8:32

Characteristics	Commandments	Creations
Us against them mentality; insistence on rigid adherence to the law; rooted in judgment	You must keep up appearances and not be an embarrassment; you will only belong if you are judged obedient	"I will create circles of welcome and grace; born of spirit; embodying truth; secure in the family of God; willing even to die"
Relationships are hierarchical; traditional marriage; devaluation of the feminine; anti-gay; anti-choice	Your sexuality is not your own and will be controlled and appropriated by men; your emotions are not important	"I will bless the body; bless the cup; bless the feminine; bless my sexuality and emotionality"
Exclusive language; women are not permitted to act powerfully or be ordained; injustice is legitimized	You will not act independently or become a mature woman	"I will exercise the power to act; realize female and male in partnership; honor the disempowered; move in God's domination-free order"
Role is valued over authenticity	You will be forced to be what others need you to be; you will not be selfish	"I will discover authenticity; love others; also love myself; believe in the power of love"
Women's voices are silenced, then co-opted for promotion of the system	You will fit in and not express your uniqueness	"I will speak up fearlessly; tell my own stories; develop my own art; own my voice"
Fear, guilt, manipulation, and literalism interrupt awareness	You will not be aware or value your intuition; you will believe what you are told	"I will judge for myself what is true and just; practice discernment; honor both reason and intuition"
"Original sin" emphasized; children are dominated, de-valued, and controlled; projection is practiced at the expense of truth	You will bear and train good, obedient children	"I will welcome children and child-likeness; become like a little child; approach mystery; truth will make me free"

Dansform Ritual

The word *dansform* is a combination of dance and transform. As you will notice, the letters of the word form an acrostic, using the first letter of each of the inheritances we wish to reclaim in each chakra. We begin with *d* for dance, *a* for ancestral inheritance, and so on up the body through all the chakras.

Dance

Ancestral Inheritance

New covenant

Support/balance

Find your heart

Open to creative expression

Recognize your authority

Marvel in mystery

Paula's Dansform collection of music is available at *ResurrectingEve.com*. The CD includes her original songs inspired by the content of each of the book's chapters, and recordings of the following dansform guided reflections.

The dansform ritual is an invitation to the reader to explore in her body how she may have been affected by fear-based, fundamentalist influences and how she can gain strength and awareness for moving beyond these effects. Rituals are part of mythology, religion, and even our daily lives. They can function as comforting habits as well as powerful, transformative tools to clarify our core values and deeply held beliefs. When we practice rituals with conscious intention, we are able to infuse our simple routines with the flame of deep meaning and depth of purpose. Explore these Dansform rituals with an awareness of their power to transform the rhythm of daily life into sacred celebration. Now we invite you to experience the magic of these rituals as you appropriate their healing power.

A pilgrimage is a journey to a sacred site. Think of this as a pilgrimage to your sacred self as you incarnate more fully into your flesh. We will focus on the colors and concepts of the body's seven chakras. We have so far introduced them from the top down. As we outline this healing journey, however, we will start at the bottom, with the root chakra. The ideas we offer for structuring this experience are only suggestions. We have framed a creative process that weaves through an entire week, but you can adapt it in any way it makes sense to you. This could be a single reflection over the course of an hour, or a daily practice repeated weekly.

Incorporate water into each day. Notice water. Keep water with you not only to drink, but also to remind yourself of God's Living Water. Experience each shower or rainstorm as a baptism. Each day you might want to wear something or everything in the color of the chakra you are exploring. You might select foods in the color you are focusing on. You can prepare a special place in your home for your time of reflection, or you can make space wherever you are. You can light a candle or burn incense. You may want to be very private, or you can enlist a friend and support each other through this week of reflection.

You may want to refer to the scripture verses and chart.

Dance

Sunday: Today, begin to bring awareness to your body. Touch your flesh with your hands. Enjoy the softness of your skin, the supple strength of your tendons and muscles beneath. Wear black, with an intention for turning mourning into dancing while knowing the week may bring plenty of both. This is a day of preparation, to think about the week ahead. Gather items you want to have available, including a book for journaling or other creative expression. Spend some time attending to your breathing.

Ask yourself, "If then, the light inside you is darkened, what darkness will that be?" Wonder about what darkness it is that might hold you back from your fullness; wonder what needs to be healed. When you notice a particular place in your body that seems to hold pain or emotion, give it a voice. What would that body part say to you? Do something today that you would consider dance. Put on a favorite or meaningful piece of music and allow your body to respond. Roll your shoulders. Curl your spine. Circle your ankles. Promise yourself to consciously put forth the effort to daily move through the impasses, the blocks, the stuck places of your life. Welcome your body into this movement adventure.

You have turned for me my mourning into dancing. (Psalm 30:11)

Ancestral Inheritance

Monday: This day is to recognize your belonging — to yourself, to your clan, to your world. It is a day for red and for paying attention to the base of your spine and your legs, the root chakra. Bring your attention today to those female ancestors who have come before you. Imagine mother after mother nurturing her child, until the child was you. Celebrate the value of the inheritance of your life, your ancestry, the qualities that make you human, and the survival of your lineage. Spend some time today in nature. Work in your garden. Eat red root vegetables. Find a place to sit on the earth and enjoy the support it offers. Appreciate your connection to the whole creation and your unique place in it. Wonder about how you have experienced belonging in your life. Notice and honor the space for belonging you have created in your home. What do you claim as your ancestral inheritance?

Referring to the chart, read the fundamentalist characteristics and commandments that relate to the root chakra. Do they resonate with your experience? Have you been affected by them? Notice memories, feelings, fears, hopes, and attachments. Focus on how these emotions affect your body. Where in your body do you notice them? This week, don't push them away. Experience them fully. Welcome them as your teachers. Allow them to move through you and out of you. Write about any insights you want to remember or reflect on further. Give yourself permission to creatively express your inheritance in any way you feel inspired. As you travel through the day, walk in confidence. Feel your feet firmly planted and supported by the earth — God's earth, your earth, the same earth where Jesus walked.

Arise, shine out, for your light has come. (Isaiah 60:1)
God forbid that I should give you my ancestral inheritance.
(1 Kings 21:3)

New Covenant / Naked Truth

Tuesday: We focus on this chakra to celebrate sexuality, emotionality, the ability to birth, our creative core. The sacral chakra involves the reproductive and sexual organs and the lower back. The color is orange, and it should be a wet and succulent day. Be sure to eat an orange today, paying full attention to the sensuality of the experience. Notice the sensations and the textures as the wrinkled firmness of the orange skin gives way to the juiciness of the fruit. Swim, wade in a creek, or take a bath. Enjoy water today. Plan something by yourself or with your partner that will nurture and spark your full, sensuous femininity. Of course, drink plenty of water. Whenever you eat and drink today, remember Jesus' blessing of the body and the cup in what we have come to celebrate as Communion. Blessed be our bodies. Blessed be our feelings. Blessed be our birth and rebirth. Blessed be our sacral chakra. Blessed be the womb. Blessed be our sexuality.

Think about what it is to commune with God, with another, with your community. Imagine the breadth and wealth of your creative life. Do you give yourself permission to acknowledge and honor all of your feelings?

Read the fundamentalist characteristics and commandments on the chart that relate to the sacral chakra. Do they resonate with your experience? Have you been affected by them? How have they affected your life and relationships? Has the integrity of your sexual self been violated in any way? How might the water in the vessel of your being be transformed to wine? Imagine a flow of release and renewal. Write about any insights you want to remember or reflect on further. Give yourself permission to creatively express your sexuality in any way you feel inspired to. As you saunter through the day, feel the freedom and the pleasure of moving your hips. Welcome the beautiful moistness and fertility of your creative womanliness and support yourself in a day of continued rebirth.

Then, taking a cup, he gave thanks and said, "Take this and share it among you, because from now on, I tell you, I shall never again drink wine until God's domination-free order comes.... This is my body given for you. ... This cup is the new covenant in my blood poured out for you." (Luke 22:17–20)

Support/Balance

Wednesday: Today we bring attention to the solar plexus chakra in our gut. The color today is yellow for the fire in our belly, our potential for action. Light a candle or a fire today and take inspiration from the dancing flame. Eat corn, yellow squash, or perhaps a spicy curry. Imagine purposefulness in how you order your day. Think about what you want to accomplish in this moment, in this day, in your life. What holds you back from successfully completing your goals? What experiences have disempowered you or left you feeling incompetent? What do you feel in your tummy? Do you have butterflies? A knot?

Imagine within yourself a balance of feminine and masculine energies. What support do you need from others to move forward? What support can you offer to yourself? How can you balance your own needs with those of the people you support? Imagine your own energy and power working in balance with that of others in your life. How can you enhance partnerships of shared power?

Read the fundamentalist characteristics and commandments on the chart that relate to the solar plexus chakra. Do they resonate with your experience? Have you been affected by them? Write about any insights you want to remember or reflect on further. Give yourself permission to creatively express your intentions in any way you feel inspired to. Recognize and delight in your power to act in your own effective way.

It was those who were poor according to the world that God chose, to be rich in faith and to be the heirs to God's domination-free order, which God promised to those who love God. You, on the other hand, have dishonored the poor. Is it not the rich who lord it over you? Are not they the ones who drag you into court, who insult the honorable name, which has been pronounced over you? ... you will love your neighbor as yourself. ... Talk and behave like people who are going to be judged by the law of freedom. Whoever acts without mercy will be judged without mercy, but mercy can afford to laugh at judgment. (James 2:5–9, 12–13)

Find Your Heart

Thursday: Green is the color for today — lettuce, broccoli, perhaps avocados? The heart chakra includes the arms and hands. As you give hugs today be aware of the full body experience as your heart and arms and hands reach out to another. The heritage of the heart is to love and be loved. As you pay attention to your heart center, remember not only who but what you love that reflects a true expression of yourself.

Bring some of nature's greenery into your home. If you like, play a beautiful piece of music and imagine your hand as a dancer interpreting the piece. Let your hand move what is in your heart to say. Try your non-dominant hand. Try both together. Appreciate the beauty and grace your heart and hands express. What people are you drawn to? What activities? When do you feel like you are most yourself? If you have the time and inclination, empty your closet. Put back in only what you really like to wear and what you feel great in. (Put the rest in a box, see if you can get by without it, and have a clothes swap someday with your friends.)

How has the authentic you been concealed by the roles you take on? By the roles expected of you? How do you allow your true self to remain veiled or hidden? In what ways has your heart been broken, denied, manipulated, or judged? How has it grown cold or hard as stone? Breathe deeply today, filling your chest fully. Expand your body, assuming an openhearted posture. Whose love do you receive? With whom do you share your love?

Read the fundamentalist characteristics and commandments on the chart that relate to the heart chakra. Do they resonate with your experience? Have you been affected by them? Write about any insights you want to remember or reflect on further. Give yourself permission to creatively express your uniqueness in any way you feel inspired to. Feel your heart reborn and refreshed today, as if it were brand new and never jaded — a fleshy, messy, woundable, renewable heart, moving from judgment to acceptance.

"Do whatever is in your heart, for God is with you." (1 Chronicles 17:2)

"You must love your neighbor as yourself." (Mark 12:31)

"In love there is no room for fear; but perfect love drives out fear."
(1 John 4:18)

Open to Creative Expression

Friday: This day is for giving voice to what lives inside you, your true blueberry self. This chakra is the throat area, where the voice is generated. Perhaps you feel tension associated with this chakra expanding through your neck and shoulders. It is your inheritance to speak your truth and to be heard. Listen today to the internal voice within you, the voice that only you know. Imagine yourself speaking to the people who never heard what you wanted to say. Say those words out loud and listen to them. Play around with your voice today. Try vocalizing in the shower. Try speaking more slowly than you usually do. Try to speak in a deeper than usual voice. Try speaking without censoring yourself. Watch yourself speaking in a mirror.

Reflect today on all the ways you express yourself. Through what medium does the clearest sense of you find voice? How can you find support for your audible voice in speaking your opinion, sharing your insights, and bringing the depth within you into the breadth of your community? What story would you most like to tell? What truths do you think most need to be told? This is a day for speaking up — writing a letter to the editor, calling your senator or representative, talking back to someone who would rather you be silent.

Read the fundamentalist characteristics and commandments on the chart that relate to the throat chakra. Do they resonate with your experience? Have you been affected by them? Write about any insights you want to remember or reflect on further. Give yourself permission to creatively express your story in any way you feel inspired to. Whether you profess, confess, or digress, may you fully express yourself today in your own resonant voice.

Pray for me to be given an opportunity to open my mouth and fearlessly make known the mystery of the gospel of which I am an ambassador in chains; pray that in proclaiming it I may speak as fearlessly as I ought to. (Ephesians 6:19–20)
Words flow out of what fills the heart. (Matthew 12:35)

Recognize Your Authority

Saturday: This is your indigo day of intuition and awareness. Maybe wearing blue jeans will support you in honoring your own point of view and opening your mind's eye. This chakra is called the third eye or the brow chakra and includes the eyes and ears and forehead. It relates to awareness, in an intuitive way as well as practically, to evaluate information, observe realities, and decide for yourself what is true and just; to use your own discretion to discern between good and evil, perhaps choosing a stance of disengagement from contact, even withdrawal when necessary.

Reflect on times in your life when you trusted your intuitive sense as a mother, or as a friend, or in a business decision. Spend some time today investigating something complicated or controversial. Go to the library, search the Internet, or listen to public radio. Honor your ability to integrate new ideas into the context of your own life experience and wisdom.

What in the past has interrupted your willingness to trust your own perspective? What darkness obscures your light? Notice light today. Dim light, candlelight, broad daylight, twilight, moonlight. What does your light look like? Ponder darkness — your own, others'. Open to developing the skill of discernment. Observe what your body experiences when you sense danger, when you discern darkness.

Read the fundamentalist characteristics and commandments on the chart that relate to the third eye chakra. Do they resonate with your experience? Have you been affected by them? Write about any insights you want to remember or reflect on further. Give yourself permission to creatively express your discernment in any way you feel inspired to. Enjoy your brilliance today, as you alone are the authority on your own life and experience. Radiate the delight of your enlightenment and celebrate your choice to shed light on darkness.

Jesus said, "Why not judge for yourselves what is upright?"
(Luke 12:57)

Marvel in Mystery

Sunday: The color for this final day is violet — a royal, regal color. The crown chakra, at the top of your head, relates to consciousness, transcendence, your connection to God, knowing. Crunch some purple cabbage today, if you like. Enjoy dark purple grapes. Incorporate any new awareness you have gained this week into your regular practice of worship and gratitude. Explore your level of comfort with the mysterious, the numinous.

Notice the uncanny wisdom of children. How might you better listen to children and pay loving attention to them, supporting them in being their spontaneous, authentic selves as much as you can? Imagine the inherent goodness and the incredible gift of a tender newborn. Wonder how you might become like a little child and so enjoy God's domination-free order. Think about the child you once were and whose wounds may live inside you still. Offer the same quality of honor and welcome to this child that is you.

Read the fundamentalist characteristics and commandments on the chart that relate to the crown chakra. Do they resonate with your experience? Have you been affected by them? Write about any insights you want to remember or reflect on further. Give yourself permission to creatively express your mystical wonder in any way you feel inspired to. Treasure and ponder all these things.

"In truth I tell you, unless you change and become like little children, you will never enter God's domination-free order." (Matthew 18:3)
"'Let the little children come to me; do not stop them; for it is to such as these that God's domination-free order belongs. I tell you the truth, anyone who does not welcome God's domination-free order like a little child will not enter it.' Then he embraced them, laid his hands on them, and gave them his blessing." (Mark 10:14–16)
"You will know the truth and the truth will make you free." (John 8:32)

It is our hope that you will find healing and renewal in your daily pilgrimage, supported in moving forward with integrity and creative resurrection into the challenges you face in yourself, your family, your church, your community, your country, your world.

About the Authors

Roberta Mary Pughe, Ed.S., is a psychotherapist in private practice in Princeton and Hillsborough, New Jersey. Licensed as a marriage and family therapist, she is a clinical member of the American Association for Marriage and Family Therapists. She also is a Reiki practitioner, a certified Gestalt psychotherapist, and a member of the faculty at the Gestalt Center of New Jersey. She has been working in the therapy field since 1980 and has extensive experience in the practice of individual, couple, family, and group work, including multi-family therapy. Her focus for years has been on women and particularly, on how religious influences have shaped women's thinking and sensed being in the world.

Roberta received her master's degree in theological studies from Gordon-Conwell Theological Seminary, graduating summa cum laude. Her ongoing primary interests and education have been the study of women's spirituality and feminist psychology. She is ordained as an interfaith minister and a minister of ancient ways through the New Mexico Theological Seminary. She received a post-master's educational specialist's degree in marriage and family counseling from Seton Hall University, also graduating with honors.

Roberta mothers her two sons—a teen and a tween—with her partner Camillo. They all endeavor to live the resurrection each and every day.

Paula Anema Sohl, O.T.R., is a homemaker, published songwriter, singer, poet, liturgical dancer, peace activist, mother of three teenagers, and an elder in her local Presbyterian (PCUSA) church. She has trained and worked as a psychiatric occupational therapist and lactation consultant, and most recently finds her calling in her home, in her dance, music, and writing, and as a volunteer in her church, community, and her children's schools. Paula has recently completed training in mediation. Her experiences in mental health and in supporting new mothers in breastfeeding add to her rich perspective and to her artistic expression. She is an English Language Learner's volunteer tutor and a peace and dance enthusiast.

Paula's other interests include yoga, biking, reading, knitting, and other fiber arts. She and her husband receive intensive and ongoing parenting instruction from the finest residential staff — their three teenagers. Paula and her family make their home in Oregon.

⌣⌢

Paula and Roberta both grew up in churches and families affected by fundamentalist dogma. They met in 1977, their freshman year at Calvin College. Through their own unique and diverse journeys, thirty years later they have both moved beyond the silencing effects of this system and are now living liberating lives. They have combined their stories, their insider knowledge, their experience, and their talents in the hope that other women may find freedom through this book.

Paula and Roberta are available to present seminars and workshops for churches, communities, and organizations throughout the United States. In their work as writers, educators, dancer and therapist, they co-facilitate the integration of body, soul, and mind, focusing on the process of unblocking and mobilizing the self to create healing, wholeness, and action. In their women's workshops, they support emergence of the authentic self.

Their passion is in supporting and guiding women uncover their authentic selves and to express themselves fully in their lives.